EVERYDAY VIOLENCE IN BRITAIN, 1850–1950

WOMEN AND MEN IN HISTORY

This series, published for students, scholars and interested general readers, will tackle themes in gender history from the early medieval period through to the present day. Gender issues are now an integral part of all history courses and yet many traditional texts do not reflect this change. Much exciting work is now being done to redress the gender imbalances of the past, and we hope that these books will make their own substantial contribution to that process. We hope that these will both synthesise and shape future developments in gender studies.

The General Editors of the series are *Patricia Skinner* (University of Southampton) for the medieval period; *Pamela Sharpe* (University of Bristol) for the early modern period; and *Penny Summerfield* (University of Lancaster) for the modern period. *Margaret Walsh* (University of Nottingham) was the Founding Editor of the series.

Published books:

Imperial Women in Byzantium, 1025–1204: Power, Patronage and Ideology
Barbara Hill

Masculinity in Medieval Europe
D. M. Hadley (ed.)

Gender and Society in Renaissance Italy
Judith C. Brown and Robert C. Davis (eds.)

Widowhood in Medieval and Early Modern Europe
Sandra Cavallo and Lyndan Warner (eds.)

Gender, Church and State in Early Modern Germany: Essays by Merry E. Wiesner
Merry E. Wiesner

Manhood in Early Modern England: Honour, Sex and Marriage
Elizabeth W. Foyster

English Masculinities, 1600–1800
Tim Hitchcock and Michele Cohen (eds.)

Disorderly Women in Eighteenth-Century London: Prostitution in the Metropolis, 1730–1830
Tony Henderson

Gender, Power and the Unitarians in England, 1760–1860
Ruth Watts

Practical Visionaries: Women, Education and Social Progress, 1790–1930
Mary Hilton and Pam Hirsch (eds.)

Women and Work in Russia, 1880–1930: A Study in Continuity through Change
Jane McDermid and Anna Hillyar

More than Munitions: Women, Work and the Engineering Industries, 1900–1950
Clare Wightman

The Family Story: Blood, Contract and Intimacy, 1830–1960
Leonore Davidoff, Megan Doolittle, Janet Fink and Katherine Holden

Women and the Second World War in France, 1939–1948: Choices and Constraints
Hanna Diamond

EVERYDAY VIOLENCE IN BRITAIN, 1850–1950

Gender and Class

Edited by
SHANI D'CRUZE

An *imprint of* **Pearson Education**

Harlow, England · London · New York · Reading, Massachusetts · San Francisco
Toronto · Don Mills, Ontario · Sydney · Tokyo · Singapore · Hong Kong · Seoul
Taipei · Cape Town · Madrid · Mexico City · Amsterdam · Munich · Paris · Milan

Pearson Education Limited
Edinburgh Gate
Harlow
Essex CM20 2JE
England

and Associated Companies throughout the world

Visit us on the World Wide Web at:
http://www.pearsoneduc.com

First published 2000

ISBN 0 582 41908 5 (cased)   0 582 41907 7 (pbk)

British Library Cataloguing-in-Publication Data
A catalogue record for this book is available from the British Library

Library of Congress Cataloging-in-Publication Data
A catalog record for this book is available from the Library of Congress

Transferred to digital printing 2004
Typeset by 35 in 11/13pt Baskerville MT
Produced by Pearson Education Asia Pte Ltd

Printed and bound by Antony Rowe Ltd, Eastbourne

CONTENTS

ACKNOWLEDGEMENTS

Our thanks to Elizabeth Stanko, the Director of the ESRC Violence Research Programme, for her support and for contributing the Foreword to this volume. John Archer would like to thank the ESRC for providing research funding for his chapter. His research, 'Violence in the North West with Special Reference to Liverpool and Manchester' (award number L133251004), is a project belonging to that programme.

A number of the chapters in this volume were first presented at the Women's History Network Northern Region conference on 'Women, Gender and Interpersonal Violence: Historical Perspectives' in February 1999. Our thanks to the School of Cultural Studies, Leeds Metropolitan University, who hosted the event, to the Women's History Network and to all who contributed papers and discussion at the conference.

Our thanks to the numerous colleagues who have read and commented on various of the chapters. My own thanks, as editor, are due to Professor Penny Summerfield, our academic editor, and, of course, to all the contributors to this book who have been a real pleasure to work with and who have produced such stimulating and scholarly chapters.

Shani D'Cruze

Publisher's acknowledgements

ABBREVIATIONS

ALR	*Ashton-under-Lyne Reporter*
AR	Annual Report
BJC	*British Journal of Criminology*
BMJ	*British Medical Journal*
BW	*The British Workman*
C&C	*Continuity and Change*
CC	*The Common Cause*
CCCSP	*Central Criminal Court Sessions Papers*
CG	*Child's Guardian*
CJH	*Criminal Justice History*
CL	*The City Lantern*
CR	*Contemporary Review*
CT	*County Telephone*
DC	*Daily Chronicle*
DE	*Daily Express*
DMr	*Daily Mirror*
DM	*Daily Mail*
DN	*Daily News*
DS	*Daily Sketch*
DT	*Daily Telegraph*
ECC	*English Chartist Circular*
EHR	*Economic History Review*
EN	*Evening News*
FR	*Feminist Review*
FS	*Feminist Studies*
FtlyR	*The Fortnightly Review*
G&H	*Gender and History*
GEPSR	*Glasgow Evening Post and Sunday Reformer*
GMPM	Greater Manchester Police Museum
GMRO	Greater Manchester Record Office
GR	*Gorton Reporter*
H&T	*History and Theory*
HJ	*Historical Journal*

HWJ	*History Workshop Journal*
IJCS	*International Journal of Cultural Studies*
IJWS	*International Journal of Women's Studies*
IPN	*Illustrated Police News*
IRLWCH	*International Review of Labour and Working-Class History*
IRP	*International Review of Psychiatry*
IRSH	*International Review of Social History*
IRV	*International Review of Victimology*
JB	*John Bull*
JBS	*Journal of British Studies*
JC&N	*Journal of Child Abuse and Neglect*
JIH	*Journal of Interdisciplinary History*
JL&S	*Journal of Law and Society*
JMH	*Journal of Modern History*
JMWF	*Journal of the Medical Women's Federation*
JSH	*Journal of Social History*
JSP	*Journal of Social Policy*
JSSL	*Journal of the Statistical Society of London*
LC	*Liverpool Courier*
LdnM	*London Mercury*
LDP	*Liverpool Daily Post*
LEE	*Liverpool Evening Express*
LHR	*Law and History Review*
LM	*Liverpool Mercury*
LWPP	Liverpool Women Police Patrols
MC	*Manchester Courier*
MCN	*Manchester City News*
MEM	*Manchester Evening Mail*
MEN	*Manchester Evening News*
MG	*Manchester Guardian*
MLR	*Modern Law Review*
MornC	*Morning Chronicle*
MPC	*Medical Press and Circular*
MQR	*Michigan Quarterly Review*
MSCH	*Manchester and Salford Co-operative Herald*
MWF	*Medical Women's Federation*
MWP	*Manchester Weekly Post*
NAPSSSP	*National Association for the Promotion of Social Science Sessions Papers*
NBR	*North British Review*
NF	*New Formations*
NSPCC	National Society for the Prevention of Cruelty to Children

OBSP	Old Bailey Sessions Papers
OWC	*Oldham Weekly Chronicle*
P&P	*Past and Present*
P&PA	*Philosophy and Public Affairs*
PMG	*Pall Mall Gazette*
PMM	*Pall Mall Magazine*
PP	Parliamentary Papers
PR	*Police Review*
PRO	Public Record Office
RCDMC	Royal Commission on Divorce and Matrimonial Causes
RH	*Rural History*
RN	*Reynolds Newspaper*
SC	*Salford Chronicle*
SDT	*Sheffield Daily Telegraph*
SH	*Social History*
SLS	*Social and Legal Studies*
SM	*Strand Magazine*
SR	*Salford Reporter*
SS	*Sunday Strand*
StPC	*St Pancras Chronicle*
TN	*Trades Newspaper*
VPR	*Victorian Periodical Review*
VS	*Victorian Studies*
WCG	Women's Co-operative Guild
WD	*Weekly Dispatch*
WFL	Women's Freedom League
WHR	*Women's History Review*
WM	*Western Mail*
WS	*Women's Studies*
WSIQ	*Women's Studies International Quarterly*
WSJ	*Women's Suffrage Journal*

Note: throughout, place of publication of cited sources is London unless otherwise stated.

FOREWORD

In 1997, I became Director of the Economic and Social Research Council's Programme on Violence. Over the past two years, I have been asked the same questions again and again. A regular query of reporters is whether violence is 'getting worse'. Another concern of journalists is to enquire about the rampaging and increasing violence of women. Interestingly, I have never been asked about police brutality, suicides in prison or the violence of prison officers (despite the recent high profile cases involving such situations). Violence, to the media and in popular culture, has become the shorthand to talk about the evil of individuals. Although there is far more awareness about child abuse, brutality against intimate partners and rape, the questions addressed to me begin with the assumption that threat and assault are 'out of the blue', removed from the mundane reality of day-to-day life. My approach to answering these queries is to move the discussion from the level of myth to the realm of the everyday. Everyday violence, a phrase I used for the title of my book in 1990, better captures the way violence is part and parcel of some people's lives. While not all of us experience threat and intimidation, far more of us do than we previously thought. British Crime Surveys regularly suggest that forms of violence are less likely to be reported to police than forms of property crime. What these victimisation studies continue to demonstrate is that harm, and the situations that regularly give rise to it, intersect daily life. The home, leisure pursuits, the neighbourhood and the workplace feature prominently as the contexts within which even the violence reported to crime researchers takes place.

This collection takes us back in time to remind us that these forms of violence were as much part of daily life in the past as now. What these articles help us see is how we came to frame 'violence' through a lens controlled by the discourse of law rather than the discourse of everyday life. The development of the state's institution of policing – with its virtual dominance in defining 'real' violence – contributed a powerful framework for skewing our understanding of and about violence. Such a framework excluded many of the injurious disputes of social life resulting in physical and sexual damage to people. The media, too, actively participated in defining serious violence. Real violence came to be associated with public violence. The rest – the bulk of what people experience – was relegated to the disputes of the deserving. To what extent this encouraged silence about the way in which your husband, your employer, your neighbour or your siblings treated you is an interesting empirical question. Certainly, today we know that such silence continues. Yet most of this violence was not hidden. The threats and abuse were known to all those around. Some intervened; many did not. Many 'knew' that danger and damage accompanied everyday life of those in their social networks. The developing institutions – the courts, welfare and caring professions – often excluded forms of so-called legitimated violence from legal definitions of criminal assault. The damage of such violence is strewn across historical documents. What is interesting is that the questions of the present – inspired by feminist inquiry into violence against women – are informing these interrogations of the past. As we see in this collection, there is much to learn from exploring the past through this new lens. In turn, we can understand how and why we continue to eschew most violence from legal judgment or state intervention. And perhaps, given the way some of its victims are treated in the process, we might begin to find ways of intervening to assist people without subjecting them to condemnation and shame.

This is an engaging and lively collection. It will add a great deal to the debates about violence.

Elizabeth A. Stanko
Royal Holloway,
University of London,
September 1999

Unguarded passions: violence, history and the everyday

SHANI D'CRUZE

A history of interpersonal violence

Historians inevitably ask questions of the past that are relevant to their contemporary circumstances. The twentieth century has closed on a world marked at all levels and in many ways by violence. The UK at the turn of the twenty-first century is a society anxious about levels of violent crime, drunkenness, vandalism, racist attacks, sexual assault and harassment, child sexual abuse, terrorism and the terrifying (if comparatively exceptional) violence of paedophiles, murderers and gunmen. Increasingly, public urban spaces are monitored by cctv cameras.[1] Our everyday behaviour is monitored regularly in the name of concerns about violence and theft. However, as recent research has shown, all these kinds of violence have a history. It seems that certain kinds of violence – for example, child sexual abuse – are subject to periods when they are not recognised and periods when they undergo moments of rediscovery and redefinition.[2] Whilst the basic physical realities of violence may be disturbingly repetitive, the socio-cultural contexts and meanings, as well as the techniques and technologies of violence, have their historical specificities.

The chapters in this volume set out to explore the history of how violence impinged on people's lives in the century before the Second World War. We are concerned here specifically with interpersonal violence; that is, violence directly administered to one person or persons by another person or people. Although some of this violence was an instrumental part of robbery or other crime, the far greater part was not. Our focus is on everyday violence; that is, violence which eventuates out of people's ordinary, routine and mundane social interaction. This involved a very wide range of violent behaviours, from domestic violence to the brawls of youth gangs and from infanticide to rape and sexual assault. We do not address violence used to further a political or religious cause, nor the organised violence of the state, either judicial or in warfare, though in avoiding these kinds of violence we do not deny that they may have fed back into the 'ordinary' behaviours of individuals.

Modern statistics show rising reported crime levels over recent decades.[3] However, over the very long term, the recorded incidence of homicide seems to have declined.[4] Victorian and Edwardian criminal statistics demonstrate a clear decline in both property and violent crime between the 1840s and the 1920s.[5] Historians of crime are rightly circumspect about criminal statistics compiled by the institutions charged with the control of crime and always acknowledge the unknown 'dark figure' of the theft and violence not included in such statistics. However, these trends do seem to indicate changes in working-class behaviour.[6] Much theft was opportunist and increased in times of economic downturn, when violence decreased. Thus, violence seems to have been an incipient part of working-class cultures, particularly when rather greater prosperity increased access to drink.[7]

Contributors to this volume take up a number of different approaches to the issues around gender, class and everyday violence. Their work is united here through its preoccupation with class and gender as intersecting modalities of power and through a concentration on violence as one outcome of contested power relations. Some approach the topic as women's historians or feminist historians; others identify themselves more closely as social historians or historians of crime. Others still, work more closely in law or literary studies. This volume has three thematic sections. In the first, contributors consider the uses of different kinds of interpersonal violence in British society during our period. Anna Clark summarises some of her key findings on the interaction of public and private, and the relationships between class and gender in nineteenth-century domestic violence. John Archer surveys the very varied ways that nineteenth-century men found themselves to be the perpetrators or the victims of violence. Also in this section, Andrew Davis examines the affrays of youth gangs in late nineteenth-century Manchester and Salford, and Meg Arnot discusses infanticide.

Our second section explores the regulation of violence by public institutions, in particular the law and the press. Kim Stevenson and Joanne Jones both use nineteenth-century newspapers to examine the treatment of sexual violence by the law. Their perspectives are rather different, however. Joanne Jones examines reporting styles in the Manchester press and demonstrates the ways that journalistic techniques comprised an ongoing interrogation of gendered femininities and masculinities, differentiating the respectable from the rough, against an urban, working-class landscape otherwise largely inaccessible to a respectable newspaper readership. Kim Stevenson uses *The Times* to examine the attitudes of higher courts to women subjected to sexual violence. She positions the silences and reticences about harm done to women against the obfuscation and confusions of statutes nominally legislated in order to afford protection against sexual violence. Jacky Burnett shows the Women's Co-operative Guild actively taking on such patriarchal constructions, in this case marital cruelty, in their evidence to the 1909–1912 Royal Commission on Divorce and Matrimonial Causes. Louise Jackson considers the role of women police officers and police surgeons in the regulation of interpersonal violence between the wars. These women developed a professional role for themselves against entrenched opposition by acquiring expertise in dealing with women and children subjected to violence. However, their middle-class identification as professional also cut across their gendered position, leading them not infrequently to collude with a disease model which could explain both male violence and women's and children's alleged propensity to victimhood.

Our final section reviews the popular representation of violence. Cat Euler considers the ways that women campaigners presented violence against women in public debates. Judith Rowbotham examines the discriminating representation of interpersonal violence in popular literature. She argues that certain kinds of violence were seen as intolerable because they were symptomatic of wider moral disorders, whereas the honourable use of violence by both middle and working-class fictional characters (particularly male) was considered praiseworthy. Julie Early's study of Dr Crippen's murder and Lucy Bland's discussion of the Madame Fahmy case demonstrate differing popular representations of notorious murderers. Crippen's dreadful violence to his wife was de-emphasised as the interest shifted to criticisms of Cora Crippen, whose domestic shortcomings virtually came to explain her murder. By contrast, Madame Fahmy was acquitted of the murder of her millionaire Egyptian husband, whose race, even more than his domestic violence, seemed to make him fair game.

Class

This book focuses predominantly on working-class violence. Middle-class and élite people, of course, committed many kinds of violence. Systems of formal and informal discipline in English public schools, the institutionalised violence of the armed forces, both at home and in the Empire, Victorian parental discipline, as well as codes of masculine chivalry provide just a few examples of violence amongst the better off. But working-class violence was constructed as a social problem, highly visible to contemporaries and well documented. Middle and upper-class offenders were certainly tried and punished, but by and large this occurred only when their offence proved impossible to ignore or redefine. In the 1970s, sociologists and historians on the Left tended to portray state institutions as trying to regulate and control working-class culture in the interests of middle-class hegemony. They often regarded working-class violence as resistance to 'social control'. However, more recent work is demonstrating that working-class people also regulated their own morality and behaviour, and used the courts for their own ends. Furthermore, feminists have demonstrated that violence within working-class communities was often a way in which working-class men exerted power over working-class women. Violence was also a way to exert power over racial minorities.

Between the later eighteenth century and the interwar period, the development and elaboration of judicial, penal and policing systems sought to construct the criminal as working class and subjected working people to new levels of scrutiny and discipline in their daily lives. Gatrell sees these trends as the development of a 'policeman state'.[8] A good deal of this effort was directed against property crime. Nevertheless, theft was associated with violence, prostitution and vagrancy as part of a more generalised moral disorder. In general, interpersonal violence gave concern *only* as part of this broader context.[9] In this section, I want to review the political and social outcomes of such an association for the interaction of working people with the 'policeman state'.

Large-scale riot and insurrection seemed to threaten social order in the late eighteenth and early nineteenth centuries when revolutionary activity on the continent caused the British political nation to glance nervously over its shoulder on repeated occasions. Before the later eighteenth century, riot and disorder had certainly been deplored. Nevertheless, it had remained an accepted and broadly non-threatening feature of society and governance. The governing classes sometimes accommodated the demands of rioters where these accorded with consensual notions of a 'moral economy' and sometimes ruthlessly put down an unacceptable disturbance. And, of course, they defended their property by the use of incarceration, transportation and the increasingly ubiquitous death penalty, inflicting terrible retribution on individuals but viewing the criminal behaviour of the lower orders as an inevitable consequence of their lower natures.[10] For the most part, neither the institutions nor the ideologies of the *ancien régime* saw the interpersonal violence that working people inflicted on *each other* as of much concern to the social order overall. In fact, interpersonal violence in general was seen as private, in the sense that it was first and foremost a matter between individuals. Élites' own codes of honour saw physical violence as an entirely legitimate way of settling disputes between men, most notably through duelling.[11] Although duelling itself was increasingly disapproved of by the early nineteenth century, the underlying principle of violence as a means of male conflict resolution remained pretty well entrenched.

Nevertheless, between the 1780s and the 1820s key changes seem to have occurred in the law's treatment of interpersonal violence where it was tried as assault. Peter King argues that magistrates' sentencing policy changed from nominal fines, indicative of the law's role in facilitating dispute resolution, to imprisonment. An increasingly plebeian population of offenders accused of assault had limited capacity to pay fines. Imprisonment was thus perceived as a more flexible and effective sentence for both violence and petty larceny at a time when prison reform movements were presenting incarceration as a corrective remedy for criminality. Thus, interpersonal violence tried as assault was positioned more firmly within the spectrum of social disorder amongst working people that reform movements increasingly wanted to address.[12] At the same time, the sensibilities which disapproved of duelling had corresponding elements in a growing distaste and nervousness about the spectacle of public hanging. The number of capital offences had been severely reduced by the late 1830s and public hanging was abolished in 1868.[13] The intention of penal policy shifted from the simple punishment of the criminal by incarceration, to a view that the penal system should extract repentance and accomplish his moral and social reform.[14] At the same time, rapid population growth and industrialisation had made the working classes a far more noticeable and apparently undisciplined element in the growing industrial towns. These social and economic changes were accompanied by vociferous demands from vocal sectors of the artisan classes, in alliance with a broad swathe of middle-class opinion, deeply critical of the *ancien régime* state and demanding inclusion in the political nation through radical parliamentary reform and extension of the political suffrage. Middle-class perspectives combined older political rights discourse with the energies of religious evangelicalism.[15]

Consequently, the debate about political citizenship contained an important moral dimension. Gatrell argues that 'the criminal' acquired a symbolic potency that 'he' didn't have earlier *and* a social identity that was primarily located in the working class. Because 'the criminal' was so strongly gendered as male, by the later nineteenth century at least the ideological confusion presented by female criminality had to be displaced by the categorisation of increasing numbers of female offenders as 'feeble minded'.[16] This notion eventually also came to have wider uses in defining the class position of 'the criminal'.

The perceived social and moral disorder of some of those asking for entry to the political nation posed a problem for their inclusion *and* established a bench mark to segregate the political nation from the rest. The boundary of the political nation was redrawn formally by an adjustment of the property qualification to include many middle-class but effectively no working-class men in 1832. Established political rights discourses had long seen property as a prerequisite for liberty and rationality. This boundary was re-debated and progressively shifted in 1867, 1884, 1918 and finally in 1928, when citizenship and the franchise eventually included all adults, women and men, and political liberties were guaranteed by the liberal state. In these debates about political rights and obligations, citizenship was increasingly constructed as an identity, rather than a proprietorial bundle of rights.[17] Such debates provided space for working people to argue for political citizenship and to construct cultures around ideals of respectability. Whilst these might have been reformist rather than revolutionary, they at least had positive political spin-offs and generated tactics to preserve dignity in the face of heavy labour, poverty and economic uncertainty. Anna Clark has traced carefully the connections between popular political discourse and its constructions of working-class domesticity through the early and mid-nineteenth century. She argues that the adoption of the breadwinner ideal by the Chartist period underpinned working men's claims to citizenship. However, the breadwinner ideal itself fuelled the possibility of domestic violence as it put heavy strains on domestic economies where wage levels and irregular working patterns meant that resources were scarce and wives' and children's earnings were frequently needed.[18]

Therefore, the boundary between those within and outside the political nation came to articulate (moral) failings implicit in people's natures as evidenced in their social practices. Interpersonal violence was important in the Victorian public sphere because public order was seen to be at risk from the *moral* damage of the interpersonal violence (most particularly) of the working class. This was the case where violence intruded on to the street and disturbed the public sphere, *and* where it disrupted the key and balancing institution in the nineteenth-century mental universe – the family. The public and the family were the two key pillars of social order. Across class, men's domestic and social conduct had consequences for their public, political identities.[19]

Where women demanded inclusion in the political nation, they often framed claims to citizenship around the importance of their family role. In fact, the state increasingly (and against considerable opposition from *laissez-faire* lobbies) intervened in aspects of the private lives of families. It curtailed the rights of husbands and fathers by legislating over divorce, separations, the custody of children and married women's property and earnings. The state's actions (and of course, the often feminist campaigns that did much to prompt them) brought to light a good deal of family violence caused by men's attempts to exert their authority at home. There were many styles of Victorian fatherhood, but an expectation of obedience was general across all classes and could be rigorously enforced.[20] Newspaper coverage of the London divorce court following the Divorce Act of 1857 and of domestic violence cases heard before magistrates' courts across the land, brought a regular diet of husbands' violence and people's marital misconduct to a broad public readership and debated the limits of legitimate male violence within the home. From this direction too, therefore, apparently private interpersonal violence had its public and political dimensions.

For the working classes, these associations had two main, related consequences in the area of interpersonal violence. Firstly, certain kinds of everyday violence came under ever increasing levels of scrutiny and discipline through the growth of the new police forces from the 1830s, the rapid increase in magistrates' summary jurisdiction under the Summary Jurisdiction Acts (1847–1855) and the development of social welfare agencies, especially from the early twentieth century. Secondly, by the later nineteenth century, codes of respectability tempered any unquestioning social or familial use of interpersonal violence for many working people. Nevertheless, working-class culture was far from rejecting the discriminating use of violence.

The police

The new police forces created after the Local Government Act (1835) and particularly following the County and Borough Police Act (1856) undertook the routine and detailed surveillance of working-class neighbourhoods. The original vision of the policeman as 'domestic missionary', imposing dominant values of neighbourhood and household order was strenuously resented. This 'plague of blue locusts', charged with keeping the streets clear and orderly, met with stiff opposition from working people from the outset, and was often resented and resisted throughout our period.[21] As Gatrell remarks, the official police rationale that their prime purpose was the detection of crime, provided a 'self-serving and convenient obfuscation' which cloaked their routine interventions in working-class life.[22] However, rank and file policemen were working class in origin, and by no means averse to making their lives a little easier by reaching accommodations with the neighbourhoods they policed. By the close of the nineteenth century, large-scale, anti-police disturbances had largely ebbed away, and for the most part working people lived with the police presence and occasionally made use of the police to settle problems, including those of violence. Nevertheless, the police had not achieved a thoroughgoing reform of working-class culture

– far from it. Gambling, drink and occasional street violence remained features of many interwar, working-class neighbourhoods. The police had simply established their routine presence and had come to 'delineate the physical arenas in which those activities might be legally pursued and supervised'.[23]

The material constraints of particularly urban working-class housing, as well as the sociabilities of working-class culture, meant that much of people's lives was lived out on their neighbourhood streets. Children saw the street as a place to play: women and men (though generally in gender-specific groups and at different times) used the street to gossip and socialise – an extension of both the pub and the home. Street gambling, courtship parades, men and boys running races and, of course, street fights, were all occasions on which working people's views of the legitimate uses of neighbourhood space came into direct confrontation with police definitions of public order.[24] The spatial dimension of the public sphere has been recognised as important in historical interpretation, for some historians replacing the earlier reliance on analysis by class.[25] Events and social interaction acquire meaning by their location in space and time. Contests for control of and access to public space are justly recognised as having political, as well as social and cultural, dimensions and involve power relations by class, gender and race.[26] Quite clearly, the new police forces from the mid-nineteenth century were engaged in a long-running struggle with working people over the legitimate uses of urban space; not only the central areas of towns but, perhaps even more crucially, the streets, courts and alleys of working-class neighbourhoods. Arguably, therefore, police activity itself, along with the resistance to it, furthered a redefinition of these spaces as part of the public sphere. Consequently, neighbourhood space, and the violence and disorder that took place there, can be related to broader contemporary contests over citizenship.

The summary courts

The second half of the nineteenth century also saw a large increase in the use of local magistrates' courts to regulate aspects of working-class life. Later nineteenth-century civic improvement often included a new police station with a purpose-built petty sessions courtroom attached.[27] These came to be known as police courts, indicating the growing police role as prosecutors of petty theft, violence and minor regulatory offences (weights and measures, obstruction, public nuisance). Previously, individuals had brought prosecutions in their own names. Though interpersonal violence was not the major preoccupation of local courts, it was an insistent presence.[28] Magistrates tried most domestic violence which came to court. The Matrimonial Causes Act of 1878, powers to grant maintenance and separation allowances for deserted wives in 1886 and the Summary Jurisdiction (Married Women) Act of 1895 led to the bench arbitrating over many unhappy, working-class marriages.[29] Magistrates had a role in the regulation of extra-marital, working-class sexuality since they awarded affiliation orders to mothers of illegitimate children. Compulsory elementary schooling from the 1870s provided yet another reason for working-class parents to have dealings with the local courts.

These courts were the point of entry for almost all working-class violence that came to the attention of the legal system. Magistrates decided whether a case should go forward to a higher court and be heard by judge and jury, or whether it fell within their own summary jurisdiction. Particular kinds of violence – garrotting (mugging) in the 1860s or domestic violence in the 1880s – became the focus of heightened concerns and even moral panics. Many highly local initiatives also targeted particular offences. Littleborough (Lancashire) police and magistrates were, for example, particularly exercised in the 1890s about working-class men defecating and urinating in the streets.[30] Magistrates (and even higher courts) exercised comparatively large amounts of discretion in defining and categorising offences, sometimes directly at odds with the evidence, to accord with normalising judgments based on the characteristics of defendants, victims, prosecutors and crimes.[31]

In the later nineteenth century, working people also made tactical use of the magistrates' courts to settle disputes and gain redress for theft and violence.[32] Working women could collude with courts' dominant projects of disciplining disorderly men in order to gain marital separations, maintenance for illegitimate children or redress for the damage to their reputations inflicted by physical and sexual violence.[33] By the interwar period, whilst working people might well be highly sceptical of the much increased disciplinary strategies of the police and local courts – and in certain neighbourhoods and amongst certain groups maintained an unremitting hostility – they were often prepared to make use of these institutions as a resource to settle the incipient difficulties of their lives.[34]

Social welfare

By the Second World War, the regulatory activities of the courts and the police were augmented and sometimes superseded by bureaucratic social agencies. Nineteenth-century philanthropy had sent the charity worker into working-class neighbourhoods. From the closing decades of the nineteenth century the new case-work techniques pioneered by the Charity Organisation Society, as well as the 'community work' approach of the settlement movement, intensified the institutional scrutiny of their working-class clients.[35] The bureaucratic proliferation of inspectors of all types, from state, local authority or voluntary agencies was produced by the adoption of collectivist state welfare policies into the twentieth century. Centralised institutions, from hospitals to approved schools, also scrutinised and categorised their clients.[36]

Working women, as household managers, deftly managed these intrusive visitors who were, nevertheless, a potential source of much-needed household resources and practical assistance in caring for the health and welfare of their children.[37] Receipt of poor law benefit disqualified men from the franchise and, thus, excluded them from the political nation. This disqualification came to apply where a man's children received free school meals.[38] By contrast, the voluntary activities of charitable agencies underlined the 'active citizenship' of the volunteers (women and men).[39] This combination of voluntary, state and local authority welfare provision, rarely addressed violence directly, but increasingly grounded understandings of family violence in the behaviours of an effectively disenfranchised social 'residuum'.

The 'collectivist' state developed legislation on education, health and welfare. The Maternal and Child Welfare Act of 1918 improved health care for infants and, by the interwar period, the school medical service, midwifery and maternity services were well established.[40] Local authorities and voluntary societies provided free milk and school meals. Such provision, fuelled in no small part by eugenic concerns about the 'deterioration of the race' was targeted particularly at infants and children and reconfigured the public interest in the working-class family. As Louise Jackson argues, professional and public attention became focused on 'new' kinds of family violence, in particular, child abuse. Consequently, domestic violence against women became marginalised as an issue. Even feminist activists concentrated on family welfare, rather than on equality for adult women in their own right.[41]

Family violence against children was originally distinguished specifically from the general laws on assault in the Prevention of Cruelty and Protection of Children Act (1889). The Custody of Children Act (1891) enabled courts to remove children from their families and subsumed family violence into a model of disorderly parenting that included neglect, poor hygiene and inadequate provision.[42] The case-work method founded the techniques of the social work professions and underpinned a medical model which targeted individuals on a case-by-case basis.[43] The behaviour of the residuum was increasingly explained as 'feeble-mindedness'. This notion combined the new discipline of psychoanalysis with eugenic perspectives. 'Scientific' understandings of defective human natures causing interpersonal violence were augmenting Victorian understandings of disorder through moral failings. The 'juvenile delinquent' was understood as a particular personality type[44] – an argument which Andrew Davies's history of late nineteenth-century gang violence does much to undermine. New kinds of arguments consequently excluded certain 'kinds' of people from citizenship. Violence was reconfigured into new constructions of identity, but remained part of the composite of behaviours that evidenced the need for such exclusion. To this extent, the policeman state and the collectivist state were interrelated.

In summary, if the 'policeman state' in the nineteenth century brought working-class neighbourhood violence into the public domain and, thus, into debates and contests around the identity of the citizen, this accompanied an increasing, if contested, willingness on the part of the state to legislate on notionally private family matters. Magistrates' courts were key sites where the problems of working-class daily life, including those of violence, encountered the institution of the law and were publicised in newspaper reporting. Although the identity of the Victorian citizen was gendered exclusively male, the suffrage movement contested and eventually overcame this view by the interwar period, though women's citizenship remained connected with their family roles and responsibilities. Citizenship for both men and women also required personal conduct that preserved social and moral order. Interpersonal violence was not a central concern in itself but was frequently seen as symptomatic of an identity which fell short of full citizenship. However, this association was neither automatic nor uncontested. Everyday violence could also be regarded as legitimate, even honourable, conduct and the potential for violence continued to underlie a good deal of social interaction. For some people, such potential was frequently realised; for others only occasionally. Yet even where violence was seldom used, the *possibility* of violence remained entrenched within the social and imaginative framework of the 'everyday'.

The everyday

My understanding of 'everyday' violence does not imply that this violence was (or is) insignificant. Rather than trivialising these experiences, the 'everyday' is a useful way of understanding the violence between people known to each other. It fixes the location of such violence in familiar places: the home and the neighbourhood, the pub or the workplace; the street or the back yard. It describes violence and aggression as a tactic in prosecuting social (or indeed sexual) relationships. According to Elizabeth Stanko, it locates violence, or the possibility of violence, at the core of people's daily lives. I also want to suggest that the actions of the law, professionals and press coverage of everyday violence also fed back; into the home, the workplace, the pub and the neighbourhood. This occurred through mechanisms of gossip and the very kinds of mundane social interaction that provided the original context for violence and, thus, formed part of broader and ongoing negotiations of respectability and social identity. We ask here what kinds of stimuli turned stressful (or pleasurable) situations into violent ones. For example, both perpetrators and commentators repeatedly explained violence through drink. Drink released inhibitions. Courts might be sympathetic to occasional drunken lapses, though repeated heavy drinking to the detriment of family obligation was a clear indicator of disorder. Alcohol was important to both plebeian and élite leisure and an important expression of masculinity. For working people, drinking was a mundane activity – if not everyday, then certainly 'every pay-day' or 'every holiday'.

Our use of the term 'everyday' violence is drawn directly from Stanko's 1985 interview-based study of violence in modern US and UK society. Stanko argues against the representation, prevalent in criminology and policing, of danger as located in certain aspects of public life, as being random and as requiring vigilance. Women are specifically exhorted to protect themselves against the public violence of male (often black and often lower-class) strangers. Stanko argues that, on the contrary, violence is neither deviant nor abnormal but 'an ordinary part of life'; a direct product of inequality in power relations, particularly by gender. According to Stanko, public and policing institutions do not provide effective protection and require the individual to devise proximate, routine, everyday tactics to 'manage danger'. She sees violence as located both in the public *and* the private and as implicit in 'modern social conditions'.[45] Across the differences of urban living since the Second World War, Stanko's argument accords in many ways with the ideological and structural outcomes of the growth of the 'policeman state' since the mid-nineteenth century. The 'policeman state' is of course also a patriarchal state and exerts its dominance by gender, as well as by class. The emphasis upon stranger violence in the public is a 'self-serving and convenient obfuscation' coinciding with the police insistence on the detection of crime as its main function; an emphasis further developed from the interwar period.[46] Arguably, a correlation of the requirement for the public to be orderly and for citizenship to be a moral status incorporating particular kinds of identities, is that public space is also constructed as threatened at its edges by danger and requiring vigilance from both the state and its active citizens.[47]

The personal costs of this have been the silence about other kinds of danger and about the ways that gender and race stereotypes act to guarantee white, masculine privilege. Such ideologies mask the ways that 'unsafety' is a proximate component of many lives and obscure the large amount of violence which is 'everyday' because it is committed by friends, family, kin, workmates, neighbours, acquaintances or lovers of the victim. A modern study has estimated that convicted sexual offenders comprised only 2 per cent of all sexual offenders in its sample.[48] As Lucy Bland shows, the sensational revelations of the 1923 Fahmy murder case disclosed violence that was everyday in the sense of being rooted in marital and household relations, even though it was made exotic through orientalist media constructions.

Everyday violence may be directed at a specific individual, or at someone targeted because they are (apparently) representative of a particular type. Stanko uses this distinction to make sense of racist violence or that directed at gays or lesbians because of their sexual orientation.[49] This kind of violence is not, of course, a modern invention. Roger Swift argues that the nineteenth-century Irish population in England were over-represented in the criminal statistics particularly for petty crime and violence.[50] This was due, in part, to violence within Irish immigrant communities rooted in patterns of sociability, poverty and fighting as dispute resolution and, thus, constituted everyday violence in the main sense of our term.[51] Irish people also experienced racist violence targeted against individuals and located in urban and often neighbourhood space, which because of its proximity to routine daily lives can also be conceptualised as 'everyday'. Irish communities were concentrated in poorer urban districts which were themselves crime 'hot spots' and because of racial prejudice of the new police forces, Irish disorderly behaviour was made particularly visible by the policeman state. Sectarian and racist violence, some pretty large scale, also targeted the Irish as a group. However, such events, like the running battles between gangs of navvies, which frequently involved many Irish, are probably best considered as 'exceptional' rather than everyday violence. Large-scale disturbances declined after 1870.[52] This might indicate a decline in racial prejudice but, particularly in specific neighbourhoods, might indicate that hostility became more localised and personal, and that other kinds of violence (verbal or psychological) replaced physical confrontations.

Everyday violence could result in serious, even fatal, harm. The 'ordinariness' of the social situations that gave rise to even the most serious violence is often so striking.[53] This implies that violence was a tactic deeply embedded in ordinary social interaction between men, women and children. Much discussion here addresses the working classes, but élite interpersonal violence features less in the historical record largely because of the privileges which élites used to protect themselves from the scrutiny of the law. In effect, they could define a much larger amount of their violence as honourable and legitimate.

Gender

We do not argue that women in our period did not employ violence. Far from it. Some women fought back physically against their husbands.[54] As Lucy Bland shows, Madame Fahmy seems literally to have got away with murder. Working women used violence to defend their own or their family's reputations. Some women were involved in gang affrays.[55] Violence against children could be understood as legitimate punishment and located within constructions of familial relationships, which also justified men's physical 'chastisement' of their wives. Women's violence to settle disputes can also be explained through the notion of the 'fair fight' – far more commonly used by men, but clearly also available to women. To argue that certain behaviours are gendered does not necessarily require that they are *exclusively* used by either men or women. Cultural constructs such as the 'fair fight' or 'legitimate punishment' could be drawn upon by individuals where specific situations seemed to warrant them. Nevertheless, for men, the 'fair fight' or parental authority had specific resonances for their identities as men. Both historical and contemporary studies have found that men commit most interpersonal violence.[56] As John Archer argues, male violence was so ubiquitous as to be considered a 'normal' characteristic of masculinity.[57] To this extent, perhaps, we can use an understanding of masculinity to explain and account for a good deal of everyday violence.

Stanko's feminist analysis sees male violence rooted in 'men's structural power and the negotiation of this power with others'. Violent behaviour is, thus, caused at the level of the social.[58] Stanko does not, of course, ignore men's (gendered) vulnerability to violence, nor does she argue that all men are (or have been) unremittingly violent. Rather, varied constructions of historically specific masculinity can be seen to operate. Certain masculinities are hegemonic and others subordinated.[59] In specific historical situations, prevailing power relations will privilege one particular way of 'being a man' and this construction will appear 'natural' and unarguable. Nevertheless, other masculinities that are less privileged or even disapproved of, will still have recognition as alternative ways of being a man.

The most stereotypical nineteenth-century examples of masculinity might be the restrained, frock-coated, middle-class paterfamilias and the hard-drinking, working man. This is, of course, an oversimplification. Much working-class culture cherished the ideal of the self-improving, working man, rooted in home and family, as well as the workplace. The romantic, extravagant figure of the artist was a clear counterpoint to the rational Victorian or Edwardian professional or businessman.[60] Nevertheless, for all these masculinities, certain kinds of violence remained a possible and often an acceptable attribute.[61] Violence employed in defence of the weak, of one's good name, of one's country or Empire was considered honourable by dominant cultures. Several chapters here demonstrate a cross-class consensus about the honourable uses of violence; in a fair fight (Archer), where a husband chastised an unruly wife (Clark) or even sometimes where a man was 'provoked' into aggression by female 'sexual ingenuities' (Stevenson). Judith Rowbotham argues that constructions of masculinity in popular literature laid claims to social realism and intentionally sought to act as guides to conduct. Discourse does not float free of social interaction nor does it hypnotise social actors into conformism any more than 'social control' terrorises them into acquiescence. Rather, individuals make situated and tactical identifications with these kinds of literatures. Popular literature was didactic, but it was also fun and provided ways of imagining masculine identities which *sometimes* could be tried out in experience. In this sense, discourse 'enables subject positions'.[62]

Subordinated masculinities actively resist the dominant construction, not only across class, but also across power differentials by age and/or race. Modern studies often emphasise that public violence is a strategy of masculinity most common amongst subordinated groups.[63] Peer approval acts as another kind of popular 'text' that provides individuals with readings that could help them shape social identities. Geoffrey Pearson has argued that the violent behaviour of teenage 'hooligans' could, despite clear disapproval, be recognised by magistrates and judges as displaying normal, if misdirected, masculinity. An identification with violence as part of masculinity was made across class difference. Hence the philanthropic energies expended on developing boys' clubs. Aggressive tendencies projected onto the sports field would hopefully be transformed into acceptable and energetic manliness.[64]

To talk of dominant and subordinated masculinities is to explain male violence at the level of the social and the cultural. My argument about the public resonances of interpersonal violence in the century before the Second World War is, in part, an attempt to map everyday violence onto the broader society, politics and culture of the period. Feminist history and social history also enjoin an interpretation that pays attention to 'experience' – that is, of everyday violence as part of the interaction between particular people. I also want to consider everyday violence as an expression of social identity and as a site of identity formation. For example, if violence is an attribute of masculinity – if it is involved in someone's way of 'being a man' – it is not only implicated in the kinds of things that person *does* but also in the kind of person he thinks he *is*.[65] Masculine identity is not something 'naturally' or 'biologically' dictated, but is 'something that needs to be accomplished'.[66] This position derives not only from feminist and other uses of social constructionism but also from psychological theory.

Feminist explanations of men's use of violence as a strategy of patriarchal power don't automatically infer that men simply don't care about or take pleasure in the harm that their violence does, though this criticism has been made of feminist theory and politics. Historical and contemporary descriptions demonstrate (some) men's dismay or remorse at the harm they have inflicted, though this does not deny the callousness of other men – or indeed of some women. However, this diversity of reactions to violence by its perpetrators signals that complex psychological processes underlie the uses of violence.

Stevi Jackson's concept of 'sexual scripts' offers a useful way into understanding how a man, working to an imaginative model of 'courtship' where women require active 'persuasion' into sexual intercourse, might disregard or neutralise any violence he used in effecting what, for the woman involved, was a rape.[67] Because such scripts are contingent and culturally constructed, however, they do not necessarily embed themselves in identity, though they certainly act imaginatively. Jefferson offers Klein's post-Freudian concepts of splitting and embedding as an explanatory bridge between violent behaviour and its location within masculine subjectivities. Meg Arnot's chapter makes rather different use of the same concepts in her discussion of infanticide. Splitting and embedding are associated with power relations around anxiety and desire. For Klein, these are defence mechanisms established before the Oedipal phase. Hence 'desire . . . [is] . . . a phenomenon that is socially produced, but also uniquely linked to individual biographies'. Splitting occurs where the ego disowns the part of itself it finds intolerable. Weakness and dependence might seem this way to a masculinity constructed around hardness and self-sufficiency. These unwanted attributes are then projected upon and embedded into an object or person which or who potentially becomes the target of aggression.[68] Thus, individuals manage anxiety by seeing attributes that they dislike in other people rather than in themselves. Where gendered identities constructed in culture through social interaction and the interplay of discourses make aggression a legitimated expression of hostility (as they have done in nineteenth and twentieth-century masculinities), then the neutralisations implied by Jackson's concept of sexual scripts can come into play and violence can result.

Kinds of violence

This raises the question of exactly what kinds of behaviours should be taken analytically to constitute violence. Much of the violence reviewed here was direct physical or sexual aggression. However, other coercive and threatening behaviours could also be considered as violence. Early Modern historians have argued that the spoken word was then also held to constitute violence and the power of the curse was tangible.[69] Physical assault can do emotional and psychological harm. Jacky Burnett's chapter, for example, describes how the Women's Co-operative Guild's evidence to the 1909–1912 Divorce Commission constructed a sophisticated argument that marital 'cruelty' should incorporate psychological, emotional, sexual and economic violence, as well as the directly physical violence which then alone provided grounds for marital separation.

The relationship between physical and sexual violence is analytically problematic. Sexual assaults not infrequently employ physical violence. Liz Kelly's modern study has suggested that a more appropriate model would be that of a continuum between sexual and physical violence and that women's culturally constructed perceptions have tended to mask the violent component in some 'normal' heterosexual sexual situations.[70] Kelly's pathbreaking study has proved very important but, by concentrating on violence within a male–female sexual relationship, necessarily cannot encompass the ways that varied kinds of interpersonal violence can have a sexual dimension. I have found even in Victorian neighbourhood quarrels, that sexual gestures and insults emphasised rage or heightened abuse from both women and men.[71] Courtroom accounts of domestic violence often stressed disputes over the management and control of household resources. However, the location of violence (in the bedroom) or its patterning (kicking the belly or genitals) can infer the totality of the control an abusive husband was seeking to impose. In a culture where female sexuality had such symbolic potency and was also such a key determinant of a woman's reputation, almost any kind of male violence could draw upon some kind of sexual metaphor to express rage or exert dominance.

Cat Euler's chapter examines the writings of nineteenth-century women campaigners against violence against women. In particular, she seeks to deconstruct our modern (feminist) readings of the historical texts generated by nineteenth-century campaigners. She focuses on the practical, political ends they sought to achieve and, in so doing, confronts the issues of the political and ethical risks around the re-presentation of violence where dominant (patriarchal) discourses legitimate, disguise or even applaud certain kinds of interpersonal violence. I have argued that issues around violence were deflected in public debates onto broader questions around political citizenship and the respectability of the working class, and later of the 'residuum'. The effect was to shift attention away from the pain and harm of violence; something which the policeman state's greater attention to property crime was also actively undertaking.[72] Stanko's definition of violence includes 'the infliction of emotional, psychological, sexual, physical and/or material damage'.[73] Violence of one 'type' causes harm of multiple types. I fully subscribe to the approach that invites us, as researchers, to understand difference, to reject naturalism and biological determinism, and to view proximate bodily experiences as historically situated. Nevertheless, a feminist politics still tells us that getting hurt amounts to just that. Cat Euler argues that nineteenth-century campaigners were actively attempting to shift the debate back to the harm of violence. She recommends that a feminist reading should keep harm in mind and this has been a priority for all contributors to this volume.

Continuity and change

The articles in this volume point to some important historical continuities in the history of interpersonal violence. There was continuity in the growth of the policeman state, though with acceleration after 1870 and increasing bureaucratisation and interaction with a welfare state composed of local authority and voluntary agencies, as well as central government. These developments increased the surveillance of 'unguarded passion'[74] amongst the working class, drawing boundaries between disorder and order, rough and respectable. Everyday violence did not sum up the 'disorder' of working people. However, the interest in disorder brought much everyday violence to the attention of the law and the courts (though of course it missed more than it noticed). This mixed people's proximate and everyday management of 'unsafety' into broader political discourses about respectability and ultimately citizenship and into cultural representations of violence which actively discriminated between acceptable (even honourable) and unacceptable violence.

The key continuity seems to have been that everyday violence kept happening, despite statistics showing a decline in recorded crime. The violence that was presented to public view by the policeman state was increasingly associated with specific groups, such as young adults or with a 'residuum' of the very poor. The growing focus on the welfare of the child made child abuse a heightened concern. Respectability came to depend more on certain kinds of physical restraint. However, the persistence of the legitimation

18

of specific kinds of violence, particularly that associated with manliness, counsels against any uncritical acceptance of the significant diminution of violence.

The growth of professionalisation around the management of welfare and social problems was accompanied by discursive shifts that constructed violence less as a moral failing and more as a product of a defective personality. Institutional change interacted with improvements in material conditions. Rising standards of living removed some people from cultures of poverty which modern studies associate with some kinds of street and family violence. Arguably, everyday violence became more private amongst certain groups. By the end of our period, developments in public housing and the growth of the housing estate had done much to change the neighbourhood spaces that many working people inhabited. Housing-estate life did not extinguish the working-class culture established in the later nineteenth century. However, the dynamics of the uses of neighbourhood space (including violent ones) were necessarily readjusted. Urban growth and social change had already created the lower middle-class suburbs around London that appeared so potentially threatening for normative constructions of gender and class, and presumably hid far more violence than that of Dr Crippen behind their lace-curtained windows.

Contributors to this volume ground their explanations in the social and the cultural. They also consider discourse and the uses of language; representations and the working of institutions. An appreciation of the body and its positioning by time and space provides yet other ways of working towards a historicised understanding of interpersonal violence. Underpinning all these investigations is an intention to untangle the workings of power, to recuperate women's and men's historical experience and to try to unravel the complex relationships between experience and subjectivity. Power relations by class and by gender have been key axes along which individuals' lives have been shaped historically. It is not, in the end, particularly helpful to debate in general terms whether gender overdetermines the effect of class, or vice versa, though in specific situations either might have a more acute effect. Overall, it is far more helpful to conceptualise historical situations through the intersections of gender and class. Furthermore, these are not the only such axes, and race, age, sexuality are among other key determinants which may, in certain historical situations, have greater importance in structuring relations of power. We also need to remember that men are also gendered, as much as white people are raced. Social identities are, thus, historically situated, are constructed and are relational. They are shaped and experienced through relations of power (and power contested) which must surely be at the root of any rigorous historical analysis of interpersonal violence.

Notes

1. Anthony E. Bottoms and Paul Wiles, 'Explanations of crime and place' in David J. Evans *et al.* (eds.), *Crime, Policing and Place: Essays in Environmental Criminology* (1992), p. 31.

2. E. Olafson, D. Corwin and R. Summit, 'The modern history of child sexual abuse awareness – cycles of discovery and suppression' *JC&N* 17 (1993), pp. 7–24.

3. Tim Newburn and Elizabeth A. Stanko, 'Introduction' in Newburn and Stanko (eds.), *Just Boys Doing Business: Men, Masculinities and Crime* (1995), p. 1; Kate Painter, 'Different worlds: the spatial, temporal and social dimensions of female victimization' in Evans *et al.* (eds.), *Crime, Policing and Place* pp. 165–166.

4. L. Stone, 'Interpersonal violence in English society, 1300–1980' *P&P* 101 (1983), pp. 22–33; 'A rejoinder' *P&P* 108 (1985), pp. 216–224; J. A. Sharpe, 'The history of violence in England: some observations' *P&P* 108 (1985), pp. 206–215; J. S. Cockburn, 'Patterns of violence in English society: homicide in Kent 1560–1985' *P&P* 131 (1991), pp. 70–106.

5. D. Jones, *Crime, Protest, Community & Police in Nineteenth-Century Britain* (1982), p. 4; V. A. C. Gatrell and T. B. Hadden, 'Criminal statistics and their interpretation' in E. A. Wrigley (ed.), *Nineteenth-Century Society: Essays in the Use of Quantitative Methods for the Study of Social Data* (Cambridge, 1972), pp. 336–396; C. Emsley, 'The history of crime and crime control institutions' in M. Maguire, R. Morgan and R. Reiner (eds.), *The Oxford Handbook of Criminology* (Oxford, 1994), p. 61.

6. V. A. C. Gatrell, 'Crime, authority and the policeman-state' in F. M. L. Thompson (ed.), *The Cambridge Social History of Britain, 1750–1950* Vol. 3, *Social Agencies and Institutions* (1990), pp. 290, 295.

7. Gatrell and Hadden, 'Criminal statistics'.

8. Gatrell, 'Crime, authority'.

9. *Ibid.*, p. 297; David Philips, *Crime and Authority in Victorian England: The Black Country 1835–1860* (1977), p. 257.

10. Douglas Hay *et al.*, *Albion's Fatal Tree* (New York, 1975).

11. Anthony Simpson, 'Dandelions on the field of honour: duelling, the middle class and the law in nineteenth-century England' *CJH* 9 (1988), pp. 99–155; R. Baldrick, *The Duel: A History of Duelling* (1965), pp. 96–101, 199.

12. Peter King, 'Punishing assault: the transformation of attitudes in the English courts' *JIH* 27 (1996), pp. 62–64, 70.

13. V. A. C. Gatrell, *The Hanging Tree: Execution and the English People, 1770–1868* (Oxford, 1994), pp. 22–23, 589–590.

14. Michael Ignatieff, *A Just Measure of Pain: The Penitentiary in the Industrial Revolution, 1750–1850* (1978), p. 213.

15. Boyd Hilton, *The Age of Atonement: The Influence of Evangelicalism on Social and Economic Thought, 1785–1865* (Oxford, 1988), Ch. 6; D. G. Wright, *Popular Radicalism: The Working-Class Experience, 1780–1880* (1988).

16. Lucia Zedner, *Women, Crime and Custody in Victorian England* (Oxford, 1991), Ch. 1.

17. Gatrell, 'Crime, authority' p. 253.

18. Anna Clark, *The Struggle for the Breeches: Gender and the Making of the British Working Class* (Berkeley, 1995) and in this volume; Keith McLelland, 'Rational and respectable men: gender, the working class, and citizenship in Britain, 1850–1867' in Laura L. Frader and Sonya O. Rose (eds.), *Gender and Class in Modern Europe* (Ithaca, 1996).

19. Martin Wiener, 'The sad story of George Hall: adultery, murder and the politics of mercy in mid-Victorian England' *SH* 24 (1999), p. 193.

20. Leonore Davidoff, Megan Doolittle, Janet Fink and Katherine Holden, *The Family Story. Blood Contract and Intimacy 1830–1960* (1999), Ch. 5; A. James Hammerton, *Cruelty and Companionship. Conflict in Nineteenth-Century Married Life* (1992), pp. 118–133.

21. R. D. Storch, 'The plague of blue locusts: police reform and popular resistance in northern England 1840–1857' *IRSH* 20 (1975), pp. 61–90; R. D. Storch, 'The policeman as domestic missionary: urban discipline and popular culture in northern England, 1850–1880' *JSH* 9 (1976), pp. 481–509; Carolyn Steedman, *Policing the Victorian Community: The Formation of English Provincial Police Forces, 1856–80* (1984).

22. Gatrell, 'Crime, authority' p. 245.

23. *Ibid.*, p. 289.

24. Andrew Davies, *Leisure, Gender and Poverty; Working-Class Culture in Salford and Manchester, 1900–1939* (Buckingham, 1992); E. Ross, 'Survival networks: women's neighbourhood sharing in London before World War 1' *HWJ* 15 (1983), pp. 4–27; E. Ross, '"Not the sort that would sit on the doorstep": respectability in pre-World War I London neighbourhoods' *IRLWCH* 27 (1985); M. Tebbutt, *Women's Talk: A Social History of Gossip in Working-Class Neighbourhoods, 1880–1960* (Aldershot, 1995); Geoffrey Pearson, '"A Jekyll in the classroom, a Hyde in the street": Queen Victoria's hooligans' in David Downes (ed.), *Crime and the City* (1989), pp. 11–20.

25. Anna Clark, 'Contested space: the public and private spheres in nineteenth-century Britain' *JBS* 35 (1996), p. 270.

26. Judith R. Walkowitz, *City of Dreadful Delight: Narratives of Sexual Danger in Late-Victorian London* (Chicago, 1992).

27. For example, in Middleton, Lancashire. S. D'Cruze, *Crimes of Outrage: Sex, Violence and Victorian Working Women* (1998), pp. 14–15, 138–139.

28. Gatrell, 'Crime, authority' p. 269.

29. T. Skyrme, *A History of the Justices of the Peace* (Chichester, 1991, 2 Vols), 2, p. 181; Ellen Ross, '"Fierce questions and taunts": married life in working-class London, 1870–1914' *FS* 8, 3 (1983), p. 590; Hammerton, *Cruelty and Companionship* pp. 47–56; J. Davis, '"A poor man's system of justice"; the London police courts in the second half of the nineteenth century' *HJ* 27 (1984), pp. 309–335; George Behlmer, 'Summary justice and working-class marriage in England, 1870–1940' *LHR* xii (1994), pp. 229–275.

30. D'Cruze, *Crimes of Outrage* p. 116; Rob Sindall, *Street Violence in the Nineteenth Century: Moral Panic or Real Danger?* (Leicester, 1990).

31. Carolyn A. Conley, *The Unwritten Law: Criminal Justice in Victorian Kent* (New York, 1991); D'Cruze, *Crimes of Outrage*.

32. J. Davis, 'A poor man's system of justice'; J. Davis, 'Prosecutions and their context: the use of the criminal law in later nineteenth-century London' in D. Hay and F. Snyder (eds.), *Policing and Prosecution in Britain, 1750–1850* (Oxford, 1989), pp. 379–426; Louise Jackson in this volume (Ch. 7).

33. D'Cruze, *Crimes of Outrage*.

34. J. White, *The Worst Street in North London: Campbell Bunk, Islington, Between the Wars* (1986), Ch. 6.

35. Pat Thane, *Foundations of the Welfare State* (1982), pp. 22–23; Geoffrey Finlayson, *Citizen, State and Social Welfare in Britain, 1830–1990* (Oxford, 1994).

36. E. Midwinter, *The Development of Social Welfare in Britain* (Buckingham, 1994), p. 72.

37. E. Ross, *Love and Toil; Motherhood in Outcast London, 1870–1918* (Oxford, 1993).

38. *Ibid.*, p. 69.

39. Finlayson, *Citizen, State and Social Welfare* p. 401.

40. *Ibid.*, pp. 67, 74–84.

41. Louise A. Jackson, *Child Sexual Abuse in Victorian England* (2000); Jan Lambertz, 'Feminists and the politics of wife-beating' in H. L. Smith (ed.), *British Feminism in the Twentieth Century* (1990), p. 46.

42. Thane, *Foundations* p. 42.

43. Midwinter, *Development of Social Welfare* p. 71.

44. Stephen Humphries, *Hooligans or Rebels? An Oral History of Working-Class Childhood and Youth 1889–1939* (Oxford, 1983), Ch. 1.

45. Elizabeth Stanko, *Everyday Violence: How Women and Men Experience Sexual and Physical Danger* (1990), pp. 5–7.

46. Midwinter, *Development of Social Welfare* p. 85.

47. Compare Nan Dreher, 'The virtuous and the verminous: turn-of-the-century moral panics in London's public parks' *Albion* 29 (1997), pp. 246–252.

48. A. Godenzi, 'What's the big deal? We are men and they are women' in Newburn and Stanko (eds.), *Just Boys* p. 136.

49. Elizabeth A. Stanko, 'Challenging the problem of men's individual violence' in *ibid.*, p. 43.

50. Roger Swift, 'Heroes or villains?: the Irish, crime, and disorder in Victorian England' *Albion* 29 (1997), p. 403.

51. *Ibid.*, p. 412.

52. *Ibid.*, p. 419.

53. L. Gordon, *Heroes of their Own Lives: The Politics and History of Family Violence: Boston 1880–1960* (1989), p. 227.

54. C. Chinn, *They Worked All Their Lives: Women of the Urban Poor in England, 1880–1939* (Manchester, 1988), Ch. 5; Hammerton, *Cruelty and Companionship* p. 46.

55. Andrew Davies in this volume (Ch. 4); also his '"These viragoes are no less cruel than the lads": young women, gangs and violence in later Victorian Manchester and Salford' *BJC* 39 (1999), pp. 72–89.

56. Gatrell, 'Crime, authority' p. 290.

57. John Archer (ed.), *Male Violence* (1994).

58. Stanko, 'Challenging the problem' p. 40.

59. R. Connell, *Gender and Power* (Cambridge, 1987), pp. 183–186.

60. J. A. Mangan and J. Walvin (eds.), *Manliness and Morality: Middle-Class Masculinity in Britain and America, 1800–1940* (Manchester, 1987); M. Roper and J. Tosh (eds.), *Manful Assertions: Masculinities in Britain since 1800* (1991).

61. Hammerton, *Cruelty and Companionship* pp. 82–101; Julie Early in this volume (Ch. 10); Wiener, 'The sad story of George Hall' p. 181.

62. Tony Jefferson, 'Theorising masculine subjectivity' in Newburn and Stanko (eds.), *Just Boys* p. 25.

63. James W. Messerschmidt, 'Schooling, masculinities and youth crime by white boys' in *Ibid.*, pp. 85–88; Kenneth Polk, 'Masculinity, honour and confrontational homicide' in *ibid.*, pp. 186, 188.

64. Pearson, 'A Jekyll in the Classroom'; Andrew Davies in this volume (Ch. 4).

65. For a helpful summary of theoretical approaches to considering masculine subjectivities see Jefferson, 'Theorising masculine subjectivity' pp. 10–31.

66. T. Newburn and Elizabeth Stanko, 'Introduction' in *ibid.*, p. 4.

67. Stevi Jackson, 'The social context of rape; sexual scripts and motivation' *WSIQ,* 1 (1978), pp. 27–39.

68. Jefferson, 'Theorising masculine subjectivity' p. 27.

69. Joanne Bailey, 'Power and privilege? Marital violence in the north of England, 1660–1800' unpublished paper, conference on 'Women, Gender and Interpersonal Violence', Leeds Metropolitan University, February 1999.

70. Liz Kelly, *Surviving Sexual Violence* (Cambridge, 1988).

71. D'Cruze, *Crimes of Outrage* pp. 19, 21.

72. For a philosophical treatment of issues around pain and harm see Elaine Scarry, *The Body in Pain: The Making and Unmaking of the World* (Oxford, 1985).

73. Stanko, 'Challenging the problem' p. 38.

74. D'Cruze, *Crimes of Outrage* p. 180.

PART I

The uses of violence

Domesticity and the problem of wifebeating in nineteenth-century Britain: working-class culture, law and politics[1]

ANNA CLARK

'Take heed of yoking yourselves with untamed heifers', the Revd William Secker warned young men looking for wives in the seventeenth century. He told them to choose hardworking, loving women who could be partners in life, but also firmly declared, 'The wife may be a sovereign in her husband's absence, but she must be subject in her husband's presence.'[2] By the nineteenth century, the softer domestic ideal of separate spheres prevailed. Husbands were to be breadwinners who supported and protected their wives, while wives were to stay at home, submissive and obedient, responsible for the smooth running of the household. Did this notion discourage wifebeating? This chapter will argue that, while the domestic ideal may have improved women's lives in some ways, it did not prevent domestic violence, and may even have excused it. The persistence of the patriarchal notion that husbands should rule the household, however softened by domesticity, could allow husbands to enforce their dominance with violence. As Methodist Adam Clarke declared, 'Superior strength gives the man domination, affection and subjection entitle the woman to love and protection.'[3] If a woman did not subject herself to her husband, she could be blamed for his battering.

During the seventeenth and eighteenth centuries, legal authorities allowed husbands to 'correct' their wives with moderate violence if they would not submit. But during the nineteenth century, wifebeating slowly became illegal. Did women owe this protection to the domestic ideal? To answer this question, this chapter will examine how women in the early nineteenth century took advantage of increasing legal disapproval of violence in general, in order to seek protection from battering. By the second half of the nineteenth century, the domestic ideal certainly inspired Parliament to pass specific laws against wifebeating, but these laws must also be understood as a response to working-class and feminist politics.

Domestic violence and working-class culture

While middle-class moralists originated the domestic ideal, working-class people had appropriated it for their own by mid-century. This ideal did, to be sure, represent an improvement over earlier marital norms. In the seventeenth and eighteenth centuries, plebeians believed marriages should be both companionate and patriarchal; husbands and wives should work together to support the family; yet ultimately, husbands should dominate their wives. The clash between husbands' desire to dominate and the assertiveness of wives, conscious of their important contribution to the family economy, could produce domestic violence. For instance, ballad-writer and collier David Love wrote that his wife 'strove to get the upper hand' but 'I . . . asserted my authority, which caused great contention'.[4]

Artisanal culture particularly could produce hostility toward women. Artisans fraternally bonded in their workplaces and clubs through heavy drinking, which robbed their families of income, and loosened inhibitions on violence. They faced competition from low-waged female labour, yet had to rely on their wives to help support the family. Domestic violence was less common among weavers, because whole families worked together at home. But when unemployment and low wages immiserated weavers, domestic violence increased.[5]

By the 1830s, radical working men denounced wifebeating as part of their larger effort to reform working-class culture and develop a disciplined working-class movement. Chartist John Watkins lamented, 'How many take that vengeance on themselves, or their wives and children, which they should take on their tyrants!'[6] Trade unionists promised women that, if they remained at home instead of competing with men at work, their husbands would bring home their wage instead of drinking it at the pub. This ideal restricted women's freedom and ignored the reality of their labour, but it did have certain advantages for women. Many women would rather stay at home than work ten hours a day in a factory, and they obviously preferred that their husbands be respectable, peaceful and sober, rather than drunken, violent and rough. By the 1860s, this ideal permeated popular culture: for instance, in his poem 'God Bless these Poor Wimmen that's Childer' [have children] Thomas Brierly, the popular Lancashire dialect poet, wrote,

> If t'maddest un'vilest o' men
> Wurn just made i' wimmen a fortneet [were just made into women a fortnight]
> They'd never beat wimmen again.[7]

But working-class people found that the ideal often contradicted reality. Working men often could not earn enough to be the breadwinner; working wives faced endless housework and childrearing, and often needed to bring in money for the family as well. The tensions between the ideal and the reality, and the difficulty of raising a family on low wages in poor housing conditions, could spark domestic violence. For instance, when a Glasgow tailor's wife told him to go look for work, he threatened to murder her.[8] When docker Michael McCarthy gave five shillings to his common-law wife, she scornfully commented, 'We are very rich – we owe three shillings for rent, and what are we to do with this small trifle?' Enraged, he demanded it back, and stabbed her when she refused.[9]

But it was not only unemployment or poverty that caused domestic violence, for employed men and even middle-class men were known to beat their wives. Rather, the ideal of domesticity itself could excuse violence. For instance, the popular song 'I should dearly like to marry' depicted the ideal wife as loving, patient, and a good wife and mother, but concludes,

> *She must always be good tempered, but never on me frown*
> *And thank me very kindly,*
> *If I chance to knock her down . . .*
> *And if I beat her with a poker*
> *She must never say a word.*[10]

The domestic ideal could excuse violence against those wives whom their husbands perceived as failing to fulfil their domestic responsibilities.[11] One working man, arriving home drunk and hungry, threw his wife down the stairs because she had not cooked his midday meal.[12] Charles McKay, a Glasgow hamcurer, stabbed his wife when she did not have breakfast ready for him.[13]

Many battered wives, however, did not passively accept wifebeating. Although a certain amount of 'rough usage' seems to have been considered normal among working-class husbands and wives, the ideals of marriage limited the extent of acceptable marital violence.[14] Conversely, a purely domestic role did not render women totally powerless, for separate spheres implied that women had agency, as well as responsibility, in running the household. As Shani D'Cruze writes, 'women's perceptions of their own social identities as household managers and defenders of their household's reputations . . . could form a basis for the complaints they brought to the courts about violence they considered to be illegitimate and unjustified'.[15] In her study of late nineteenth-century London, Ellen Ross portrays homes and streets divided into distinct male and female worlds, husbands and wives with separate social lives and financial responsibilities. But conflict erupted on the border between masculine and feminine space, when husbands interfered in the wives' domestic domain or wives tried to prevent husbands from spending their wages at the pub.[16]

When women were dependent on their husbands, they found it difficult to resist domestic violence and to demand help from magistrates. Wives who continued to engage in paid labour may have had a greater ability to assert themselves against violent husbands, although husbands still had a legal right to all their wives' earnings.[17] On trial for stabbing his estranged wife Phoebe, Abraham Moss asked her, 'Did I not bring up the children for thirty-one years, and provide for you in respectability, and with hardwork and honesty?' She retorted, 'I . . . stood in frost and snow with fruit to support my children – I supported them.'[18] However, married women's wage-earning came under increasing disapproval by the second half of the nineteenth century.

Wifebeating and the law in the nineteenth century

Until 1853, legal authorities did not decisively pronounce that wifebeating was illegal. In the eighteenth century, wives could swear out 'articles of the peace', similar to a restraining order, against violent husbands, but these documents were often ineffective in gaining help from authorities. The author of the most influential handbook for magistrates, Richard Burns, vaguely advised magistrates that 'some say' a man could 'correct' or 'chastise' his wife without forfeiting his sureties under an article of the peace.[19] The notion that a man could beat his wife with a stick as big as his thumb was not a legal precedent, but people widely believed it to be so.[20] Nonetheless, many women came to magistrates to charge their husbands with assaulting them; they had their own notion of justice, and believed they deserved protection from violent husbands. Magistrates could do little, however, partly because in general the laws against violence mandated only slight punishments for any assault short of rape or murder.

During the early nineteenth century, the legal system did begin to provide some protection for battered women because violence in general became less acceptable. The weakness of the laws against assaults began to threaten the legitimacy of the state as violent offenders escaped with light sentences. Inspired by the French revolution, radicals declared that the discrepancy between harsh penalties for property crimes and leniency toward violence proved that the law excluded all but the propertied from its benefits.[21] In response to these threats to state authority, Parliament passed

Lord Ellenborough's Act in 1803 which, for the first time, imposed death sentences on attempted murder and grievous bodily harm.

The state moved toward more extensive regulation of violence as the middle class, motivated by Evangelicalism and humanitarianism, demanded rational, efficient protection. Middle-class men rejected the old notion of honour and hierarchy defended by violence; instead, they espoused rationality and self-control, achieving manhood through hard work in the public sphere, rather than aggression within personal relations.[22] Furthermore, for the middle class, private morality necessarily accompanied public, political virtue. While they upheld the sanctity of their own homes, they believed that they should interfere in the private lives of working people, for the perceived disorder and crime in working-class families and communities threatened society as a whole. In response to these concerns, by the 1830s, police surveillance and long prison sentences replaced the threat of death as the means for the state to regulate violence.[23] By 1837, the death penalty was removed as the punishment for grievous bodily harm, in order to increase the prosecution and conviction rates for this offence.

The new protectionist intrusion into working-class lives had ambiguous consequences for women. The law now offered women potential protection from violence through the police and through greater sanctions against serious assaults. But it also diminished women's control over the prosecution process. And women's increasing economic dependency limited their ability to envision prison for their husbands. By the mid-nineteenth century, working-class wives were less likely to work outside of the home, and female occupations were scarce and miserably paid. Despite these constraints, some battered wives still struggled to use the law for their own ends. They found that different levels of the criminal justice system varied in their responsiveness to women; from the police, to the magistrates' courts, which settled cases or passed them on to the higher courts; finally to the Old Bailey, the London higher court where juries tried felony cases.

Battered women could now call upon the police for help during an assault, but the police, then as now, probably refused to interfere in most domestic violence cases. In 1834, the radical *Weekly Dispatch* complained of the 'inefficiency of the new police' who were nowhere to be seen when a husband chased his wife into the street and beat her with a poker.[24] Yet the working-class press also criticised the police for interfering in domestic relations. In 1830, the *Weekly Dispatch* indignantly exposed the 'over officiousness of the new police' who charged a man with 'quarrelling with his own wife!'[25] Regarding the police as outsiders, some women resented their attempts to interfere.

Women could bypass police constables, however, by going directly to the magistrates' courts for a warrant. Nineteenth-century Londoners in general and battered women in particular seem to have resorted to the magistrates' courts with enthusiasm. For instance, Elizabeth Cooney demanded protection one week after marriage because her husband 'tyrannised' her.[26] As Jennifer Davis writes, working-class people expected the magistrates' courts to provide them with justice on their own terms and regarded the legal system as oppressive when they did not.[27] In fact, the jurisdiction of the magistrates' courts over assaults was extended in 1828, due to popular demand, especially for 'disputes between man and wife'.[28] Although magistrates could now impose two-month gaol sentences for assault, they continued to focus on mediation rather than punishment. In 1837, a magistrate called Rawlinson told Martha Taylor to reconcile with her husband, a journeyman paper hanger, after he beat her. She declared in a passion, 'Make it up! Never! I'll suffer death first!' When asked what she wished the magistrate to do, she asked the magistrate to bind him up 'neck and heels to keep the peace, or let him go to prison if he can't find bail'. The magistrate, however, only bound him over to keep the peace on his own recognisance, asserting there were 'faults on both sides'.[29] As this example reveals, the magistrates varied in their willingness to provide protection. Furthermore, even if the full sentence were imposed, two months was not long for very serious assaults.

Although women could prosecute husbands who committed grievous bodily harm in the Old Bailey Sessions, where judges could impose sentences of several years' duration, they seemed reluctant to do so. Old Bailey judges were concerned with demonstrating state control over violence and crime, and they intimidated battered women. However, in cases of severe grievous bodily harm, the police could also now prosecute violent husbands, even if their victims were unwilling, so that women who earlier would not have sought protection were now forced to testify in the well-documented Old Bailey Sessions. Even if women initially wished to prosecute, the great expense and trouble, the likelihood that their husbands would promise reform in the intervening time, and their economic dependency often produced an ambivalence which comes through in the Old Bailey testimony of battered wives. For instance, when William New was tried for stabbing his wife Sarah, she testified 'I do not think he meant to hurt me', and refused even to appear before the magistrate. It was the police who arrested him and committed him for trial. Her ambivalence may have had something to do with the fact that she was out of work at the time, and therefore needed his support.[30] Bridget Barrett, whose husband kicked her while she was pregnant, testified, 'I know he did not intend to injure me – I wish to grant his pardon as much as possible – I have a child five years old, and we are dependent on him.'[31]

Women's interests in gaining separations and the court's interests in imposing punishment conflicted. Ellen Donovan declared, 'I do not wish to hurt him – I only want peace and quiet and a maintenance.' But her testimony also reveals a typical conflict between self-blame and desire for revenge. At first she said that his beating, which put her in the hospital for two weeks, was 'perhaps . . . my fault as much as his', but after he insulted her in the trial, she burst out, 'he is a great murderer, and I should like him punished . . . and I should not have given him in charge now but for the women in the same house'.[32] Alone, she could not have stood up for herself, but the other women did not want to see a violent husband go free.

By the 1840s, the reluctance of wives to prosecute and juries to convict for domestic violence threatened to undermine the legitimacy of the law, complained law-and-order advocates in a public newspaper debate.[33] *The Times* noted indignantly that a man who beat and tried to strangle his wife was convicted only of common assault, though he had previously threatened to kill her.[34] The *Daily News* pointed out 'how much safer it is to stab one's wife than to defraud one's master'.[35] However, the solution for this injustice, according to the journalists, was to remove domestic violence from the conventions of the common law of manslaughter and murder, and increase chivalrous state control over prosecutions. Some commentators felt frustrated at the reluctance of women to prosecute violent husbands, and wished to take this decision out of women's hands. 'A Lover of Justice' wrote that 'it is worth serious consideration on the part of legislators to see whether a law may not be framed to meet these cases – to remove from the tender hands of the wife the power of shielding a ruffianly husband from the offended laws'.[36] The *Daily News* argued that wifekilling should be defined as manslaughter because juries refused to return verdicts of murder despite clear evidence of express malice; if the crime were defined as manslaughter, argued the paper, at least there would be a greater chance of a conviction.[37] Manslaughter was homicide caused by provocation, and did not incur the death penalty. By defining all wifekillings as manslaughter, this proposal implicitly judged wifekilling not as a violation of an individual's right but as an excessive use of normal domestic violence. A husband's duty was to protect, and a wife's to submit. If he killed her, it could be excused as provocation, and the full public sanction would not fall on him.

In 1853 the reluctance of women to prosecute, and juries to convict, in the higher courts, and the inadequacy of the sentences magistrates could impose, impelled legislators to adopt the Aggravated Assaults on Women and Children Act, which allowed magistrates to impose six-month sentences for such crimes. But the Act had a limited effect because wives could not fully prosecute their husbands if they were financially dependent on them. When they appeared before the magistrates' courts, sometimes mangled and bloody, they still testified reluctantly. Women apologised for their husbands' beatings by saying 'he was in liquor', or 'he was not in the habit of ill-using her'. One woman began with these excuses, explaining her injury by saying her husband's foot 'slipped' on her stomach, but later admitted he had kicked her and often beat her. The magistrates' action in committing him for six months would protect her from assault, but also deprive her of a breadwinner.[38] Furthermore, the domestic ideal promised protection only to those women seen as 'obedient, submissive, and incapable of defending herself', as Carolyn Conley observes.[39] If a woman asserted her own rights, magistrates would stigmatise her as a shrew who did not deserve protection. Of course, in order to escape a violent husband, a woman needed those very qualities of defiance, economic resources, a sense of self-worth and independence which alienated magistrates.[40] As a result, the Act was mainly used to punish violence committed by men on women and children unrelated to them.[41]

The politics of wifebeating

In the second half of the nineteenth century, moral concerns about wifebeating became symbolically linked to political debates over the citizenship of women and working-class men. Parliament overcame its long opposition to interfering in the private sphere of the home by defining wifebatterers as working-class brutes who did not deserve the right to privacy and their victims as passive creatures who could not determine their own fates. During working-class agitation, conservatives often attacked the morality of the working class in order to discredit their claims to suffrage.[42] If working men were irresponsible husbands, they could not claim the privilege of the vote. The conservative religious journal *The British Workman*, dedicated to turning working men away from radical action, told them,

> Gentlemen, there are two ways of governing a family: the first is by force, the other is by mild and vigilant authority . . . . A husband deserves to lose his empire altogether, by making an attempt to force it with violence.[43]

Working men, therefore, had to earn the privilege of control over women, just as the journal admonished them to prove their respectability before they demanded political rights.

Middle and upper-class legislators and moralists presented themselves as the protectors of poor wives against violent husbands. In an editorial on wifebeating *The Times* fulminated against the lower classes as 'a race of barbarians, ignorant alike of their duty to God and man, and stimulating the most ferocious passions by the most brutal excesses'. It called for education to 'elevate' the lower orders, but went on to say that 'if we will not teach we must punish, and the lessons which ought to be impressed by reason must be inculcated by fear' in the form of the flogging of wifebeaters.[44] The wifebeater was now a brutal other of the urban lower depths, who could only be treated with terror, not rational regulation. In 1856, a Parliamentary measure allowing the flogging of wifebeaters stirred up public indignation at 'unmanly brutes', but the women of Leicester opposed it, fearing it would inspire men to even worse violence and, therefore, deter women from prosecuting.[45]

Feminists developed entirely different arguments to oppose wifebeating by pointing out the flaws in the domestic ideal of separate spheres. In the 1840s, women such as Caroline Norton and Caroline Napier tried to critique violent husbands without entirely undermining domesticity itself. The polemicist Caroline Norton, who herself had had to face her husband's threats, took on the popular notion that husbands 'govern by law, [wives] by persuasion'.[46] Norton demonstrated that, if a wife could not persuade her husband to stop being violent, she had no status in law. When a man beat his wife, she argued, 'he is no longer the administrator and exponent of the law, but its direct opponent'.[47] Another middle-class writer on women's issues, Caroline Napier, declared that a false notion of male authority 'leads men to indulge their tempers at the expense of female happiness, who would shrink from doing so, if they saw their conduct in the light of injustice, or discerned that their claim to submission rested on no better basis than force'. She asserted that women had the right to protection from abuse on the basis of justice, not merely humanity.[48] But both Norton and Napier persisted in upholding the principle that the male is the head of the household and rightfully dominant. Thus, wifebeating could be criticised without challenging patriarchy itself.

In contrast, as Lambertz states, feminists such as Harriet Taylor Mill and John Stuart Mill asserted that women lacked adequate protection from the law because they were deprived of their rights as citizens.[49] An editorial in the *Morning Chronicle* by Taylor and Mill explained women's reluctance to prosecute by declaring that 'punishments are so inadequate women feel it is useless to pursue a case'. The editorial pointed out that 'at present it is very well known that women, in the lower ranks of life, do not expect justice from a bench or jury of the male sex'.[50] Mill and Taylor also critiqued marriage itself, for as another editorial proclaimed 'the vow to protect thus confers a license to kill'.[51] And Harriet Taylor Mill went beyond the sexual contract of marriage, declaring that women would only be safe if they did not depend economically on their husbands.[52]

By the 1870s, women in the suffrage movement and reformers such as Frances Power Cobbe began agitating for more effective protection for battered wives. In 1872, Lydia Becker claimed that women needed the vote, among other reasons, to protect them from wifebeating: 'a cry of distress has gone up from around the land.'[53] They repudiated suggestions such as flogging, instead favouring separation orders which would allow women an independent maintenance so that they could escape violent men. Interestingly enough, Frances Power Cobbe was joined in her campaign by Henry Labouchere, a paternalist reformer angry at the class bias of the legal system. Together, they were instrumental in persuading Parliament to pass an act in 1878 which did allow such maintenance orders.[54] Women resorted enthusiastically to the courts to demand separations.

The 1878 Act did not solve the problem of wifebeating, however. Many jurists and magistrates continued to believe that battered wives had provoked their husbands and refused to allow maintenance or separation orders. To justify such actions, jurists reasserted patriarchal authority against the feminist critique of marriage. Liberal but authoritarian jurist James Fitzjames Stephens, for instance, linked force in government to a rigid patriarchy in the home. For Stephens, marriage was parallel to the government in its ultimate dependence on force. He argued that since men were stronger, they should have authority, while wives should submit: 'submission and protection are correlative, withdraw the one and the other is lost, and force will assert itself a hundred times more harshly.'[55] By these statements, he implicitly defended as acceptable what feminists had pointed out as the flaw in the theory of chivalry (wifebeating) and denied women's claim for the vote.

Conclusion

During the nineteenth century, the problem of wifebeating was ameliorated somewhat by a replacement of older more brutally patriarchal attitudes which blatantly sanctioned wifebeating, with a newer ideology of separate spheres in which men were to love and protect their wives, and wives were to submit affectionately. Working-class radicals tried to discourage domestic violence among their communities by promulgating this more harmonious, domestic model of marriage. Many battered wives refused to accept their husbands' violence and demanded protection from the courts. The legal system began to provide more avenues for the prosecution of wifebeaters, first, as part of a wider effort to control violence in society, and second, with specific measures such as the 1853 Act mandating six-month sentences for assaults on women and children.

The domestic ideal of separate spheres, however, mandated female submission and dependence; factors which exacerbated domestic violence and made it difficult for women to seek help. Hard times made it difficult for men to live up to the breadwinner ideal, and caused domestic tensions. Middle and upper-class legislators attempted to criticise wifebeaters as working-class brutes in order to portray themselves as chivalrous protectors of poor women. However, by doing so, they also deflected women's and working men's claims to citizenship, and ignored the marital problems of the middle and upper classes. Feminists, however, pointed out that what women needed was not chivalrous protection, but the economic independence and legal guarantees which would enable them to leave violent men.

While Nancy Tomes cites statistics to show that wifebeating declined considerably during the late nineteenth century, as the means for prosecuting husbands expanded, Ellen Ross argues that wifebeating continued to be very common in the late nineteenth century, and A. James Hammerton does not see firm evidence of a decline until 1914.[56] Women's economic dependence on men and the persistence of a domestic ideology mandating their submission limited the effectiveness of legal changes of the nineteenth century in significantly reducing the incidence of domestic violence.

Notes

1. Some of the material in this chapter has appeared, in different frameworks, in Anna Clark, 'Humanity or justice? Wifebeating and the law in the eighteenth and nineteenth centuries' in Carol Smart (ed.), *Regulating Womanhood: Historical Essays on Marriage, Motherhood and Sexuality* (1992) and Anna Clark, *The Struggle for the Breeches: Gender and the Making of the British Working Class* (Berkeley, 1995).

2. Revd William Secker, *A Wedding Ring, Fit for the Finger, Laid Open in a Sermon, Preached at a Wedding in St. Edmond's* (Glasgow, n.d.) in John Cheap, *The Chapman's Library* (Glasgow, 1877), pp. 11, 20; see also William Whateley's *Directions for Married Persons* (1763 [1619]), p. 47.

3. Adam Clarke, *Christian Theology, with a Life of the Author* by Samuel Dunn (2nd edn., 1835), p. 299.

4. David Love, *Life and Adventures* (Nottingham, 1823), p. 37.

5. For a detailed development of this argument see Anna Clark, *The Struggle for the Breeches* Ch. 5.

6. *ECC* 1 (1841), p. 49.

7. Thomas Brierly, 'God bless these poor wimmen that's childer' in John Harland (ed.), *Lancashire Lyrics* (1866). See also A. James Hammerton, *Cruelty and Companionship: Conflict in Nineteenth-Century Married Life* (1992), p. 32.

8. *The Thistle, or Literary and Police Reporter* 14 May 1831.

9. OBSP Sept. 1830, Vol. 3, p. 767.

10. 'I should dearly like to marry' in London, British Library, Collection of broadsides, 11621.k.4, fol. 326.

11. See also Nancy Tomes, '"Torrents of Abuse": crimes of violence between working-class men and women in London, 1840–1875' *JSH* 11 (1978), p. 331; Jan Lambertz and Pat Ayers, 'Marriage relations, money and violence in working-class Liverpool' in Jane Lewis (ed.), *Labour and Love* (Oxford, 1986), p. 197; Shani D'Cruze, *Crimes of Outrage: Sex, Violence, and Victorian Working Women* (1998), p. 68.

12. *TN* 30 July 1820.

13. *GEPSR* 24 Dec. 1842.

14. D'Cruze, *Crimes of Outrage* p. 75.

15. *Ibid.*, p. 80.

16. Ellen Ross, *Love and Toil: Motherhood in Outcast London, 1870–1918* (New York, 1993), p. 576.

17. Leah Leneman argues that as urbanisation increased working opportunities for women in late eighteenth-century Scotland, they became more able to protest domestic violence. 'A tyrant and tormenter: wifebeating in Scotland in the seventeenth and eighteenth centuries' *C&C* 12 (1997), p. 40.

18. OBSP 1840, Vol. 4, p. 922.

19. Richard Burns, *Justice of the Peace* (1776, 4 Vols), 4, p. 268. For a full discussion of the legal precedents, see Maeve E. Doggett, *Marriage, Wife-Beating and the Law in Victorian England* (Columbia, S.C., 1993), p. 15.

20. This notion was attributed to Judge Francis Buller, known as 'Judge Thumb'. It was not a legal precedent, but may have been a quip he 'blurted out' which reflected his general attitude. See Alan Simpson, *Biographical Dictionary of the Common Law* (1984), p. 88 and William C. Townsend, *Lives of Twelve Eminent Judges* (1846).

21. Peter Linebaugh, 'The Tyburn riots against the surgeons' Douglas Hay *et al.* (eds.), *Albion's Fatal Tree* (New York, 1975), p. 65.

22. Leonore Davidoff and Catherine Hall, *Family Fortunes. Men and Women of the English Middle Class* (1987), p. 21.

23. Sir Leon Radzinowicz, *A History of the English Criminal Law* (1948, 4 Vols), 1, p. 583.

24. *WD* 21 Dec. 1834.

25. *WD* 12 Dec. 1830.

26. *WD* 25 July 1841.

27. Jennifer Davis, '"A Poor Man's System of Justice"; the London police courts in the second half of the nineteenth century' *HJ* 29 (1984), p. 310.

28. Commissioners on Police, Report, PP (1828) Vol. 6, p. 147.

29. *LdnM* 22 Jan. 1837.

30. OBSP 20 Sept. 1844, Vol. 3, p. 771.

31. OBSP 1 Dec. 1842, Vol. 1 (1842–1843), pp. 16–18.

32. OBSP 6 April 1843, Vol. 2, p. 994.

33. Margaret May, 'Violence in the family; an historical perspective' in J. P. Marton (ed.), *Violence in the Family* (Chichester, 1978), p. 143.

34. *Times* 24 Aug. 1846.

35. *DN* 24 Aug. 1846.

36. *RN* 21 Dec. 1851.

37. *DN* 28 Aug. 1846, also *Times* 22 July 1847.

38. *Times* 5 Jan. 1854.

39. Carolyn Conley, *The Unwritten Law. Criminal Justice in Victorian Kent* (New York, 1991), p. 71.

40. For a discussion of magistrates' attitudes see Hammerton, *Cruelty and Companionship* p. 62.

41. *Returns relating to Assaults on Women and Children, from Each of the Metropolitan Police Courts* PP liii (1854–1855).

42. For a fuller discussion of these themes see Anna Clark, 'Gender, class, and nation: franchise reform in the long nineteenth century' in James Vernon (ed.), *Rereading the Constitution* (Cambridge, 1996).

43. *BW* 1 Oct. 1855.

44. *Times* 20 Aug. 1852.

45. J. M. Kaye, 'Outrages on Women' *NBR* 25 (1856), p. 256.

46. J. J. S. Wharton, *An Exposition of the Law relating to the Women of England, showing their Rights, Remedies and Responsibilities in Every Position of Law* (1853), p. 467, quoting Lord Kaimes.

47. Caroline Norton, 'English Laws for Women' in *Selected Writings of Caroline Norton* (New York, 1978), p. 167.

48. Caroline Napier, *Women's Rights and Duties* (London, 1844), p. 201.

49. Jan Lambertz, 'The politics and economics of family violence, from the late nineteenth century to 1948' (Manchester University M.Phil., 1984), p. 80.

50. *MornC* 28 Oct. 1846.

51. *MornC* 28 Aug. 1851.

52. Harriet Taylor Mill, 'The enfranchisement of women' in A. Rossi (ed.), *Essays on Sex Equality: John Stuart Mill and Harriet Taylor* (Chicago, 1970), p. 105.

53. Lydia Becker, 'The political disabilities of women' *Westeminster Review* Jan. 1872 in Jane Lewis (ed.), *Before the Vote was Won; Arguments for and against Women's Suffrage* (1987), p. 118.

54. Hammerton, *Cruelty and Companionship* p. 65.

55. James Fitzjames Stephens, *Liberty, Equality, Fraternity* (2nd edn., 1874), p. 284.

56. Tomes, 'Torrents of abuse' p. 345; Ellen Ross, ' "Fierce questions and taunts": married life in working-class London, 1870–1914' *FS* 8, 3 (1983), p. 590; Hammerton, *Cruelty and Companionship* p. 41.

CHAPTER TWO

'Men behaving badly'?: masculinity and the uses of violence, 1850–1900[1]

JOHN E. ARCHER

Most interpersonal violence was, and is, carried out by men and most of their victims have been or are male. These seemingly obvious facts have not attracted much academic attention from sociologists, criminologists, psychologists or historians. Male-on-male violence has been assumed or taken for granted. Philips, Emsley and Conley, for example, all address the theme of violence, but the closest any of them come to gendering explicitly violent behaviour is when they consider domestic and sexual violence.[2] Many of the chapters in this book provide ample testimony to men's violence against women and children. The meaning and significance of that violence will be different from male violence directed at other men. Moreover, male-on-male violence was, as will be shown, remarkably varied both in terms of location – street, home, pub, workplace and, in rural areas, game covers – and in terms of relationships – family members, work mates, figures of authority and total strangers. This very variety probably accounts both for the lack of research on the subject and the acceptance of male violence. To put it simply, violence is very much a male attribute, a fact feminist historians have long since known and researched. But when men hit, stab, kick and shoot other men their actions may also be casting light on another under-researched theme, that of masculinity or masculinities. Unlike Roper and Tosh's *Manful Assertions* this chapter will be examining largely, but not exclusively, working-class men and notions of working-class masculinity and manliness which often diverged from middle-class conceptions in the second half of the nineteenth century.[3]

It is notoriously difficult for historians to quantify the amount of male-on-male violence.[4] First, criminal statistics in this country only date back to 1805 and, even then, they only enumerate crimes coming before the upper courts, such as the assizes and quarter sessions. The more frequent forms of assaults and woundings which came before the magistrates' courts were officially counted from 1857. These summary offences did not require trial by jury. Offences against the person ranged from murder and manslaughter at one extreme, to common assault and intimidation at the other. When compared with the more common offences against property, offences against the person represented only a small percentage of all offences reported or prosecuted.

Philips and Wiener found that 90 per cent of those committed for trial for crimes against the person were men.[5] Nowadays, aggravated assaults by men in the USA and Great Britain range between 86 and 91 per cent.[6] The figures would appear, therefore, to change little over time, but variations could and did occur between one city and another, and between one year and another. In Liverpool, for example, summary and indictable violent offences perpetrated by men were in the order of 83 per cent between 1850–1900; the remaining 17 per cent suggests a relatively high level of female violence.

All these figures omit to tell us the other crucial detail, namely the sex of the victims. Hardly any official government criminal statistics exist for this period which actually identify the victim's gender. However one parliamentary paper, *Reports to the Secretary of State for the Home Department on the State of the Law Relating to Brutal Assaults* identifies and differentiates the number of convictions for summary and indictable assaults on men, and on women and children between 1870 and 1874. Although these figures are incomplete, the percentage of brutal assaults on men in the first five years of the 1870s was 62 per cent.[7] Even this report, however, failed to identify the gender of the assailants. The surest way of determining the gender of both victims and assailants is to research magistrates' court records for minor assaults and the assize and quarter sessions records for the more serious cases of interpersonal violence.

Quantifying crime cannot overcome one fundamental problem – the dark figure. Historians deal with reported crime but, as we know from research conducted on domestic and sexual crimes of violence, much criminal violence went unreported and hence unprosecuted. Even today, crimes of sexual violence that come to the attention of the police and courts represent a minority of such cases that are actually perpetrated. Male-on-male violence was probably more under- and unreported than domestic violence for reasons which are, in part, historical and bound up with notions of masculinity.

Prior to the nineteenth century, male violence was frequently not prosecuted since men were expected to defend their honour, status and manhood through fighting. Only towards the end of the eighteenth century and the beginning of the nineteenth, do we see male violent behaviour being increasingly frowned upon and prosecuted. This growing intolerance was reflected not only in the increasing number of prosecutions but also in changes in punishment for assaults. Short prison sentences, rather than financial compensation to victims, became the norm. This growing social intolerance towards male violence, it has been argued, led to an increasing criminalisation of men during the nineteenth century. Violence is, thus, a historical concept which changes over time.[8]

Deeply embedded beliefs, attitudes and values with regard to a man's right to fight remained evident, even though the law proscribed such violent acts. Moreover, these residual beliefs were held not only by the working classes but even by some of those in positions of authority such as magistrates, judges and the police. The scales of the criminal justice system could be weighted in favour of a defendant who behaved in traditionally accepted male ways. Neither the newspapers nor the courts necessarily labelled violent men as evil, nor branded them as working-class roughs. Men perceived to be respectable and in white-collar occupations could, thus, end up in courts without losing their respectability. Although duelling, with its complex codes of male honour, had effectively disappeared by 1850, the idea of the duel lingered on. However, it was increasingly ridiculed. Through his choice of language and ironic tone, this reporter made it plain how he felt about the topic. 'Two gentlemen' from 'the delightful suburbs of Ben Johnson Street' (one of the roughest streets in Liverpool) fought over 'a well-known basket girl (street trader). The choice of weapons, that of a life-preserver and a pair of knuckle-dusters lacked the style and class of pistols or swords, the preferred weapons of officers and gentlemen.'[9]

Working-class combatants possessed their own codes of honour and manner of fighting known as 'the fair fight' or 'up and down fight'. The crucial ingredients were that the fight was mutually agreed upon, no weapons were used, and that only two combatants were involved. Such fights could be almost formal affairs. In 1896 neighbours Edward Wilson and James Duxbury fought because a physical dispute between their respective wives had been cut short by the intervention of the police. Later, after an altercation in a pub, the two men went to a coach builder and sought his permission to have 'a friendly set-to' in his stables. The fight, one eyewitness at the coroner's court recalled, 'was more hugging and falling together' than punching, and ended after five rounds. They left the stable by separate exits and went to their respective homes where Wilson complained of a serious injury to his abdomen. His bowel had ruptured during the fight. All the witnesses agreed the fight was a 'fair one' but the coroner's jury returned a verdict of manslaughter which led to Duxbury's arrest. The case was later dismissed and Duxbury discharged because Wilson had initially issued the challenge and had forced Duxbury to respond to the verbal insults of 'cur' and 'coward'.[10] It was not unusual for cases to be dismissed in court because 'a fair stand-up fight took place', but in another case, the Liverpool stipendiary magistrate told Stephen M'Dermot, charged with stabbing another man, 'If you fellows would confine yourselves to the use of your fists, it would be a good thing for the town . . . . If you had used your fists I might have discharged you; but I wish all you fellows to understand that as soon as ever you use a knife you shall be dealt with according to the law.'[11]

The notion of men, stripped to the waist, fighting fairly with clenched fists within a circle formed by their peers, and then walking away afterwards with honour restored all- round, contains a number of mythical qualities if the evidence from the nineteenth-century courts is anything to go by. What may have started out as a fair fight could degenerate into a stabbing and wounding case very rapidly, if one of the combatants appeared to be gaining the upper hand. When in Liverpool in 1872 two men named Chambers and Derricott moved their quarrel from the pub out into the street, they were watched and supported by a group of sailors and dock labourers. During the fight Chamber's 'backer' or second called out that his man 'was not getting fair play' and invited his friends to remove their belts and beat the crowd back to form a larger circle. These actions led to a stabbing fatality and a more general fight. In another case in 1896, a day of quarrelling and sparring between two labourers culminated with Robert Devine calling out to John Donnolly, 'If you want to fight me, come now and fight fair.' Both men drew weapons from their pockets; a stick and an open knife. Crucial eye witness reports of Devine shouting, 'Come on, Donnolly, come on', before being stabbed in the neck by Donnolly were enough to get the charge reduced from murder to manslaughter.[12]

Bare-knuckle fighting was considered 'manly' and 'English' compared to foreigners' supposedly devious and underhand use of knives. The Irish too were thought to prefer weapons to fists. Whether these beliefs were more pronounced in a port like Liverpool, which was visited by thousands of sailors and immigrants every year, than in inland towns is difficult to judge. The idea of the fair fight was kept alive by the belief that the English placed a high value on human life and, as a consequence, preferred to use fists which only bruised. In defending an Argentinian sailor who had stabbed a German with 'a long Spanish knife', his counsel maintained, 'foreigners too frequently settled their quarrels with knives, and unfortunately did not look on life so seriously as Englishmen did'.[13] Englishmen who resorted to such weapons were considered cowards. English xenophobia underpinned one of the worst nineteenth-century Lancashire cases of wounding with intent to commit grievous bodily harm. Colliers from St Helens made an extraordinarily vicious and racist attack on an eighty-year-old Irishman and his wife. Shouting, 'kill the whole Irish lot', they knocked out the old man's eye,

44

poured hot lime into the socket, and forced lime up his nostrils and down his throat. Justice Addison saw these as more the kind of acts 'done amongst Red Indians than people residing in this civilized country and calling themselves Christians'.[14]

Racism was also apparent in assaults on black seamen like John Williams, who got struck by 'a black bottle' for singing 'nigger songs' in a pub. In a mutual altercation between a Brazilian seaman and a black sailor, the former was reported as saying, 'Look at the young Zulu coming.' This was met with the reply, 'If I'm a Zulu, you are a Diego', apparently 'a term of reproach amongst sailors'. Racism might also be associated with 'coloured seaman' John Charles's claim that he stabbed a dock labourer in self-defence because 'a crowd of "them" turned on him and would not let him pass'.[15] Sectarian assaults between the Irish Catholics and indigenous poor also took place in many towns and cities after 1850. Whilst such assaults tended to peak around St Patrick's day on 17 March and 12 July when Orangemen celebrated the Battle of the Boyne, evidence of underlying tensions throughout the year exists. This can be complicated for historians by the fact that inter-Irish disputes could take place in which groups of men from one county might fight another group from another Irish county. Many Irish rows also involved women as well as men.[16]

The choice of weapons in attacks on men by men was not, it could be argued, specially selected. As studies of domestic violence have demonstrated, drunken men or men acting on sudden impulse either used their fists or selected the nearest item to hand, like a poker. The same observation could be made of male-on-male violence, the only difference being that, because violence occurred in many different locations such as the workplace, street, pub and so forth, men used a wider range of offensive weapons – not only knives but also cotton hooks by dockers, shovels and hammers by labourers, bottles and glasses by drinkers. Virtually all nineteenth-century men carried either penknives or tobacco knives and, if seamen, sheath knives. No laws existed against the carrying of knives. Firearms were also legal until 1920, when the Firearms Act restricted their availability and use. In large towns, such as Manchester and Liverpool, a surprising number of firearms were both in circulation and used in offences against the person. Many Liverpool publicans, for example, kept revolvers behind the counter, presumably to frighten aggressive drunks into leaving the premises.

Lancashire was infamous for one particular form of fighting known as 'purring'. 'The common tendency' reported the *Liverpool Mercury*, 'to substitute the clog for the fist in Lancashire has no parallel in any other county in the kingdom.'[17] In August 1874 alone, seventeen cases of kicking came before the county courts. Judges and magistrates often punished defendants who had kicked in a similar fashion to those who had used knives. It was seen as a 'brutal' and 'unfair' method of combat that could kill or maim. In the 1874 Tithebarn Street murder in Liverpool in which three 'roughs' kicked Richard Morgan to death, the assault lasted about ten minutes. No one in the large, holiday crowd intervened to save Morgan, even though cries of 'the man is kicked to death' were heard.[18] The other formidable working-class weapon, and one again carried by all men, was the leather belt. Scuttling gangs, as Andrew Davies has shown, placed great store on their highly ornamental belts which, when used as weapons, were swung with the buckle end inflicting the damage, usually to the face. Michael Mullen, for example, received a compound fracture to the back of his skull when set upon by four men wielding their belts.[19]

Why were men violent and what situations led to violent confrontation? Whilst historians cannot enter contemporary criminological debates centred around psychology or the 'nature versus nurture' argument, it is possible to deploy insights based on present day studies.[20] One concept, the notion of the 'real man' who is tough, capable of taking care of himself in a fight, defends his mates and protects his family through violence if need be, can be identified in many nineteenth-century court cases. Man as the protector may seem cruelly ironic given the subject matter of other essays in this book, but evidently that is how some men viewed themselves. When Patrick Scholes, for example, came into his daughter's house and found his son-in-law 'ill-using' her, he hit him about the head.[21] In a more tragic episode, James Hanney asked his wife for another sixpence for more drink on returning home from the pub. This she refused and was assailed with offensive language and a chimney ornament. Hanney's adult son asked his father to be quiet, which only further enraged him. In the ensuing fight out in the court, the son knifed his father, who died six days later.[22] In another case, George Sheldon took exception to his father's advertisement in the local press which announced his separation from his mother and his lack of responsibility for any of her debts. In a very cool encounter at a pub doorway, George asked his father, Thomas, 'What does my mother owe you?' The contemptuous answer of 'who are you?' from his father led George to shout, 'I am a man, and am come to know.' In the ensuing struggle he shot at his father with a revolver, bought especially for the confrontation. Here, defence of the family extended beyond protection from physical assault and could include, as in one example, an attack on an employer by the brother of a woman whom he had sacked. Intervention in family rows tended to come from the immediate family circle or a close neighbour, whereas interference from strangers in any fight between men and women was unusual and dangerous. When Daniel Caine told a man whom he found beating a woman, 'it was a shame to ill-treat women', the incident culminated in his being knifed by the man's son.[23]

Acts of male violence contain many different meanings, and messages, and a single assault might well be motivated by more than one impulse. Attacks on figures of authority (policemen, bailiffs or estate agents for example), might involve a combination of saving face, protecting oneself or family and asserting the right to stand on a street corner. Such authority figures could be viewed as a challenge to a man's masculinity which had to be confronted and, if necessary, beaten. This brings out an important characteristic of male violence, namely that men regard violence as a solution to a problem; arguments could, in fact, be cut short and ended with a punch, kick or a stab. In this context the outcome of the fight is not necessarily relevant. So long as the man was seen to fight, his status and role as a man were assured. Meeting the challenge and confronting the danger were important. A man named Fitzpatrick successfully prevented a bailiff from entering his house and kicked him in the street. The following day, the bailiff returned with five colleagues and two police constables who proceeded to load up a cart with Fitzpatrick's furniture. Workers from a neighbouring steel works came out in force, beat the police and bailiffs and rescued the furniture. The police, determined to arrest one of the ringleaders, went in force to the steel works where they were attacked by 20 to 30 men carrying red-hot iron bars. What had started out as a standard distraint of goods ended with two men being sentenced to twenty years' penal servitude. This unusually heavy sentence contrasts sharply with the three years' penal servitude William Blacklodge received for stabbing two bailiffs who had come for goods to pay off a mere £2 back rent.[24]

During the nineteenth century, scenes of confrontation and challenge between local men and the police most frequently took place on the city streets. In his seminal articles, Storch outlined the hostility to the police from the time of their inception in the 1830s and 1840s and their continuing unpopularity into the post-1850 period.[25] High levels of anti-police violence were often triggered when urban police attempted to stop crowds of working-class men from congregating on the streets. Such confrontations addressed the fundamental question of who controlled local neighbourhoods. Thus, the police forces' 'move on' policy contained the potential for serious trouble. Police constable Stratton, while patrolling the notoriously tough Scotland Road area of Liverpool, ordered 'a large assemblage of roughs' standing at a street corner to move on. One man, Roberts, objected, knocked down the constable and stabbed him five times in the neck and head. Roberts, it should be noted, fought the constable on his own and in front of his mates. Contemporary criminologists have argued that men readily take up a fight or a challenge if there is an audience of male friends present. It seems that Roberts was attempting to enhance his reputation among his peers as a 'hard' man.[26] In a city like Liverpool, with its high levels of casual labour, underemployment, slum housing and deep poverty, men had few avenues open to them for gaining status, reputation and self-esteem. The local press saw such 'street cornermen' as 'loafers', 'roughs' and even 'gorillas', 'for they more resemble such than human beings'. Many things about these men upset the press and the respectable inhabitants of the city, not least their lack of obvious employment, their street gambling and their loud, insulting and 'foul language'. These 'man-hawks' stood watching, eyeing up passers by, weighing up their chances to insult, mock, fight or rob. As a group they were probably responsible for much stranger violence, although their strength was such that they could attack their more law-abiding and equally poor neighbours with impunity.[27]

Analysis of cornermen and roughs establishes how seemingly trivial incidents and banter could escalate into fatal quarrels. As journalist Hugh Shimmin reported, 'the transition from a coarse word or a ribald jest to a kick, from a poker to a knife, are made with alarming rapidity'.[28] Through their actions and words, cornermen would appear to have been inviting a violent confrontation. Violence was to some extent fun; it was sport with which to display one's toughness. The scenario for the confrontation could be quite insignificant, like helping oneself to someone else's chips, or a push on the pavement. 'He shoved against me and knocked me off the footwalk', complained Stanley Ralph, 'and I struck him.' When two men pushed against James Burns one Saturday night, after remonstrating with them Burns was stabbed in the stomach. Nowhere is the laying down of the challenge with a provocative act more explicit than in the knocking or pushing off of someone's cap or hat.[29] Such behaviour was known as 'bonneting' and was sometimes a prelude to a street robbery.

Violence in this context was instrumental; it was being deployed for a robbery. Of all the forms of interpersonal violence, robbery with violence, often termed 'garotting' during the moral panic of the 1860s, was the most feared, and most heavily prosecuted and punished by the authorities.[30] Nevertheless, more often it was mundane and everyday robbery and street violence which could and did lead to fatalities. Again the circumstances surrounding such incidents were trivial enough; in many cases there was a request for either a drink or money to buy a drink. When Isaac Miller of Manchester refused such a request from a 'professor of pugilism' he had his face punched. In the 1874 Tithebarn Street murder, the victim Morgan was accosted for sixpence to buy some ale.[31] Twenty years later, two 'rough-looking' young men – Spring (18) and Staging (23) – accosted a private in uniform for a penny for half a pint. On being refused, they knocked him down but the soldier stood up and offered to thrash them. Following the street code of preparing for a fight, the soldier removed his top coat, body coat, shirt and belt, whereupon the two men ran off with them.[32]

Most male-on-male crimes of violence were alcohol fuelled and, as has been shown, many robberies with violence were undertaken with a view to getting more drinking money. While it is possible to find examples of apparently random and motiveless violence by men so drunk that they did not recall fighting, it would be wrong to write off drunken brawls as lacking any significance. After the street, the pub or beerhouse represented the next most dangerous place for a working man. The heavy concentration of men, not all of whom were sober, made for a hostile environment in which a wrong word or look could develop into a row. Previously loose regulation of beerhouse opening hours was tightened up in the 1870s when times for Sunday openings and earlier evening closing were introduced.[33] These changes, it could be argued, increased the danger of assault for beerhouse and pub staff, who not only had to enforce the new laws but also now had to decide whether customers had had enough to drink. Refusal to serve already inebriated drinkers led to minor scuffles, stabbings and broken bottle woundings. Publicans and barmen could be equally aggressive. Publican Thomas Bell, for example, shot a customer who had the temerity to ask for his change. Bell, who was drunk, insisted on having a whisky out of the money.[34] These violent exchanges between staff and customers represented, to some extent, a power struggle for control of drinking space. The former were increasingly being pressurised by the police and magistracy to tighten up on how they ran their establishments, since failure to conform meant the loss of their licence. The drinking public were equally demanding of their right to drink when and as much as they liked. During the 1870s the temperance campaign on the licensing laws and drunkenness was considered the most effective way of tackling crime, particularly violent crime. Half of all violent crime, according to the recorder of Birmingham in 1876, arose from quarrels in pubs, whilst in Manchester 45 per cent of all men arrested for all types of crime were drunk. What disturbed the authorities as much as anything else was the apparent relationship between economic prosperity, increased alcohol consumption and rising levels of violence. If, therefore, the authorities could break the chain, then interpersonal crime would drop. Such an experiment had been carried out at Luton, where liquor licences were not renewed for disorderly houses. It was claimed that violent crime had dropped by 75 per cent in five years through such a scheme.[35]

The link between alcohol and violence was an important one. Most assaults on the police in the second half of the century occurred when they were attempting to arrest drunk and disorderly individuals. Many urban police forces did not have a policy of arresting all drunks, only those who were disturbing the peace. This may account for the slightly older age profile of violent criminals in the nineteenth century when compared with the present day.[36] Taking a number of years at random after 1850, it was found that 75 per cent of those charged with assaulting the Liverpool police were over 20 years of age. Nowadays, the age cohort in their late teens is considered the most violent.

The pub, both in town and countryside, might have its dangers, but it was also the most important place for male socialising. It offered warmth, comfort, conversation and the company of other like-minded men. It was, in short, a place of male bonding. The pub, not surprisingly, figured greatly in accounts of poaching and poachers, who instead of pursuing a regular daytime occupation, spent their time in 'dissipation and idleness'. Poaching was a test of skill against nature and the men paid to protect the game. It was the archetypal male activity of hunting and providing for the family. Some poachers might have been trying to feed their families either directly by putting food on the table, or indirectly by selling the game and using the money to support their household. In court, poachers would occasionally cite the excuse of having a large family to support, but magistrates rarely accepted this argument. There was, however, another side to poaching which, as yet, has received little attention from historians, namely that poaching was a male pastime that provided an income for men to drink and remain in the company of other men. Poaching could, in other words, lead husbands and fathers to neglect their families. Victorian parliamentary enquiries were certainly keen to make such a connection and it was one that contained a large measure of truth. In an interview with the Preston prison chaplain John Clay, a poacher graphically described how a beershop keeper not only bought the game from him, but also supplied traps and snares. 'That beershop was the ruin of me', he bemoaned, for he met up with other young men there and went in for more serious gang poaching. They would spend all the money from the sale of the game on drink and when that ran out, return to the game covers for more pheasants. When his wife came looking for Clay, the landlord would hide him in a backroom.[37] It was in this kind of environment that poaching gangs were formed, expeditions planned, oaths of loyalty to stand by one another in a fight sworn. It was also the point of sale and credit in which drink could be bought on the promise of game. Drink was the provider of courage before the poaching trip and a relaxant on their return, when they wove stories of their fights and sung the many popular poaching songs which emphasised comradeship and physical courage. The harshness of the laws on night poaching and assaulting game-keepers probably encouraged violence. Gaol sentences of between 12 and 18 months were usual for assaulting a keeper at night, whereas an assault on a policeman carried a penalty of two months. The concept of a fair fight was not apparent during nocturnal clashes between poachers and keepers in the game covers. Both sides were armed and poachers operated in large groups, since safety in numbers was their best defence. There was the added danger that gang poachers tended 'to stimulate each other into acts of violence in their determination to obtain game, or in their fondness for excitement'.[38]

The history of trade unionism has tended to emphasise the peaceful and progressive characteristics of Victorian labour organisations. Just occasionally, violence associated with trade unionism, the Sheffield Outrages of the 1860s for example, is given a place in the narrative.[39] By concentrating solely on such high profile disputes, historians may have missed much more mundane and common forms of interpersonal violence between workmen. Court cases reveal the threats, fights and intimidation that were often directed at 'blacksheep' and strikebreakers. Carting disputes at the Liverpool docks also meant assault and intimidation against men who worked for wages below the going rate. Though most assaults were of a relatively minor character,[40] some were far more serious. Stonemason James Burnes, it was reported, went 'in fear of his life' from other unionised masons while working at a Salford gas works. He was assaulted and killed in broad daylight by two men who were thought to have been brickmakers. The chief witness to the killing was clearly frightened and unhelpful when cross-examined.[41]

Not all workplace assaults arose out of union disputes. Verbal exchanges, so-called banter or 'chaffing' which is typical of men, could go one stage too far and lead to fist fights and knifings. Presumably, such joking had upset and angered some butchers at St John's Market in Liverpool. One group of butchers had been calling two others 'bulldogs' and 'gorillas' all evening and this led to a fight. Butchers, it should be noted, were considered to be 'a desperate and vicious set of men'. 'Their neighbours', noted *The Porcupine*, 'fear and avoid them, and policemen know them too well to interfere too freely with their quarrels.' Their access to and skill with knives, coupled with their meat diet which gave them thick-set bodies that conformed to prevailing notions of manhood, made them formidable opponents.[42]

'There is some good, yes, much good in a man developing his muscular power, and being able skilfully to apply it in his own defence' but, as was noted at the time, it may have been difficult in finding the dividing line between 'the manly art of "self-defence" and downright ruffianism'.[43] Certainly, in the working-class slums of cities like Liverpool, 'violence and brutality are the accepted signs of manliness'.[44] But it would be wrong to ascribe violence solely to working-class males. Men from all social groups could and did admire fighting and accepted that physical prowess was a key component of masculinity, and one which could provide a solution to a problem. Many men had, after all, been on the receiving end of violence from childhood, either from their fathers, their peers, later in the century from their teachers, and no doubt from their workmates. Physical violence would have therefore seemed an effective strategy with which to defend their reputation and honour if challenged, or through which to enhance their status. Witnesses were often necessary to verify a defence of personal reputation or the enhancement of status. Fighting was, therefore, an important facet of masculinity for many men, and one which was used freely in the street, pub and, in the context of domestic violence, the home. Whether men who used their fists or clogs on other men were the same men who treated women with equal disdain is perhaps a question worth investigating. It is hoped this short essay has highlighted the very prosaic character of male-on-male violence in which the largely male territories of the pub, the street, the workplace and the woods were the scenes of daily conflict. It may be not so much men behaving badly as men behaving normally.

Notes

1. This chapter is based on examples drawn from a project on 'Violence in the north west with special reference to Liverpool and Manchester 1850–1914' funded by the Economic and Social Research Council (award number L133251004) as part of the Violence Research Programme.

2. Carolyn A. Conley, *The Unwritten Law: Criminal Justice in Victorian Kent* (New York, 1991); Clive Emsley, *Crime and Society in England 1750–1900* (1996); David Philips, *Crime and Authority in Victorian England: The Black Country 1835–1860* (1977).

3. Michael Roper and John Tosh (eds.), *Manful Assertions: Masculinities in Britain Since 1800* (1991).

4. See V. A. C. Gatrell and T. B. Hadden, 'Criminal statistics and their interpretation' in E. A. Wrigley (ed.), *Nineteenth-Century Society: Essays in the Quantitative Methods for the Study of Social Data* (Cambridge, 1972).

5. Philips, *Crime and Authority* p. 266; Martin J. Wiener, 'The Victorian criminalization of men' in P. Spierenburg (ed.), *Men and Violence: Gender, Honor, and Rituals in Modern Europe and America* (Ohio, 1998), p. 209.

6. Anne Campbell and Steven Muncer, 'Men and the meaning of violence', in John Archer (no relation) (ed.), *Male Violence* (1994), p. 332; Archer, *ibid.*, p. 3.

7. 'Reports to the Secretary of State for the Home Department on the State of the Law Relating to Brutal Assaults, &c' PP lxi (1875), pp. 169–172.

8. Wiener, 'The Victorian criminalization of men' pp. 197–212; Peter King, 'Punishing assault: the transformation of attitudes in the English courts' *JIH* 27 (1996), pp. 43–74.

9. *Porcupine* 4 July 1874. On the decline of duelling see Antony E. Simpson, 'Dandelions on the field of honor: dueling, the middle classes, and the law in nineteenth-century England' in *CJH* 9 (1988), pp. 99–155.

10. *LM* 10 and 17 July 1896.

11. *LM* 23 Dec. 1874.

12. *LM* 25 May 1872 and 1 Aug. 1896.

13. *LM* 6 Aug. 1890; see also 22 June 1895 or Philips, *Crime and Authority* p. 265.

14. The attack sent the old man insane, see *LM* 11 and 16 Dec. 1874.

15. *LM* 26 April 1876, 18 Oct. 1879 and 19 July 1870.

16. Frank Neal, *Sectarian Violence: The Liverpool Experience, 1819–1914* (Manchester, 1988); Roger Swift, 'Heroes or villains?: the Irish, crime, and disorder in Victorian England' *Albion* 29 (1997), pp. 399–421 and 'Anti-Irish violence in Victorian and Edwardian England' *CJH* 15 (1994), pp. 127–140.

17. *LM* 1 Sept. 1874.

18. *LM* 6 Aug. 1874.

19. Andrew Davies, 'Youth gangs, masculinity and violence in late Victorian Manchester and Salford' *JSH* 32 (1998), pp. 349–369; see also *LM* 26 Nov. 1874 and 12 April 1876.

20. Archer, *Male Violence*; Elizabeth A. Stanko, *Everyday Violence: How Women and Men Experience Sexual and Physical Danger* (1990); Tim Newburn and Elizabeth A. Stanko (eds.), *Just Boys Doing Business: Men, Masculinities and Crime* (1995), especially their introduction.

21. *LM* 19 Jan. 1872; see also 16 Oct. 1877.

22. *LM* 18 Aug. 1874.

23. *LM* 19 June 1877, 22 Dec. 1874 and 11 July 1871.

24. *MC* 23 and 30 Aug. 1862.

25. R. D. Storch, 'The plague of blue locusts: police reform and popular resistance in northern England, 1840–1857' *IRSH* 20 (1975), pp. 61–90 and 'The policeman as domestic missionary: urban discipline and popular culture in northern England, 1850–1880' *JSH* (1976), pp. 481–509.

26. *LM* 23 Aug. 1876; see Kenneth Polk, 'Masculinity, honour, and confrontational homicide' in Newburn and Stanko (eds.), *Just Boys* p. 177.

27. Such groups were common in the north end of Liverpool and in Bootle. See *The Porcupine* 24 Oct. 1874 when there was much public concern about roughs.

28. *Porcupine* 22 May 1875.

29. *LM* 21 Sept. 1878, 19 Oct. 1875 and 18 Nov. 1872.

30. J. Davis, 'The London garotting panic of 1862: a moral panic and the creation of a criminal class in mid-Victorian England' in V. A. C. Gatrell, B. Lenman and G. Parker (eds.), *Crime and the Law: A Social History of Crime in Western Europe Since 1500* (1980), pp. 190–213; Rob Sindall, *Street Violence in the Nineteenth Century: Moral Panic or Real Danger?* (Leicester, 1990).

31. *MC* 30 Jan. 1858; *LM* 6 Aug. 1874.

32. *LM* 22 Nov. 1894.

33. Under the Licensing Acts of 1872 and 1874 pubs closed at 10.00 pm on Sundays and by 11.00 pm on other days. Brian Harrison, *Drink and the Victorians: The Temperance Question in England 1815–1872* (1971), pp. 328–329.

34. *LM* 5 May 1892.

35. See the report published by the Howard League, *LM* 15 April 1876. For Manchester see the Chief Constable's Reports, 'Criminal and Statistical Returns of the Manchester Police 1847–1913', Manchester Local History Unit, 352.2 M1; Gatrell and Hadden, 'Criminal statistics' pp. 369–371.

36. Stanko, *Everyday Violence* p. 121; see also the ESRC Violence Research Programme, *Taking Stock: What Do We Know About Violence?* (1998), p. 15.

37. W. L. Clay, *The Prison Chaplain: A Memoir of the Rev. John Clay, B. D. late Chaplain of the Preston Gaol* (1861), pp. 566–568; John E. Archer, 'Poaching gangs and violence: the urban-rural divide in nineteenth-century Lancashire' *BJC* 39 (1999), pp. 25–38.

38. For example, Seed's beerhouse in Blackburn.

39. Charles Dickens, 'The last Sheffield outrages' *Once a Week* 14 Dec. 1861, pp. 679–683; see also Richard N. Price, 'The other face of respectability: violence in the Manchester brickmaking trade 1859–1870' *P&P* 66 (1975), pp. 110–132.

40. *MC* 29 March 1851.

41. *MCN* 16 Oct. 1869; see also *LM* 20 and 22 Jan. 1873.

42. *LM* 20 Feb. 1871; *Porcupine* 19 Feb. 1870.

43. *Porcupine* 16 March 1861.

44. *LM* 27 Feb. 1869.

CHAPTER THREE

Understanding women committing newborn child murder in Victorian England

MARGARET L. ARNOT

At six o'clock on a summer evening in 1847, 38-year-old Elizabeth Cornwell was working in the kitchen of the Windsor Castle Public House in Albany Street, London, where she lived and worked as a servant. A story about what happened on that evening, and subsequent days, can be found in the records of the Central Criminal Court. Elizabeth complained of 'being very ill with spasms'.[1] Mrs Rich, her mistress, sent her to bed after giving her a little brandy and water, and called the doctor.

A little later, Mrs Rich found Elizabeth clearly in distress, sitting on a chamber pot and throwing up into another one. However, as 'she said she was better', her mistress left immediately.[2] Perhaps Mrs Rich had heard what she wanted to hear and did not want to inquire further. Very soon afterwards, Elizabeth bore a child. She left it in the chamber pot where it was delivered, the umbilical cord uncut. After covering it with the wash basin and pushing it under the bed, she lay down to recover. Soon afterwards, Mrs Rich returned with the doctor. Though a suspicious little noise came from under the bed, Elizabeth managed to hide the nature of her illness. She told the doctor she was much better and he left without examining her. She arose the same evening and recommenced work. The next day, she took the infant's body down to the water closet in the slop pail. She used a stick kept in the house to poke it down as low as she could in the closet.

Elizabeth concealed her pregnancy, delivered herself alone and successfully covered the bloody traces of birth: even the doctor walked into and out of the room without suspicion. No one saw her disposing of the body in the privy, and no one caught sight of it in the ensuing days. So her tragic act may well have remained hidden, had she not become her own accuser. Six days after the birth, she confided in another servant that 'she was very much distressed in her mind'.[3] This servant replied that nothing distressed her except poverty – and she was very concerned that she would not have any clothes organised for her expected baby. Elizabeth replied, 'I had plenty of things with my baby.'[4] Here, for the first time, she acknowledged to both herself and another person that she had actually had a baby, though the notion of having 'plenty of things' was a fantasy. At last, the isolation, the solitary bearing of the burden, was over. But the consequence of that very unburdening was that Elizabeth Cornwell was charged with murder and found herself facing the full might of the law, though she was eventually found guilty of concealment only and imprisoned for twelve months.

We cannot determine the precise extent of neonaticides that occurred in Victorian England. According to some Victorian commentators, England was awash in rivers of infant blood. Some medical coroners especially had an unfortunate tendency to assume that most infant bodies that came before them were murdered. Edwin Lankester, for example, calculated that in the 1860s there were about 20,000 women in London alone who had committed infanticide.[5] Such interventions were sensationalist and unfounded. Many considerations suggest that, even amongst those few cases reaching the courts, there were many that did not involve actual neonaticide.[6] On the other hand, as Elizabeth's story indicates, there was much potential for the crime to remain hidden. Concealing pregnancy is a major accomplishment in denial and some women may well have successfully carried that denial through to the post-partum period. If the testimony of Elizabeth's mistress is to be believed, she walked into and out of the room where a woman was in the late stages of labour without any acknowledgement of this reality, and the medical man saw nothing that caused him to examine her body. Potential witnesses in other cases may also have chosen not to 'see' an unpalatable reality. Though many infant bodies were discovered in privies,[7] there were other more anonymous places where bodies could be abandoned. In many rural areas, woods and hedgerows were plentiful, though in the cities secret disposal became more difficult. Even when discovered, few abandoned infant corpses were ever traced to their parents.[8] And it was also difficult to determine with certainty the cause of death of most of these anonymous infants. Many may have been still births. Even if a coroner brought in a finding of murder, complex evidential issues ensured that few charges of murder for neonaticide were substantiated in criminal courts.[9]

Only a small proportion of deaths of newborns resulted in formal criminal proceedings. Between 1840 and 1879 an average of about ten such cases was heard each year before the Central Criminal Court.[10] Most women were charged with concealment of birth – 306 indictments during this period. There were also sixty indictments for murder of newborns, ten women appeared in the same period on the Coroner's inquisition only, five on manslaughter indictments, and twelve people, including two men, on other indictments charging various offences against the person.[11] In 1859, for example, there were 137 cases of concealment known to the police in England and Wales,[12] but it is impossible to determine national judicial statistics for neonatal homicide because figures for all children between the ages of newborn and seven are aggregated. Homicide and concealment were heard in the assizes, the highest courts. Although provincial assizes had less business than the Central Criminal Court in London, the number of concealment and neonaticide cases heard there, together with the extensive number of infant bodies that were discovered elsewhere in Victorian England, suggest that there was more neonaticide during the Victorian period than currently occurs in Britain. Today between about six and ten cases enter the criminal justice system each year.[13]

Was there anything particular to the Victorian period that helps us understand why there was probably more neonaticide than there is today? And are there any continuities that can help us understand some of the similarities between modern and Victorian cases? In order to understand these very particular acts of family violence, this chapter will examine a range of social, economic, political and cultural contexts. The final part of the chapter begins with a story of a 1990's neonaticide and explores the possibility that some of the insights gained from modern forensic psychiatry might well enrich our understanding of women committing infanticide in Victorian England.

The particular circumstances surrounding nineteenth-century illegitimacy need consideration. Contemporary observers consistently linked illegitimacy and infanticide, and studies of court records indicate that this was no illusion.[14] Participating enthusiastically in the debate about the effects of the New Poor Law, a *Times* leader argued, along with many other critics, that the draconian Bastardy Clauses placed full moral responsibility for illegitimacy on the mother, who was also forced to carry the financial burden through the shortcomings of legal affiliation proceedings.[15] This was seen as an important cause for a perceived increase in infanticide. Such criticisms continued even after the 1868 Poor Law Amendment Act enabled Poor Law Guardians to initiate affiliation proceedings on behalf of the mothers of illegitimate children and the 1872 Bastardy Act increased the sum paid for maintenance.[16] Gaining support from the father of an illegitimate child remained a difficult procedure throughout the Victorian period and was successful only in a minority of cases.[17]

Victorian criticisms of the bastardy clauses also focused upon the harsh conditions in workhouses that deterred some women from living and giving birth there. Severe poverty was undoubtedly a factor contributing to some unmarried mothers destroying their infants. Conditions were harsh for women attempting to support themselves and dependants. Women's wages in mid-century London could be less than half of men's.[18] Such wage levels were based upon a deeply entrenched assumption that women remained dependent on men throughout their lives, whether these men were fathers, brothers, husbands or sons. When Sarah Cooper stood before the Central Criminal Court charged with murdering her newborn in 1847, she and her two illegitimate children, aged about five and two, had been living in lodgings. Her circumstances at the time were 'very bad indeed': several witnesses deposed to her distress.[19] She seems to have had no regular occupation to earn a living. For one child she received an allowance of 2s. 6d. a week, but she had no support for the other. In June of that year, a decomposing body of a male infant was found in the privy of the house where she lived. No one but her landlords, Cooper and her children used the privy. The extent of decomposition of the body undermined the medical evidence. She may or may not have killed her child, but her words to a police officer that 'she should not plead guilty to the murder; that it would be the death of her poor mother' certainly implicated her in court.[20] After she was in custody she explained to a police sergeant that,

> . . . it would not have happened had she not been in such a bad state of poverty, that she and her children had been starving all the winter . . . she said that the child was hers . . . that she must have fainted after she was delivered, and she had put it where it was found.[21]

Denial of pregnancy to the local midwife and the choice to be delivered alone also indicated a wish that her child should not survive, especially considering that she had the midwife for her previous delivery. Evidence was given that 'she appeared a very kind mother to her two children – she was very fond of them'.[22] Arguably, this mother's neglect or murder at birth of her third infant was, in fact, a necessity if she were to continue a family life with her other children outside the workhouse. Perhaps it can be seen in retrospect as an act of love for the two children already living, of charity for the newborn, thus preventing it suffering, and of resolute independence. The mother's confession of concealment gave the jury little choice but to convict, resulting in a sentence of one year's imprisonment.

But poverty is only one relevant consideration here. Let's return to Elizabeth's circumstances, for not only were most of the alleged neonaticides that eventually came to court committed by unmarried women: a very large number of them were also servants.[23] Historians have pointed to customary pre-marital sexual activity in rural areas in nineteenth-century Britain.[24] In stable, rural society, family and community policing of sexual relationships usually ensured that marriage followed prenuptial pregnancy, or birth outside of marriage was in itself acceptable, as was also the case in some urban, working-class communities. But women who took advantage of increasing mobility during industrialisation and moved away from home to work in service, lost such support. While some employers provided a protective environment for their servants, many had to survive in harsh, exploitative conditions.[25] It may well be that such conditions resulted in feelings of both isolation and a crushing necessity for complete self-reliance that could culminate in the experience of giving birth unassisted. Furthermore, the contradictions between the conditions of service in well-to-do-families – immobility, strict supervision, demands of propriety and often a strict 'no followers' rule – and servants' desires for courtship and making a good marriage, led to higher than average levels of illegitimacy amongst servants.[26] These same conditions could perhaps also make concealment of birth and infanticide more likely.

One astute correspondent to *The Times* in 1865 had a remarkably down-to-earth attitude to women servants' sexuality, which he implored others of his class to adopt. 'Do not let us think that by forbidding followers we change our blooming housemaid into a cold Diana. She will have her male friends in spite of us; let her have one with our permission.'[27] He went even further, encouraging readers of *The Times* to allow servants to marry while they remained in service, thus enabling wife and husband to live honourably and preventing the temptation to commit infanticide.

Concealment of pregnancy was a rational strategy for servants. Even for a betrothed woman in service, discovery of pregnancy could result in instant dismissal. Staying in service for as long as possible meant her employer absorbed the cost of her room and board. For the less-established liaison, discovery by the master and mistress was a disaster. For, even if they continued to tolerate the pregnant, unmarried woman in their household – which was unusual – there was no hope that her lover would be tolerated: almost all chance of following the pregnancy with marriage would be lost. Most of the unwed mothers who entered London's workhouses had worked as servants.[28] The confusion and uncertainty caused by pregnancy in such circumstances, combined with the culture of concealment and the moral opprobrium attached to unmarried motherhood by the employing class, could well have led many women to deny the nature of their condition, even to themselves.

There was another important consideration that influenced all Victorian women: the crushing burden of maternity in an age with little reliable knowledge of birth control. The testimonies of working women sent in 1914 to the Women's Co-operative Guild, tell a composite, bleak tale of inadequate care, hunger, overwork, exhaustion, illness, self-sacrifice, ignorance and despair that was the lot of poor, working-class mothers.[29] These life stories suggest that knowledge of birth-control techniques was minimal. Family size was far greater than it is today. The 1911 census indicated that, of those women who had completed their childbearing by that date, almost 20 per cent had eight or more children.[30] Angus McLaren has argued that women in nineteenth-century England had less control over their reproductive function than at any other time. Folk knowledge of means of prevention of conception and abortion had been lost as traditional social structures by which this knowledge had been communicated broke down. Only with the twentieth-century spread of the modern birth-control movement and the improvement in medical abortion techniques did women regain some choice over when they bore children.[31] It is therefore not surprising that socially and economically disadvantaged Victorian women like Sarah Cooper sometimes used infanticide as an alternative means of family limitation. There are other cultural factors that could have contributed to the practice of neonaticide as late abortion. In order to explore them, let's return to Elizabeth Cornwell's story.

There is little evidence of Elizabeth suddenly facing the 'reality' of giving birth to a baby. She sat on the chamber pot alone in her room and as she explained to the court, 'I never saw it; as it came from me in the chamber utensil, so it remained.'[32] She had not acknowledged the presence of a potential child in her body, nor had she spoken about a baby. Now, at birth, she did not look at it: for Elizabeth at this point in time, a baby did not exist. She left it in the chamber pot, still attached to the placenta, with as little regard for it as for a pile of excrement. And the next day, still in this frame of mind, she carried the body in a slop pail to the water closet, pushing it down amongst the soil, where in her mind it belonged.

There are some broader issues that help us explain the fact that Elizabeth and women like her did not suddenly recognise something called a 'baby' as the product of their labour. Several aspects of the experience of pregnancy are worth consideration. First is the question of physiological knowledge. Might Elizabeth not have 'known' she was pregnant? Certainly, this is what she claimed before the court. One of the most striking elements of Victorian cases of illegitimate neonaticide is that, in almost all cases, the women never acknowledged their pregnancies. If questioned about weight gain by family or neighbours, these pregnant women would dismiss suspicions in various ways. Having dropsy was a popular explanation. The culture of concealment inherent in conditions of service provides part of an explanation for such concealment, but there are other issues. It is difficult to assess the full impact of the stifling moral climate in which middle-class, evangelical opinion determined that discussion about and knowledge of their bodies and sexuality was inappropriate for women. There is some evidence that sexual ignorance probably increased during the Victorian period for some working-class as well as middle-class women.[33] It is likely that in Victorian England, some women – especially young women – would not have actually had the physiological understanding to know they were pregnant and may well have proceeded through a whole pregnancy without full knowledge of what was going on. Here we can only begin to imagine the sheer terror that might have been caused by the onset of labour.

Whether thirty-eight-year-old Elizabeth Cornwell could have retained this level of ignorance is debatable. However, she had gone through pregnancy telling no one of her circumstances, and afterwards denied that she had known her condition. She had not prepared any baby clothes – a routine enquiry in such cases. In the Victorian period there were no reliable pregnancy tests, and no foetal monitoring or ultra-sound. Women continued to be their own judges of whether or not they were pregnant. Until clear evidence of life inside was established by feeling the kicking of the infant – or 'quickening' – in women's minds, what was 'wrong' was that their menses had been temporarily interrupted. Barbara Brookes's work suggests that this was the case up to the early twentieth century.[34] So, the length of time that it was conventional for women to be anticipating and preparing for the big event was considerably shorter in the Victorian period than it is today. Furthermore, with much less external 'evidence' available for what occurred within a pregnant woman's body, there was then a considerably wider canvas for a woman's subjective, imaginative engagement with her own body. Similarly, the foetus was not a potential person in women's minds until considerably later in pregnancy than is now the case. It is not difficult to imagine how easy it was for a foetus to remain unacknowledged until birth, when the appearance of a child would cause quite impossible dilemmas for the woman concerned.

These factors were strengthened by others which contributed to definitions of life and meanings of infant death. In Victorian Britain, both fertility and mortality were high. Infant mortality rates in some poor, urban areas were as high as 55 per cent, and the rate for illegitimate children ranged between 60 and 90 per cent.[35] Nineteenth-century parents simply had to face infant death with at least some degree of equanimity in order to continue functioning.[36] Anthropological study has shown that, in societies with these demographic facts, viewing infant death as a misfortune rather than a tragedy, and facing it with equanimity and resignation are the norm.[37] This attitude is often reflected in the stories about infanticide in the Victorian Central Criminal Court records. Furthermore, in the minutes of evidence of these cases, the word 'it' was used pervasively by everybody when infants were referred to – and that included parents, neighbours, other family members, medical men and workhouse officials. Such linguistic devices surely indicate a reticence to grant full human individuality to very young children.

There is other nineteenth-century evidence that newborns were regarded as different from older persons. Inquiries by the Lincoln Coroner revealed that it was common practice for infants who died before they were baptised to be simply nailed up in a box and handed over to the sexton, together with his one-shilling fee. The child would not be given a Christian burial because she or he had not been baptised. Apparently, in popular belief, the child between birth and baptism occupied a liminal space: if it died before baptism, it was not accorded the rites of those who had lived, and to all intents and purposes, was treated as still-born.[38]

It is not only from the working class that evidence can be found for different value being attached to infant life. Among other things, the Royal Commission on Capital Punishment held in 1866 was trying to establish the feasibility of removing infanticide from the capital classification of murder. The Commission considered whether a boundary could be drawn between infants whose murder warranted the capital penalty and those whose murder was somehow less heinous. A number of eminent men on the Commission agreed that infanticide was often a less serious crime than murder of older people. The Commission debated whether the first breath gave the newborn a 'soul' or whether it only attained full human status later, as it developed rationality.[39] Some modern liberal defences of abortion and infanticide make very similar arguments.[40]

Anthropologist Nancy Scheper-Hughes argues that, even in modern societies, attributes of 'personhood' and 'humanness' 'must be understood as culturally constructed and historically situated in each instance'.[41] While today's major cultural contestations in the West about this boundary have retreated backwards in foetal life and focus on abortion and scientific use of fertilised eggs and human foetal material, the continued practice of infanticide may well provide evidence that cultural consensus has not been achieved about the status of neo-natal life. Traces of nineteenth-century attitudes may well remain today, contributing to the commission of infanticide. For example, Dr Margaret Oates, Consultant Perinatal Psychiatrist explaining what happens after the birth in modern cases of neonaticide, said: '. . . or . . . you want to kill the baby before it has started to live – in some way that's less bad than killing a baby that has lived.'[42] The suggestion here is that the popular understanding that 'life' begins when the baby takes its first breath (when it cries for the first time), which exercised the 1866 Royal Commission, may still have some influence on behaviour.

Feelings that infants are something 'other' have not vanished. Rather, different economic, social and cultural contexts have ensured that different peoples and classes at different times and places have placed different moral interpretations on the otherness of infants. It is doubtful whether there has ever been consensus on the matter throughout a whole society. In the nineteenth century, the sense that newborns were not wholly persons appears to have been more pervasive than it is today, and probably contributed more to the commission of infanticide then than it does now – but it is important to note that today this boundary remains contested.

The meaning of infant life is not the only area concerning infanticide where remarkable continuities between the Victorian period and the present can be located. In the early 1990s in England, 'Kate' gave birth alone in a room where she was lodging. She had told no one about her pregnancy. About this concealment she explained:

> It wasn't that I'd formulated a plan from start to finish, I didn't – I wasn't thinking oh, I'm not going to tell anyone on purpose or anything like that. It was like I'd lost my voice – I couldn't speak . . . – it was like somebody had erased something.[43]

Eventually, the time of delivery arrived. Her landlord was away and she endured the seventeen-hour labour alone. During this labour she became quite desperate, thinking to herself, 'I wish I was dead . . .'.[44] The birth was difficult and blood was everywhere. Kate managed to go downstairs to find a knife to cut the umbilical cord. She experienced immense feelings of sadness, held the baby for a little while, but then smothered her. She kept the body with her in her room for several weeks, yet to the external world she was carrying on as normal, going to work every day. Then she had to move house and realised she had to get rid of the body. She put little thought into this disposal, but did it with deep emotion and sadness. She put the body in a bag and simply walked into a field near her home in broad daylight and left the bag where anyone could find it. Someone saw her, became suspicious and looked in the bag. Kate was charged with infanticide, effectively a form of manslaughter that has been on the statute books in England since 1922. She was sentenced to three years' probation.

This story is so remarkably similar to stories in Victorian court records that it demands some consideration. The broad pattern is precisely the same: concealment of pregnancy, a secret delivery and very rapid dispatch of the infant. Kate's keeping the baby's body in her room was also a very frequent practice in Victorian cases: numerous infant corpses were found in servants' boxes, the places where they kept all their personal belongings.[45] These similarities may well provide a clue that helps meet a fundamental dissatisfaction that remains after all the explanations so far outlined in this chapter are considered. The dissatisfaction is this: the social, economic and cultural considerations discussed help to contextualise the experience of women committing neonaticide and to understand some of its general parameters. But they do not explain why one woman facing unmarried pregnancy concealed it, gave birth alone and killed the child while another woman bravely faced the consequences, acknowledged her child, bore it in safer circumstances and struggled to support it. The explanatory power of all analytic tools available in the standard social-historical and textual analysis tool box are left wanting when one is seeking as full an understanding as is possible of the human experience of infanticide. To loosely quote film critic Laura Mulvey, 'a certain kind of history takes one inexorably into psychoanalysis'.[46] The questions 'why did neonaticide occur?' and 'what did those acts mean for the women who committed them?' constitute just this kind of history.[47]

The remainder of this chapter makes some attempt to compare Kate's story with those of some Victorian women, in the light of a modern psychiatric explanation. One psychiatrist explained in an interview the mental process that she thinks accounts for Kate's concealment and secret delivery:

> Splitting is a mental mechanism which results when a person is under very, very great stress and instead of dealing with that distress and the very high level of anxiety, they split it off from consciousness in the way a small child would say it was the bad person who broke the window, it wasn't me. The minute you talk about it to somebody else it becomes real. If it becomes real then she is expecting a baby. She has to make plans, she has to do something about it. It becomes a real issue whereas as long as the process of concealment, denial and splitting goes on it remains a fantasy.[48]

'Splitting' in its various forms provides a key defence mechanism used by infants to cope with a confusing and contradictory world.[49] But even in the healthy adult personality, such early attitudes can come into play as 'the manifold defences which the ego uses in order to combat anxiety'.[50] There is a wealth of evidence in psychological literature from many countries, from many generations and from across the socio-economic spectrum that unconscious defence mechanisms are universally used by people as coping strategies. Accepting that there is a limit beyond which human beings cannot be reconstructed does not somehow invalidate the historical enterprise, rather, it enriches understanding that can be reached from historical enquiry. If there is a certain unity between ourselves and actors in the past, there is also an immense diversity in the many ways in which what we share has been shaped and mediated by historical conditions and the very cultures and societies that people construct. Arguably, history is the task of understanding the rich interplay between that unity and diversity.

Taking on board the modern view of concealment and neonaticide can help us to glimpse some of the deepest human dimensions of infanticide in the Victorian period. In so doing, I am assuming that the dynamic unconscious and use of defence mechanisms that psychoanalysts have described were part of the lives of Victorians of all classes.[51] So, even if a Victorian woman had the physiological knowledge to recognise pregnancy on a rational level, it may well have been that for some women the condition carried with it so many unbearable consequences that they split it off from their conscious minds. If this occurred more often in the Victorian period than it does today, which the figures discussed earlier suggest, the diverse social, economic and cultural factors discussed in the first part of the chapter explain why more women at that time would have found unwanted pregnancy so unbearable as to force splitting. At the same time, the common acknowledgement of pregnancy so much later in gestation than is the case today would have made the sustaining of splitting and denial for the whole pregnancy more possible. The stories of neonaticide across the generations are so strikingly similar, though the historical conditions have changed so much, that positing a core of psychic continuity seems to make sense.

There are striking similarities between Kate's experiences and those of Elizabeth Cornwell and other Victorian women in similar circumstances. In Elizabeth's case, it is interesting that the words that are frequently repeated are that she was not 'aware' that she was pregnant – a subtlety that allows for the possibility that 'knowledge' of her condition resided in her unconscious. As well as explaining away physical symptoms, labour was also often constructed as 'violent spasms' in the way that Elizabeth did. As in the modern cases, what remained crucial was that pregnancy itself and the presence of a potential child were never admitted. The symptoms of the body could be translated and explained by the mind in any number of ways. Whatever might have been occurring in fantasy, the refusal to speak, to name, to put into language, is shared by women across this 150-year period. This must be one of the most extraordinary testaments to the power of language to shape consciousness.

There may well be another continuity, suggesting the power of the psychosomatic connection: the refusal of the mind to accept the possibility of pregnancy may contribute to the suppression of physical symptoms of pregnancy. This occurred in a recent American case.[52] In the nineteenth century, stories of women sharing a bed without one woman knowing the other to be pregnant were quite common. Obviously, there are many possible explanations for such evidence given in a court room: lack of physical knowledge on the part of the witness; successful disguising of the physical symptoms, even in shared rooms and beds; and the other woman refusing to 'see' because of her own inner conflicts, to name a few. But the possibility that the pregnant woman felt and displayed no physical symptoms must also be considered.

Like 'Kate' in the 1990s, Elizabeth Cornwell became her own accuser, effectively giving away her secret to another servant. Lyndal Roper has written about the infanticide case of Appolonia Mayr in a culture distant from Victorian Britain: seventeenth-century Germany. Here, too, a woman's words spoken from grief provided the grounds for her own prosecution.[53] In modern Britain, 'Kate' took her baby's body outside in a bag and left it in a field, in public view. Modern psychiatrists have spoken of the immense suffering of young women who have concealed a pregnancy and killed their child.[54] The acts and words of self-revelation of such women suggest across the centuries that that pain could become too much to bear alone. The pain of Appolonia Mayr, of Elizabeth Cornwell and of 'Kate' was made of the same stuff, and bound to similar traumatic, physical experiences of giving birth alone, and neglecting or killing their babies and disposing of their bodies.

In conclusion: a significant number of neonaticides with many characteristics similar to those occurring in Victorian Britain continue to happen in modern Britain, where contraception and abortion are widely available and little stigma attaches to bearing children outside of marriage. While the politics of sexuality and reproduction in the Victorian period may well have contributed to the extent of infanticide, general social, cultural and economic explanations are not sufficient to illuminate fully any particular case of infanticide, nor to explain why one servant responded to the crushing burden of fertility by dutifully entering the workhouse to bear her child, then supporting it through appalling deprivation, whilst another committed infanticide. Understanding psychological interpretations of infanticidal women today provides us with an additional tool with which imaginatively to explore the mysterious regions between the lines in our historical texts. We will not find a mirror of the present – but it may well help us with that very difficult process of moving from general explanation based on conventional social, cultural, economic and political phenomena, to understanding the particularities of one woman's tragedy. And perhaps more than anything, the notion of splitting helps us to imagine a woman's pain when she at last acknowledges in her conscious mind that, in fact, she bore an infant and killed it.

Notes

1. Elizabeth Cornwell, *CCCSP* 10th Session, 1846–1847, p. 731.

2. *Ibid.*

3. *Ibid.*

4. *Ibid.*

5. Edwin Lankester in discussion, *NAPSS Trans* (1864), p. 580.

6. Ann R. Higginbotham, ' "Sin of the age": infanticide and illegitimacy in Victorian London' in Kristine Ottesen Garrigan (ed.), *Victorian Scandals: Representations of Gender and Class* (Athens, 1992), pp. 257–288.

7. Margaret L. Arnot, 'Gender in focus: infanticide in England 1840–1880' (PhD, University of Essex, 1994); and compare Regina Schulte, 'Infanticide in rural Bavaria in the nineteenth century' in Hans Medick and David Warren Sabean (eds.), *Interest and Emotion: Essays in the Study of Family and Kinship* (Cambridge, 1984).

8. Lionel Rose, *Massacre of the Innocents* (1986), pp. 38–39.

9. D. Seaborne Davies, 'Child-killing in English law' *MLR* 1 (1937), pp. 203–223.

10. This statistic is derived from a complete manual search of the *Central Criminal Court Sessions Papers*, Jan. 1840–Dec. 1879. Compare similar figures discussed in Higginbotham, 'Sin of the age'.

11. *CCCSP* Jan. 1840–Dec. 1879.

12. Judicial Statistics, PP lxiv (1860), p. 525.

13. Calculated from figures provided in M. N. Marks, 'Characteristics and causes of infanticide in Britain' *IRP* 8 (1996), pp. 99–100.

14. *CCCSP* Jan. 1840–Dec. 1879; Higginbotham, 'Sin of the age'.

15. *Times* 8 Aug. 1842, p. 6, c. 3; John Knott, *Popular Opposition to the 1834 Poor Law* (1986), Ch. 10; Frances Trollope, *Jessie Phillips: A Tale of the Present Day* (1843); U. R. Q. Henriques, 'Bastardy and the new Poor Law' *P&P* 37 (1967), pp. 103–129.

16. For example: 'The increase of infanticide' *BMJ* 2 (1865), p. 409; 'Committee for amending the law in points wherein it is injurious to women' *Infant Mortality: Its Causes and Remedies* (Manchester, 1871); Elizabeth Wolstenholme, *WSJ* 2 Sep. 1872, p. 123.

17. Anne Digby, *Pauper Palaces* (1978), p. 154; Barry Reay, 'Sexuality in nineteenth-century England: the social context of illegitimacy in rural Kent' *RH* 1 (1990), p. 234.

18. 'Report of an investigation into the state of the poorer classes of St George's in the East' *JSSL* Aug. 1848, p. 203, cited in Sally Alexander, *Women's Work in Nineteenth-Century London: A Study of the Years 1820–50* (1983), p. 22.

19. Sarah Cooper, *CCCSP* 8th Session, 1846–1847, pp. 247–250.

20. *Ibid.*, p. 247.

21. *Ibid.*, pp. 248–249

22. *Ibid.*

23. *CCCSP* Jan. 1840–Dec. 1879; Arnot, 'Gender in focus'; Higginbotham, 'Sin of the age'.

24. Reay, 'Sexuality' Table 1, p. 221.

25. Pamela Horn, *The Rise and Fall of the Victorian Domestic Servant* (2nd edn., Gloucester, 1986), Ch. 7.

26. John Gillis, 'Servants, sexual relations and the risks of illegitimacy in London, 1801–1900' in Judith L. Newton, Mary P. Ryan and Judith R. Walkowitz (eds.), *Sex and Class in Women's History* (1983), pp. 114–145.

27. *Times* 10 Aug. 1865, p. 7, c. 6.

28. Ann Higginbotham, 'The unmarried mother and her child in Victorian London' (PhD, Indiana University, 1985), pp. 53–54.

29. Margaret Llewelyn Davies (ed.), *Maternity: Letters from Working Women* (1915, 1978).

30. Ellen Ross, 'Labour and love: rediscovering London working-class mothers, 1870–1918' in Jane Lewis (ed.), *Labour and Love: Women's Experience of Home and Family, 1850–1940* (Oxford, 1986), p. 76.

31. Angus McLaren, *Reproductive Rituals: The Perception of Fertility in England from the Sixteenth Century to the Nineteenth Century* (1984).

32. Cornwell, *CCCSP* p. 732.

33. Janet Blackman, 'Popular theories of generation: the evolution of *Aristotle's Works*' in John Woodward and David Richards (eds.), *Health Care and Popular Medicine in Nineteenth-Century England: Essays in the Social History of Medicine* (1977), pp. 56–88.

34. Barbara Brookes, *Abortion in England 1900–1967* (1988).

35. John Brendon Curgenven, 'The waste of infant life' National Association for the Promotion of Social Science Sessions Papers (NAPSSSP) (1866–1867), pp. 222–235.

36. Ivy Pinchbeck and Margaret Hewitt, *From the Eighteenth Century to the Children Act 1948* Vol. 2, *Children in English Society* (1973), p. 349; Edward Shorter, *The Making of the Modern Family* (New York, 1975), Ch. 5.

37. Nancy Scheper-Hughes, 'The cultural politics of child survival' in her *Child Survival: Anthropological Perspectives on the Treatment and Maltreatment of Children* (Reidel, Dordrecht and Lancaster, 1987), pp. 2, 9–12.

38. 'Letter from J. W. Hitchins, Coroner, to Home Secretary' Lincoln, 3 April 1844, HO45 OS 641, PRO, Kew.

39. 'Royal Commission on Capital Punishment' PP xxi (1866), p. 290, q. 2193; p. 59, q. 422.

40. Michael Tooley, *Abortion and Infanticide* (Oxford, 1983); also his 'Abortion and infanticide', *P&PA* 2 (1972), pp. 37–65. Compare Jonathan Glover, *Causing Death and Saving Lives* (Harmondsworth, 1977); L. W. Sumner, *Abortion and Moral Theory* (Princeton, 1981), pp. 60–61.

41. Scheper-Hughes, 'The cultural politics of child survival' p. 13.

42. 'Deadly Secrets', *QED* broadcast BBC1, 5 Aug. 1998.

43. *Ibid.*

44. *Ibid.*

45. See also Duncan Campbell, *A Stranger and Afraid: The Story of Caroline Beale* (1997).

46. Laura Mulvey, 'Freud, war trauma and film in the late 1920s and 1930s' paper presented to the Psychoanalysis and History Seminar, Institute of Historical Research, 4 Feb. 1999. Compare the historical work of, e.g. Peter Gay, *Freud for Historians* (Oxford, 1985); Lyndal Roper, *Oedipus and the Devil* (1994).

47. See also M. N. Marks, 'Characteristics and causes' p. 105.

48. Dr Margaret Oates, 'Deadly Secrets'.

49. On splitting see especially Melanie Klein, *Envy and Gratitude and Other Works 1946–1963* (1988), *passim* but see especially 'Notes on some schizoid mechanisms' (1946), pp. 1–24. On defence mechanisms more generally see Anna Freud, *The Ego and the Mechanisms of Defence* (1936; Engl. trans., 1937). On defence mechanisms and crime see Christopher Cordess and Murray Fox (eds.), *Forensic Psychotherapy: Crime, Psychodynamics and the Offender Patient* (London and Bristol, 1996).

50. Melanie Klein, 'On mental health' (1960) in *Envy and Gratitude* p. 273.

51. On the unconscious see for example Sigmund Freud, *Studies on Hysteria* written with Josef Breuer (1895) in *The Standard Edition of the Complete Psychological Works of Sigmund Freud* (trans. and ed.) James Strachey (1953); and his, 'The unconscious' (1915) in *ibid.*, Vol. 14.

52. 'Deadly Secrets'.

53. Roper, *Oedipus* Introduction.

54. 'Deadly Secrets'.

CHAPTER FOUR

Youth gangs, gender and
violence, 1870–1900

ANDREW DAVIES

The late nineteenth century saw widespread reports of gang violence among working-class youths in Britain's major conurbations. Local newspapers in London, Manchester, Liverpool, Birmingham and Glasgow reported confrontations between rival gangs and brutal assaults by gang members upon 'respectable' citizens and the police. By the late 1890s, the problem of 'hooliganism' captured the headlines of the national press, and hooligan exploits were freely evoked in music-hall songs and in popular literature.[1] Gang violence was generally discussed by contemporary journalists and social commentators in terms of disorder among young males. Middle-class concern with the increasing lawlessness of working-class youths led to the development of the Lads' Club movement, which saw the establishment of recreational clubs for boys and young men in many of the poorer districts of Britain's cities. Lads' Clubs were intended to instil the values of 'muscular Christianity' by fostering religious observance alongside team sports, and thus to provide a new form of social discipline for young working-class males. In the reformers' vision, lawless youths were to be lured off the streets to find a new sense of manliness in the Christian comradeship of the clubs.[2]

Social commentators rarely featured young women in their accounts of gang violence. Indeed, when young women did appear in commentaries on youth gangs, they generally featured as 'molls' (the ornamental property of violent young males), rather than as gang members in their own right. It was sometimes alleged that young women incited the conflicts by switching their affections from a member of one gang to a member of another. Moreover, it was acknowledged that young women formed part of the audience for male displays of fighting prowess, and concern was frequently expressed that male gang members were shielded from the law by false alibis provided by their molls. Nonetheless, young women were generally accorded non-combative roles in what were seen as essentially masculine conflicts.[3] The contemporary preoccupation with young males was further reflected in the slow development of schemes to provide recreational clubs for girls and young women along the lines of the Lads' Club movement.[4]

Stephen Humphries and Geoffrey Pearson have argued that the emergence of street gangs with a shared sense of style points to the existence of a distinct 'youth culture' in nineteenth-century cities.[5] Along with Rob Sindall, Pearson and Humphries have also highlighted the role of the press in raising fear of street violence among the middle classes.[6] Close attention has been paid to the relationship between youth, crime and social class, and Humphries in particular has provided a forceful analysis of street gangs as channels of resistance to middle-class authority among working-class youth.[7] Less attention has been paid to gender in these pioneering studies. Indeed, historians have generally reproduced the widespread contemporary assumption that youth gangs should be characterised as all-male associations. In the most detailed examination of gangs and gender relations, Humphries principally identified young women as the girlfriends of male gang members. According to Humphries, young women in poor districts were sometimes willing to trade sexual involvement for the status and excitement provided by relationships with members of violent gangs.[8] Young women were, thus, brought into focus largely through discussion of their sexuality.

Humphries, Pearson and Sindall all gathered examples of gang activity from a range of British cities. In contrast, this chapter is derived from a case-study of the Manchester conurbation.[9] It draws upon a sample of 250 cases of gang violence reported in the local press between 1870 and 1900. Of the 717 young people prosecuted in these cases, 672 (93.7 per cent) were male and only 45 (6.3 per cent) were female. In the light of these figures, it is perhaps not surprising that contemporary commentators and subsequent historians have characterised gang conflicts as masculine concerns. Moreover, some of the best-documented affrays appear to have been fought between all-male gangs. Young men's participation in gang fights was rooted in a wider association between toughness and masculine status which permeated working-class culture, and for many of those aged in their mid to late teens, gang membership formed part of the transition to manhood. Considerable kudos was derived from displays of fighting prowess, and boys and young men continually tested each other's mettle in order to prove themselves, and thus their masculinity, in the eyes of their peers. Confrontations between rival gangs were invested with enormous significance by the participants. Gangs issued challenges in order to spark confrontations in which honour and reputation might be acquired by defeating, and thus shaming, their rivals. Equally, gang members were obliged to meet challenges issued to them in order to defend their honour. As contemporary observers frequently noted, this male bravado was also intended to impress young women, and male gang members assumed a chivalrous obligation to avenge perceived insults to their female associates.[10]

In view of the prevailing gender norms in working-class districts in the late nineteenth century, it is perhaps unsurprising that only a very small minority of those convicted following outbreaks of gang violence were female. Working-class notions of respectability incorporated central components of the middle-class ideal of womanhood. Working-class women, like their middle-class counterparts, were expected to devote themselves to their domestic concerns as wives and mothers, and were generally expected to adhere to far higher standards of decorum than their husbands.[11] Moreover, working-class girls were trained for their future domestic roles and versed in the codes of respectability from an early age.[12] Nonetheless, it is important to acknowledge that violence was not an exclusively masculine trait in working-class districts. Although women who fought in public risked losing their claim to respectability, married women sometimes fought in the street in order to avenge insults or resolve disputes, whilst in private, many actively resisted violent and domineering husbands.[13]

Equally, the extent to which the behaviour of girls and young women conformed to dominant conceptions of femininity must not be overstated. Young women, like older married women, sometimes settled their grievances by fighting one-to-one in the streets. Such fights were far less common than brawls among young men, but their relative rarity ensured that they attracted large crowds.[14] Young women's active involvement in gang conflicts, albeit in a small minority of cases, is less surprising once it is acknowledged that there was no masculine monopoly upon violence in working-class neighbourhoods. It is possible to discern clear patterns in cases involving female gang members. I have been unable to locate a single report of an affray between opposing all-female gangs in the Manchester press. However, the press did report both occasional confrontations between gangs comprised of young people of both sexes and a series of cases in which young women took part in collective assaults by gang members upon local people and the police. Female gang members were denounced as 'degraded' and 'unwomanly' by magistrates and journalists alike. Yet, paradoxically, they tended to receive less stringent sentences than their male counterparts, perhaps reflecting the widespread contemporary view of young women as marginal figures in the local gang conflicts.

Youth gangs in Manchester in the late nineteenth century

From the early 1870s to the late 1890s, the Manchester press carried frequent reports of fighting between rival, neighbourhood-based 'scuttling' gangs in the working-class districts across the conurbation, from the borough of Salford to the West of the city to the manufacturing districts of Gorton and Openshaw to the East.[15] Gang conflicts were not confined to the poorest 'slum' districts, and some of the most notorious gangs were drawn from the relatively prosperous industrial districts such as Gorton. It is possible to trace both long-running feuds between gangs drawn from adjacent neighbourhoods and confrontations between gangs drawn from districts three or four miles apart. 'Scuttles', or fights between rival gangs, usually took place in the streets or on patches of open ground within working-class residential districts, although on Friday and Saturday nights, gangs also clashed in and around the music halls and nearby beerhouses in Manchester city centre.

Gang members, or 'scuttlers', were drawn overwhelmingly from the fourteen to nineteen age group. They were employed in a wide range of unskilled manual occupations, and it would be highly misleading to characterise scuttlers as belonging to the lumpenproletariat or a distinct 'criminal class'. Indeed, scuttling gangs were clearly viewed by local social commentators, magistrates and police officers alike as fighting gangs, rather than as criminal gangs in any broader sense.[16] For the most part, gang members lived with their parents, although as wage-earners they enjoyed a degree of independence in their leisure activities and associations. Scuttlers distinguished themselves from other young people in working-class districts by adopting uniforms that signified their toughness and their willingness to take part in street fighting. Male scuttlers wore pointed, brass-tipped clogs, flared trousers, and brightly coloured silk scarves. They grew their hair into long fringes, which were parted and plastered down upon the forehead. Peaked caps were worn tilted to the left to display their fringes.[17] Female gang members 'all dressed as much alike as possible. Those of one gang might wear straight striped skirts and shirt blouses, while those of another wore full shirts decorated with coloured braid.'[18] Contemporary press reports suggest that they sometimes wore their hair in long fringes, matching those of their male counterparts.[19]

I have only been able to trace five homicides attributed to members of scuttling gangs in the Manchester conurbation between 1870 and 1900.[20] Nonetheless, reports of woundings inflicted during clashes between rival gangs were commonplace. Gang members customarily fought with bricks, stones, knives and belts with heavy brass buckles.[21] Clashes between rival gangs prompted many lurid headlines, but the local press also frequently reported assaults by gangs upon individuals. In some of the most brutal cases, isolated gang members were set upon by members of rival gangs, but assaults were also made upon people who had no connection with the gangs. These included both local people who complained about a gang's activities and, occasionally, passers-by who strayed into territory to which a scuttling gang laid claim. Reports in the Manchester press suggested that scuttling declined in frequency and severity during the late 1890s, just as London's hooligans were capturing national headlines. Social commentators attributed the decline of Manchester's gang conflicts to the success of police campaigns against the local gangs.[22] However, further research is needed, both to ascertain whether the reported decline was more apparent than real, and to identify shifts in police strategy which might explain the demise of a pattern of street violence which had gravely concerned local civic leaders for almost three decades.

'When I am a man I would like to be able to fight like that': masculinity and gang violence

Boys growing up in working-class neighbourhoods in Manchester in the late nineteenth century were faced with a range of role models reflecting the very diverse local conceptions of what being a man entailed. As the principal wage-earners in most families, men claimed the status of bread-winner, stressing their capacity to provide for their wives and children and, thus, deriving their standing as men in part from their role within the household. Men who devoted themselves to their families and restricted their personal spending on beer and betting were regarded as 'good' husbands and 'family' men. Other notions of 'respectable' manliness were derived from occupational identities (such as those of skilled artisans), from religious affiliation, or from the 'self-improving' culture of autodidacts, and political and union activists. However, another pervasive working-class conception of manliness was centred upon a very different set of masculine virtues, including toughness (expressed both in a man's physical labour and in his everyday public conduct) and the capacity to drink heavily, which could earn a man peer recognition as a 'hard' man, or a 'man's' man. Of course, these differing conceptions of manliness were not mutually exclusive. Many men subscribed to more than one of these notions of what it meant to be a man, adopting different personas in different contexts.

Others, however, were more clearly identified, either as 'respectable' working men, or as heavy-drinking 'hard' men.[23]

Working-class boys learned from a young age that violence was a customary means for men to vent their anger. Boys were themselves frequently the victims of adult male violence. Retrospective accounts of working-class family life in the late nineteenth century suggest that many households were characterised by high levels of domestic violence, mainly perpetrated by adult men against their wives and children.[24] Moreover, adult men who fought in public could earn powerful local reputations and considerable status from displays of courage and fighting prowess. 'Fair fights', in which men fought only with their fists, often in front of large crowds, were an established means of settling grievances in working-class districts.[25] At pub closing time and weekends, such fights assumed the status of a spectator sport and provided lessons in manly conduct for those boys who joined the watching crowds. As William Bowen, who grew up in Salford during the 1880s, recalled:

> I can remember as a boy one Sunday afternoon, after closing time, a glorious summer afternoon, a crowd came out of a public house with two men stripped to their naked waists who began to fight and they fought until their naked bodies were streaming with blood. I thought, when I am a man I would like to be able to fight like that.[26]

Watching these displays, boys were left in little doubt that toughness was one of the core masculine virtues.

Fathers taught their sons to assert themselves by always accepting challenges to fight, and this emphasis upon the need to demonstrate a willingness to fight was further consolidated by peer pressure among boys. Joe Toole, who was born in Salford in 1887, reflected upon the emergence of a succession of famous local boxers:

> You had to fight to survive in my early days in Salford. If you were not fighting for a living, you had to periodically defend your skin, which included your honour; if you declined a challenge to fight, you took a back seat at all games; and if you didn't swear vigorously, nobody believed what you said.[27]

Thus boys learned by example that violence was both a necessary and legitimate means of self-assertion. Upon entering the world of work, boys were again expected to demonstrate their readiness to 'stand up for themselves'. Challenges to fight had to be accepted in order to gain peer-group acceptance in the workplace, and retrospective accounts of working-class life in Manchester in the late nineteenth century suggest that young workers continually tested each other's mettle.[28] Moreover, in a milieu in which young men tended to regard their 'sweethearts' as their property, fights also frequently stemmed from quarrels over the affections of young women. The local press frequently reported assaults committed by jealous suitors upon their rivals. In such cases, notions of the 'fair fight' were frequently abandoned and revenge was sought with knives.[29] Chivalry clearly had its limits. Mirroring the behaviour of many older working men, those aged in their mid to late teens were at times violent in their treatment of both their 'sweethearts' and their own female relatives.[30]

This broader culture of male violence formed the backdrop to young men's involvement in violent gangs. Public displays of aggression and acts of violence in clashes between rival gangs allowed those on the brink of adulthood to imagine themselves as 'hard' men. Full-scale confrontations between opposing gangs were frequently prompted by territorial infringements. Gangs staked control over territory through the occupation of strategic street corners and public houses, and incursions by one gang into the territory of another were treated as deliberate acts of provocation, leading to vendettas between rival gangs across the Manchester conurbation. In collective encounters between rival gangs, it was understood that weapons would be used by both sides, and from the mid-1880s onwards, reports of stabbings inflicted by scuttlers appeared with increasing regularity in the local press. In June 1890, the Salford police told how the Hope Street and Ordsall Lane gangs had clashed repeatedly over a period of eighteen months. The feud resulted in a series of knifings, which led in turn to a spate of trials. Hostility between the two gangs was perpetuated as both attempted to salvage their honour by avenging stabbings inflicted by their adversaries.[31] Although scuttlers appear to have sought to wound rather than murder their opponents, feuds between rival gangs generated intense hostility and the use of weapons such as belts and knives was customary in the pursuit of status and reprisal.

Assaults were also frequently made by a number of scuttlers belonging to one gang upon an isolated member of a rival gang.[32] Gangs were quick to interrogate young men from rival districts who ventured alone into their territory and appear to have regarded all such territorial infringements as challenges to their honour, even when they were undertaken by individuals. Again, the notion of the 'fair fight' was abandoned when gangs made collective assaults upon lone rivals. Particularly brutal assaults were made as acts of reprisal, and it is significant that on the rare occasions when scuttling conflicts did lead to fatalities, the victims tended to be isolated and outnumbered in attacks of this sort.[33]

As indicated above, territorial encroachments were not the only perceived insults which precipitated gang violence. Male gang members also claimed ownership of their female associates. Charles Russell, one of the pioneers of the Lads' Club movement in Manchester and an influential local social commentator, claimed that, 'The gravest troubles generally arose from attentions paid to the sweetheart of a member of one gang, by a member of another.' Local journalists, following police officers and, on occasion, gang members themselves, were quick to blame young women for inciting gang conflicts.[34] However, male scuttlers, who clearly viewed their 'sweethearts' as their possessions, required little encouragement to interpret the actions of young men from rival districts as challenges.[35]

Contemporary commentators claimed that scuttling gangs were led by 'captains', or 'kings', who had distinguished themselves in affrays.[36] By combing reports of scuttling cases in the local press, it is possible to identify a number of prominent individuals, such as John Joseph Hillyar of Salford, whose reputations appear to have spanned the working-class districts across the Manchester conurbation. Hillyar was involved in at least eleven court cases during the late 1880s and 1890s, facing charges ranging from disorderly conduct to attempted murder.[37] By the time he was aged seventeen, Hillyar was well known to rival scuttlers and was singled out by the members of opposing gangs during affrays. In May 1891, he was severely injured in a clash outside the 'Cass', a music hall in Manchester city centre. Thomas Callaghan, 'King' of the London Road scuttlers, was reported to have threatened Hillyar inside the music hall. In the subsequent affray, which occurred in the streets outside, Callaghan struck Hillyar on the head with an iron bar. Hillyar fell to the ground, and was surrounded and kicked by the rival gang.[38]

In November 1893, Hillyar was charged with stabbing Peter McLaughlin in Salford. According to the police, Hillyar initially admitted that he had committed the offence, declaring that, 'McLaughlin thinks he is the champion scuttler in Salford, and he has got to see there is some one who can . . . take him down.' Hillyar, now labelled 'King of the Scuttlers' by the Salford press, was gaoled for six months.[39] In February 1895, Hillyar was indicted for the attempted murder of a Salford collier. The police officer who apprehended Hillyar stated that he had admitted to the offence. However, at the trial Hillyar claimed, 'He had a knife, and I did it in self-defence. They keep following me from all nations. I could only go in one part of Manchester, and then certain people were not satisfied until they had got me in prison again.' Hillyar thus claimed that he was a marked man, harassed by rivals from across the conurbation. Nonetheless, he was gaoled for five years.[40] Clearly, whilst the leaders of scuttling gangs enjoyed considerable prestige, they also faced the constant risk of assault. Just as Hillyar stabbed Peter McLaughlin, he in turn was subject to assaults by rivals who sought to enhance their own reputations at his expense.[41]

It is important to stress that participation in gang conflicts was not universal among young, working-class males. Some young men, like Joe Toole, were willing to risk ostracisation by their erstwhile peers. Telling how he was increasingly drawn to the local libraries in his youth, Toole recalled how 'The lads at the street corner began to miss me. They now referred to me as a snob, who was learning more than was good for him.' When the local gang appealed to Toole to join them in a forthcoming confrontation, to save the 'honour' of the gang, 'They received no assistance from me. A new world had opened up for me which was quite unknown for them.'[42] Toole eschewed the street corner for a lifetime of activism in the labour movement, and his account usefully reminds us that the transition to manhood could take a number of different forms for young men in working-class districts in the late nineteenth century.

'They acted like Amazons, and were very active in the fray': young women and gang violence

Female gang members, like their male counterparts, tended to be single and aged in their mid to late teens. In court, they were almost invariably described as factory operatives (usually as mill workers). Young working-class women led relatively independent lifestyles between starting work and getting married. Most obtained full-time, paid employment in factories upon leaving school, and this marked the beginning of a new stage in the life cycle, as a young adult. In general, young women were likely to enjoy less free time and less freedom of movement than young men, as females were expected to perform more household chores and parents tended to make more strenuous efforts to regulate the leisure-time associations and movements of girls and young women. Nonetheless, single, female factory operatives tended to enjoy a level of disposable income and a degree of freedom of movement which enabled them both to dress fashionably and to attend places of amusement.[43]

Young, single women spent much of their free time in peer-group activities. Time was spent both in all-female groups and mixing with groups of young men, whether in beerhouses, dancing saloons, music halls and cheap theatres, or on the streets. Young women, like young men, spent much of their free time in informal gatherings on street corners, and casual congregations of scuttlers frequently involved young people of both sexes. Moreover, on the Saturday and Sunday evening parades, the principal thoroughfares of the two cities of Manchester and Salford were taken over by young people, who promenaded in same-sex groups with the aim of meeting members of the opposite sex. As public spaces, the streets were, therefore, colonised by young women as well as by young men. Their presence on the streets inevitably brought young women into conflict with the police, as beat constables attempted to break up street-corner gatherings in order to keep the pavements clear for pedestrians and to prevent annoyance to 'respectable' householders.[44]

Press reports of scuttling provide a series of glimpses of young women's involvement in gang violence. The local press occasionally reported full-scale confrontations between gangs comprised of young people of both sexes. In Bradford in East Manchester in 1877, frequent disturbances were reportedly caused by two rival gangs of scuttlers 'of both sexes, perhaps 200–300 in all' skirmishing with bricks, stones and sticks.[45] Similarly, in June 1889, a confrontation between opposing gangs from Gorton and Openshaw involved one hundred or more 'lads and lasses' hurling stones at each other according to police testimony in court.[46] Press reports frequently failed to differentiate between the roles played by young men and young women in clashes between rival gangs, but it is clear that female gang members were often far from passive in these confrontations. In January 1885, for example, Ann Flannaghan, an eighteen-year-old factory operative, was tried alongside two male scuttlers following an incident in the Manchester district of Ancoats. Flannaghan and her companions were sitting on the steps outside a public house when members of a rival gang passed by. Challenges were exchanged and a fight ensued in which a young man was stabbed. Flannaghan reportedly kicked the victim of the stabbing as he lay on the ground.[47]

By far the most notorious female scuttler was Hannah Robin, the 'sweetheart' of sixteen-year-old William Willan who was sentenced to death on 20 May 1892 for the murder of a rival scuttler in Ancoats. Robin was one of four young women who were apprehended following a disturbance in Manchester city centre at 11.00 p.m. on 27 May. According to the police, she was drunk when taken into custody and found to be armed with a 'formidable-looking belt with the usual heavy buckle at the end'. A tattoo on her right arm proclaimed 'in loving remembrance of William Willan'. A police inspector claimed in court that Manchester city centre was currently 'infested by gangs of "scuttlers"', which were actively supported by girls like the prisoners'. Robin and her companions were each sentenced to a month's imprisonment with hard labour. These were exceptionally harsh sentences for 'disorderly conduct', and it is likely that the magistrate was swayed as much by Robin's association with Willan (whose trial had generated enormous outrage in the local press) as by the police account of events on the night of 27 May.[48]

Only a small minority of the reports of affrays between opposing gangs in the local press highlighted the participation of young women. More commonly, however, young women featured in reports of assaults carried out by scuttling gangs within their own neighbourhoods, whether upon passers-by or upon local people against whom the gangs bore grudges. In January 1890, members of the self-styled 'Buffalo Bill's gang' from Pendleton in Salford assaulted a local collier named John Cunliffe late on a Saturday night. Two eighteen-year-old colliers were charged with the assault, along-side two female mill workers, Amelia Higginbottom, aged seventeen, and Agnes Garforth, sixteen. In court, Cunliffe told how he was initially as-saulted by the male prisoners, one of whom struck him on the head with a belt, knocking him to the ground where he was kicked repeatedly. Cunliffe told how he struggled home and told his two brothers what had happened. When the three of them went out to confront the gang, the two girls rushed at them and struck them with their clogs. The two male gang members were both gaoled for six months. Amelia Higginbottom and Agnes Garforth were gaoled for three months. The *Salford Chronicle* called for the male scuttlers to be flogged, then added:

> How to deal with the 'scuttleresses' – it would be too palpable a mockery to talk of such creatures as the 'gentler sex' – is more difficult. According to what the police say, these viragoes are no less cruel than the lads for whom we advocate flogging, and, therefore, perhaps, some arrangement might be made by the prison matron for a similar bestowal of the principal mark of disapproval of their vixenish behaviour.[49]

Female gang members were also sometimes actively involved in collect-ive assaults on the police by members of scuttling gangs. The feud between the Ordsall Lane and Hope Street gangs in Salford culminated in a trial on 6 June 1890 in which seventeen young men were charged with riot and wounding.[50] The trial, which followed a clash between male members of the two gangs, was followed by a series of further incidents in Ordsall Lane involving both male and female scuttlers. At 10.00 p.m. on Saturday 14 June, a police constable who was patrolling Ordsall Lane was beaten un-conscious and almost killed in what appears to have been an act of reprisal against the police following the trial.[51] Eight members of the Ordsall Lane gang (five males and three females) were charged with the assault. At a subsequent court hearing, a working man who had witnessed the assault, testified that:

> ... [he] saw the whole of them strike the officer Chapman, and if they had not been prevented [they] would have killed the officer. The girls were the

chief cause of the disturbance . . . they acted like Amazons, and were very active in the fray.[52]

This description of the female gang members as 'Amazons' is significant as it illustrates how older working men, like middle-class newspaper editors, resorted to a highly exotic vocabulary to describe violent young women. The magistrate who heard the case declared that two of the gang's female members had prompted the assault. They were sentenced to three months imprisonment. The five male scuttlers, who were judged to be 'equally guilty', nonetheless each received the maximum sentence for assaulting a police officer of six months.[53]

Young women were also involved in the systematic intimidation of witnesses by gang members. George White, a local youth and one of the principal witnesses to the assault upon the police constable in Ordsall Lane, suffered persistent harassment intended to deter him from testifying in court. In one incident, White was chased through the streets of Ordsall by a gang of young women brandishing knives. Detectives apprehended Elizabeth McGregor, Matilda McStay and Alice McEwen, three fourteen-year-olds, who were charged with breaching the peace. In court, White confirmed that the 'girls' had 'threatened to rip him up with a knife, if he gave evidence against the Ordsall Lane gang'.[54] However, after lecturing the prisoners on 'the state of depravity into which they had fallen', the magistrate, who did not appear to be convinced that fourteen-year-old girls could be a menace to society, bound them over them over to keep the peace for six months and released them. The magistrate was in turn severely admonished by the *Salford Chronicle*, which judged that harsh words from the bench were worthless if knife-wielding 'girls' could escape gaol so easily.[55] Salford's *County Telephone* labelled McGregor, McStay and McEwen 'girl "rippers"'. Less than two years after the Whitechapel murders of 'Jack the Ripper', this was a quite sensational inversion of one of the most clearly gendered labels adopted by the late Victorian press.[56]

Gender and violence

Once gang activity in Britain's major conurbations in the late nineteenth century is analysed in relation to the prevailing gender norms in working-class districts, then it is possible to suggest a new interpretation of 'hooliganism'. Those young men who joined street gangs sought to embody the working-class ideal of the 'hard' man and, thus, reproduced a deeply entrenched pattern of manly behaviour. From this perspective, it is tempting to reverse Humphries's characterisation of male gang members as 'rebels', and to view them instead as archly conservative in cultural terms. By contrast, the much smaller number of young women who took part in gang violence clearly transgressed the notions of feminine decorum embedded in working-class codes of respectability. In terms of their active violation of dominant gender norms, female gang members were far more rebellious than their male counterparts.

This is perhaps reflected in the language deployed to describe gang members in the local press. Male scuttlers were denounced in terms which were deeply familiar to the readers of the local press, as 'roughs', 'ruffians' and 'brutes'. However, this was a gendered vocabulary. These terms were rarely applied to violent young women, who did not fit within gendered stereotypes of the perpetrators of street violence centred on literary clichés and cartoons of masculine figures such as the street rough. In the absence of a stereotype of the violent, young, working-class woman, male magistrates and journalists and disapproving, older, working men adopted a more exotic vocabulary – 'virago', 'vixen', 'Amazon' and even 'girl "ripper"' – for the apparently anomalous figure of the female scuttler. Magistrates loudly condemned the behaviour of these 'degraded' young women, yet, paradoxically, often imposed comparatively lenient sentences upon female gang members. Ultimately, magistrates viewed young women as marginal figures in Manchester's gang conflicts.

Scuttling was pre-eminently a youthful activity. Young people tended to join gangs during the stage of the life cycle between leaving school and getting married and, for many young men in unskilled occupations, membership of violent gangs appears to have formed a rite of passage into manhood. However, gang violence was not an exclusively masculine concern and a minority of young women took advantage of the relative freedoms available to them before marriage to take an active part in the often tumultuous street life of working-class neighbourhoods. Unfortunately, in the absence of autobiographical accounts by former gang members, it is impossible to ascertain whether male gang members attempted to prevent young women taking part in affrays in order to preserve their function as arenas in which masculine prowess was asserted. Equally, it is difficult to chart the life experiences of former gang members into adulthood, and thus to assess the extent to which youthful reputations for criminal behaviour were cast off in the quest for respectability during adulthood. For those in their mid to late teens, however, it is clear that considerable peer-group prestige was at stake in scuttling affrays and many young people of both sexes risked serious injury in pursuit of the status and excitement derived from confrontations between rival gangs.

Notes

1. Stephen Humphries, *Hooligans or Rebels? An Oral History of Working-Class Childhood and Youth 1889–1939* (Oxford, 1981); Geoffrey Pearson, *Hooligan: A History of Respectable Fears* (1983); Rob Sindall, *Street Violence in the Nineteenth Century: Media Panic or Real Danger?* (Leicester, 1990).

2. Charles E. B. Russell and Lilian M. Rigby, *Working Lads' Clubs* (1908).

3. *MG* 13 Dec. 1890, 5 Feb. 1898; *SR* 5 May 1894.

4. Russell and Rigby, *Working Lads' Clubs*.

5. Pearson, *Hooligan* pp. 94–101, Steve Humphries, *A Secret World of Sex. Forbidden Fruit: The British Experience 1900–1950* (1988), pp. 142, 158–160.

6. Pearson, *Hooligan* pp. 76–81; Humphries, *Hooligans or Rebels* pp. 174, 176; Sindall, *Street Violence passim*.

7. Humphries, *Hooligans or Rebels* Ch. 7.

8. Humphries, *Secret World of Sex* Ch. 6.

9. For fuller treatments of the themes raised in this chapter see Andrew Davies, 'Youth gangs, masculinity and violence in late Victorian Manchester and Salford' *JSH* 32, 2 (1998), pp. 349–369, and ' "These viragoes are no less cruel than the lads": young women, gangs and violence in late Victorian Manchester and Salford' *BJC* 39, 1 (1999), pp. 72–89.

10. *SC* 12 July 1890.

11. Lucia Zedner, *Women, Crime, and Custody in Victorian England* (Oxford, 1991), pp. 15–18.

12. Carol Dyhouse, *Girls Growing Up in Late Victorian and Edwardian England* (1981); Anna Davin, *Growing up Poor: Home, School and Street in London 1870–1914* (1996).

13. Ellen Ross, 'Survival networks: women's neighbourhood sharing in London before World War I' *HWJ* 15 (1983), pp. 4–27, and *Love and Toil: Motherhood in Outcast London* (Oxford, 1993); Shani D'Cruze, 'Sex, violence and local courts: working-class respectability in a mid-nineteenth-century Lancashire town' *BJC* 39, 1 (1999), p. 40.

14. Davies, 'These viragoes' p. 77.

15. The term 'scuttling' was widely deployed in the Manchester press to describe gang fighting from 1871 onwards. The origins of the term are obscure, but it was peculiar to the Manchester conurbation.

16. A. Devine, *Scuttlers and Scuttling: Their Prevention and Cure* (Manchester, 1890), p. 2; *MG* 13 Dec. 1890.

17. *MG* 5 Feb. 1898; Charles E. B. Russell, *Manchester Boys: Sketches of Manchester Lads at Work and Play* (Manchester, 1905), p. 51.

18. *Times* 3 Oct. 1964.

19. *MC* 17 June 1890.

20. The most widely publicised homicide occurred in the Manchester district of Ancoats in 1892; see *MEN* 9 May 1892.

21. Devine, *Scuttlers and Scuttling* p. 2.

22. Russell, *Manchester Boys* p. 53.

23. Andrew Davies, *Leisure, Gender and Poverty: Working-Class Culture in Salford and Manchester, 1900–1939* (Buckingham, 1992), Ch. 2.

24. Paul Thompson, 'Voices from within' in H. J. Dyos and Michael Wolff (eds.), *The Victorian City: Images and Realities* (2 Vols, 1976), 1, pp. 73–79.

25. Davies, 'Youth gangs' pp. 354–356.

26. Henry Hill, *The Story of Adelphi: Sixty Years' History of the Adelphi Lads' Club* (Salford, 1949), p. 121.

27. Joe Toole, *Fighting through Life* (1935), pp. 5–6.

28. Davies, 'Youth gangs' pp. 355–356.

29. *SR* 13 Jan. 1894.

30. *SR* 8 Feb. 1890; *SC* 22 May 1897.

31. *SC* 13 July 1889, 8 Feb. 1890, 7 June 1890; *MC* 7 June 1890.

32. Devine, *Scuttlers and Scuttling* p. 3.

33. *MG* 12 May 1892.

34. Russell, *Manchester Boys* p. 52; *MG* 5 Feb. 1898; *SR* 3 June 1899.

35. Davies, 'Youth gangs' pp. 358–359.

36. Russell, *Manchester Boys* p. 53.

37. Davies, 'Youth gangs' pp. 360–363.

38. *MG* 5, 13, 20 May, 13 June 1891; *SR* 9 May 1891.

39. *SC* 18 Nov. 1893; *SR* 13 Jan. 1894.

40. *SR* 2 March 1895.

41. *MEN* 9 May 1892.

42. Toole, *Fighting through Life* p. 48.

43. Davies, 'These viragoes' p. 78.

44. *CL* 6 Aug. 1875; *MCN* 31 Jan. 1885.

45. *GR* 25 Aug. 1877.

46. *ALR* 22 June 1889.

47. *MCN* 31 Jan. 1885.

48. *MC* 21, 30 May 1892; *MEN* 28 May 1892.

49. *SC* 25 Jan. 1, 8 Feb. 1890; *MG* 5 Feb. 1890.

50. *SC* 7 June 1890.

51. Davies, 'These viragoes' pp. 84–85.

52. *MC* 17 June 1890.

53. *SC* 28 June 1890.

54. Davies, 'These viragoes' pp. 85–86.

55. *SC* 21 June 1890.

56. *CT* 21 June 1890; Judith R. Walkowitz, *City of Dreadful Delight: Narratives of Sexual Danger in Late-Victorian London* (Chicago, 1992).

PART II

The regulation of violence

'Ingenuities of the female mind': legal and public perceptions of sexual violence in Victorian England, 1850–1890

KIM STEVENSON

In August 1851 at Gloucester Assizes, Richard Kear, aged twenty-four years, and four other young male colliers appeared, charged with the rape of Mary M'Carthy. Altogether nine men had been involved. Finding Mary 'exhausted and resting' in the Forest of Dean they directed her towards a house for some water. She refused to enter but was threatened with a shovel and with being burnt alive. Afterwards, she went to the workhouse where the doctor 'confirmed her injuries'. All five charged were found guilty of rape and either 'transported for their natural lives' or sentenced to fifteen years imprisonment. Twenty-five years later, in the same month and at the same court, Richard Morgan and nine other men aged between seventeen and twenty-seven appeared before Mr Justice Grove, charged with raping, or aiding and abetting the rape of Jane Goodall. She was also walking through the Forest of Dean with one of the defendants, William Barrett, but left him, apparently drunk, to rest. Nine men then accosted her; four 'committed the outrage' while the others held her down. Barrett 'offered no assistance' to her, but on 'hearing her screams', several other men did. They later identified the prisoners and the 'individual outrages committed'. One man was acquitted, two were convicted of rape and sentenced to fifteen years. The rest received ten years imprisonment as accessories to the crime, as the judge believed that 'all would have committed the full act' had it not been for the intervention of the witnesses.

The impression provided by the case summaries in the court reports section of *The Times* for 16 August 1851 and 10 August 1876 is (for the modern researcher) of two fairly brutal incidents of 'gang' rape. But expressions used in the reports, such as 'committed the outrage', 'committed the act' and the bland 'confirmation of her injuries', make it very difficult to recover what actually happened. Euphemisms like these, constantly used in reporting, act to disguise the true events. Consequently, an amount of interpretative ingenuity is needed to decode the language used. Court reports were hugely popular, in local and national newspapers. During the latter half of the nineteenth century, as Jo Jones's chapter in this book confirms, newspapers printed a constant stream of representations of sexual violence, indicating that, while such incidents did not occur every day, they were by no means exceptional. But the ambiguity of the discourse turned everyday violence (in the sense that ordinary women might be attacked during their normal, daily lives), into something altogether more aberrant and deviant. However, despite reports of some fairly horrific and brutal sexual assaults, and an increase in the reported incidence of sexual violence during the period 1850–1890, the wider significance of violence on this scale was generally disregarded, largely because public attitudes reproduced gendered norms and stereotypes about male and female sexuality. In the courtroom in particular, gender stereotypes often operated to the detriment of any woman involved, especially female complainants. Thus, the spontaneous reaction of a woman trying to protect herself from sexual attack became for the defence lawyer an instance of the 'ingenuities of the female mind'.[1] Such feminine 'ingenuity' was often interpreted in the courtroom as sexual deviance or fabrication, rather than a praiseworthy attempt at resistance. Female ingenuity was underpinned by a woman's sexuality which itself posed a hazard to men's respectability and restraint. This chapter examines the effectiveness of the legal and public response to sexual violence, and considers the extent to which public adherence to gendered stereotypes influenced the practical operation of the law.

The study is underpinned by over 200 cases of sexual violence reported in *The Times* newspaper between 1850 and 1885, mainly from the assizes, but also the London police courts. In each daily edition at least one whole page, and frequently up to three, was devoted to court reports. As the 'voice of the nation', *The Times* was highly influential in communicating establishment views and providing an indication of the representation of crime in terms of contemporary ideology.[2] *The Times* was comparatively restrained in its reporting of sexual violence, unlike the more robust, and sometimes 'sensationalist', coverage of some provincial papers.[3] Such discretion was commended by Sir Francis Jeune, who concluded that while the administration of justice should be given suitable publicity, *Times* 'newspaper reports today are pretty much as they should be'. *The Times* was a gauge of the contemporary respectable perspective.[4] *The Times* coverage of these cases, especially those reaching the higher courts, highlighted certain aspects of such violence for public consumption – in particular, those aspects emphasising either female unrespectability and male respectability or vice versa.

This served to hide, or at least marginalise, the majority of those ambiguous cases where blame could be less clearly apportioned.

Between 1850 and 1890 the incidence of sexual violence was believed to have increased, while indices of other types of physical violence (except domestic violence) systematically decreased. Statistical accuracy here is highly problematic. Not only are there difficulties of definition in terms of what did or did not constitute a sexual crime but the language used in the reporting of such crimes was often ambiguous. Equally, in the historical record, sexual offences were not always segregated from other physical assaults but included under general returns categorised as 'offences against the person', 'crimes of violence' or 'crimes of morals'. For example, many police court assault cases reported in *The Times* turn out to be failed charges of sexual assault with the (lesser) conviction for common assault being substituted.[5]

A statistical analysis published in the 1898 *Pall Mall Magazine* shows that, as a generic group, the average yearly number of committals for persons tried for 'offences against the person' at both the assizes and quarter sessions, decreased from 9.5 per cent in the period 1876–1880 to 8.9 per cent in 1891–1895.[6] Modern statisticians corroborate this decline. Amongst modern historians, Gatrell concludes that, from 1856 onwards, all indices of violence 'unambiguously declined' until the end of the century; yet simultaneously the incidence of sexual assaults increased. He estimates that the rate of trials for non-sexual assaults fell by 71 per cent from the late 1850s to the beginning of the 1900s.[7] However, his summary for sexual assaults based on the annual criminal statistics suggests a very different picture. Here, the number of committals to trial systematically increased from an annual average of 189 in the period 1836–1840 to 846 (of 1318 cases known to the police) by 1896–1900. The annual average peaked at 944 in 1886–1890 (of 1255 cases known to the police), probably due to the legislative reforms introduced by the 1885 Criminal Law Amendment Act. Gatrell is dismissive of the statistical integrity of this data, arguing that it is distorted by the 'prevailing legislative and attitudinal changes'. He assesses its value as merely 'incidental', simply demonstrating the relative infrequency with which such cases appeared before the courts. But it is likely that the data relating to physical assaults could have been similarly distorted, for example by the Aggravated Assaults Acts 1853 and the Offences Against the Person Act 1861. This increase in sexual violence cases should not be so easily dismissed, especially given the inherent difficulties in bringing such cases to trial. Not only might the victim be understandably reluctant to prosecute but, as Home Office papers underline, except in cases of rape, the law required that the injured person bear the financial cost of prosecution. This raises the question of how many cases involving sexual violence were not completed, as they were not transferred from the (virtually free) summary jurisdiction of the magistrates court to a higher court competent to deal with them.[8] Many sexual assault cases were only prosecuted in higher courts if financially sponsored by some society or public body, such as the Institute for Improving and Enforcing the Laws for the Protection of Women, the Associate Institute for the Protection of Females or the National Vigilance Association.

Establishment attitudes towards certain crimes can clearly limit or increase their seriousness in public and legal perceptions. 'The Crimes of England', an 1898 official classification of all existing indictable crimes, ordered all offences against the person hierarchically, from murder down.[9] Rape appeared in nineteenth position followed by indecent assault and defilement. Unnatural offences appeared at sixteen, and other more general assaults at eight and nine, thus giving some indication of contemporary public perceptions as to the gravity of sexual crimes overall. In this analysis, sexual violence was categorised as a moral offence. The statistical range of sexual crimes seems to indicate that the highest proportion of such 'moral crimes', as reported to the police, took place in the 'agricultural counties' of southwestern England, with the lowest averages being in the 'manufacturing' and 'pleasure' towns'.[10] Such statistics should be regarded with some scepticism. Certainly, contemporary commentators were more preoccupied with the sexual dangers of Victorian towns and cities.[11]

Sexual ingenuities

The newspaper depiction of certain types of sexual violence actively masked the occurrence of other kinds. The legal discourse, both through the legislative function and the trial process, tended to objectify women, downplaying their individuality and sexual identity. Press reporting colluded in this phenomenon.[12] As Arnaud-Duc argues, 'women were at the center of the law's ambiguities, which resulted from the gap between the legal discourse and the social reality the law claimed to regulate'.[13] This dichotomy is reflected in the recent debate over the actual operation of the concept of gendered separate spheres within the period.[14] Despite the dominant gender stereotypes, women's and men's daily experience could blur boundaries between public and private. As Kent comments, women were identified by their sexual function as 'the Sex', but the resulting contradiction between the ideal mother and the degraded prostitute trading her sexuality in public was too extreme to apply in real life.[15] Dominant ideologies attributed moral status to the idealised and necessarily sexually chaste woman in the private sphere and denied it to her symbolic opposite, the 'fallen woman'.

These ideological constructions of morality had wider connotations than the status of individual women, however. The sexually chaste woman anchored in 'the family' became the guarantor of a much wider social morality. Consequently, the transgression of the 'fallen woman' was likewise seen as a generalised social and moral danger. The problem for individual women bringing cases of sexual violence to a court was that the law used such gendered divisions as a basis for making both courtroom judgments and enacting legislation. According to Clark, working women who had been raped were regarded as deviant by, amongst others, doctors, lawyers and journalists.[16] A woman could rely on the law's (limited) protection only to the extent that she conformed to dominant stereotypes. As Frost comments, rape was the ultimate limit to women's sexual freedom. Any suggestion that a woman had been 'sexually assertive' meant her case was more likely to fail.[17] If her behaviour offended against the doctrine of separate spheres, as it was understood by the legal system, then instead of being 'victim' she often became 'offender'. Legal and moral discourse colluded to define the practical limits of these gendered spheres – with direct consequences for women in court.[18]

One way in which legal professionals in court reinforced the impact of dominant gender norms was through the rhetoric of ingenuity. When used to describe masculine actions, ingenuity implied that a man had acted in a positive, even creative, manner. Manifestations of masculine ingenuity can be found in the strategy and conduct of the defence. William Ballantine QC, a regular defender of men charged with sexual offences, and 'the most brilliant cross-examiner',[19] was praised when he used such rhetorical devices. Defending Alfred Willis, a Queen's Messenger in the Home Department charged with indecent assault, Ballantine conducted a 'very ingenious defence' of an undoubtedly guilty man by throwing doubt on the complainant's motivation, resulting in a lenient sentence of two months imprisonment.[20] However, *feminine* ingenuity was associated with deceit. Hale's warning that rape was an accusation 'easy' to make was always uppermost in the mind of the court.[21] At Middlesex Assizes John Champ, a police constable, was alleged to have taken 'indecent liberties' with a woman. She had struggled violently, but Champ only let her go when she claimed she had just miscarried. Ballantine (defending) made a 'humorous speech' suggesting it was a 'trumped up charge', 'one of the ingenuities of the female mind'. Ballantine's defence undermined the seriousness of the case by diminishing the integrity of the victim.[22]

The importance of 'ingenious' defences was great. In 1860, Joseph Lock appeared before Marlborough Street Police Court charged with indecently assaulting Elizabeth Webb, the thirteen-year-old daughter of one of his employees. She was examined personally by the defendant and his first lawyer but neither could shake her testimony. Sir Robert Carden, presiding magistrate, was strongly impressed with the respectability of her parents and was convinced that, despite very rigid cross-examination, the facts 'remained unshaken'. However Lock, recently married, was represented as a man of the 'highest moral character' and respectability, so Carden sent the case to jury trial. There, an 'inspired' defence ensured that the Central Criminal Court viewed the complainant less positively. The jury accepted the defendant's claim that he had kissed her with 'her consent', making her guilty of 'wilfully misrepresenting' the situation. Lock was found not guilty to the applause of the court, which was hushed by the judge.[23] Under the Criminal Procedure Act 1865 defendants could represent themselves and regularly adopted such 'ingenious' tactics, often successfully. Charged with the 'rape of a semi-idiot girl' and robbing her of money which had been the 'gift of pitying friends', Henry Scott represented himself at Monmouth Crown Court in July 1876. He tearfully addressed the jury, asking them to believe that the money was his and that the girl had been trying to rob him, 'tempting him with advances of an indelicate nature'. His 'ingenious defence' might have succeeded, had it not been for the presence in court of the girl's clergyman, testifying to her good character.[24] The legal system itself, therefore, reinforced this gendered concept of ingenuity, pitting the complainant against its masculine force and identifying any demonstration of female 'ingenuity' as suggestive of her unreliability as a credible witness.

The press further reinforced the patriarchal notion of the law that female complainants were less reliable. Often journalists reporting cases of sexual violence singled out for praise those lawyers who conducted 'searching examinations' of these women. The rhetoric used was also coded in other ways. *Times* reporters habitually censored details as being 'too disgusting for publication' or 'unreportable'. As in the two cases cited at the outset of this chapter, sexual violence offenders 'effected their purpose', 'committed the outrage', 'attempted to violate the person' or 'had connexion', thus disguising the specific nature of the assault. Witnesses too were apparently schooled in the correct language.[25] In cases of indecent assault, the precise nature of attack is less obvious: deciphering the much-used phrase 'taking liberties' would test the most competent cryptographer. In 1853, Henry Scott, who claimed to be a doctor, was charged with rape but convicted of indecent assault. A young woman sought his advice for a malady but was 'abused and taken advantage of'. In contrast, as Sue Lees's work has shown, the modern courtroom hears highly explicit details about the specific parts of the body touched.[26]

Euphemisms used to describe the effects of an attack upon a victim acknowledged her precarious position and so removed her from the 'everyday' sphere. Modesty required that victims simply 'fainted', 'suffered ill-health', or 'complained of being ill'. As Lucy Bland argues, modesty was an inhibitory force that ensured female purity; an unconscious quality, which once 'outraged' was morally destroyed and could not be regained.[27] This desexualisation of intimate words and descriptors was a constant element in Victorian respectable discourse.[28] Such euphemisms purportedly protected morals – of the women involved, of those in court and, of course, of the wider readership of the court reports. However, this discretion of language also screened from public view the shocking realities of the physical (and emotional) harm that sexual violence caused to women and girls.

Protecting the person?

Such ambiguity of language was also emphasised by the law's consistent reluctance to define clearly the constituent elements of sexual crimes. As Bland argues, to feminists, the law was seen as having the potential to be both empowering and protective. While 'the vote was seen as the panacea for most women's ills', until attained, there was an immediate need for protective legislation of women and children which addressed the dangers of sex.[29] The two major legislative enactments of the period were the Offences Against the Person Act 1861 and the Criminal Law Amendment Act 1885. Arguably designed and intended as protectionist measures, in the sense of aiming to facilitate prosecution and conviction, the former manifestly failed even to consider the desirability of protecting women from sexual violence. The latter concerned itself more with the 'moral panic' associated with the white slave trade and the sensational exposé of child prostitution in the *Pall Mall Gazette* than any considered approach to effectively policing sexual violence.[30]

As its title suggests, the 1861 Offences Against the Person Act was the first major consolidating statute to codify all crimes likely to cause injury or harm, and made rape a statutory crime. Hitherto, interpersonal violence had been largely dealt with under the common law, that is, the law derived by judges from the precedents set by previous cases. The use of the word 'person' might lead one to believe that its protection would effectively extend to the sexual 'personhood' of a woman. In the courtroom, the word 'person' was used with a very clear sexual connotation as a euphemism for both male and female genitalia. However, the purpose of the Act was much broader than this, encompassing all conceivable actions where any part of the whole person might be injured. Clauses cover not only general physical assaults, such as causing actual or grievous bodily harm, but offences of endangering passengers on trains, workers on the railway, and attacking specific individuals in the course of their duty, such as the clergy, magistrates and seamen. The statute clearly defined the necessary constituent elements of *mens rea* (criminal intent) and *actus reus* (unlawful conduct). Sections 18 and 20 governing serious physical assaults, for example, required the prosecution to prove 'unlawfully and maliciously (*mens rea*) wounding, causing or inflicting any grievous bodily harm (*actus reus*)'. Detailed clauses, often running to fifty words or more, were drafted for most of the three dozen or so crimes in the Act, except rape and murder.

Despite considerable debate, the legislators could not agree a common clause for murder. By contrast, rape barely featured in the debates and no thought appears to have been given to its definition. Section 48 simply provided that 'whosoever shall be convicted of the crime of rape shall be guilty of a felony' and sentenced to penal servitude for life, or not less than three years. In rape, criminal intent depended upon the woman's refusal of consent and the offender's knowledge of this. However, the statute did not define these elements but left them to the judges' discretion, based on existing common law. Consequently, judicial attitudes influenced and shaped the law. Victims were expected to make 'every resistance they could', regardless of circumstances.[31] In failing to define explicitly the requisite elements of rape, the 1861 Act was arguably less effective in controlling such violations. The mystification remained about whether rape was a property crime (infringing another man's rights over a woman's sexuality), a physical crime of violation, or a 'moral' crime undermining female sexual chastity. Such mystification is particularly apparent in the clauses dealing with the 'lesser offence' of the 'defilement' of young girls. There was a widespread belief that 'natural' sexual innocence and purity would protect young girls, suggesting that formal legal protection might have been unnecessary. Where a girl had been sexually abused, it was consequently self evident that her sexual innocence had already been corrupted. Therefore, there could be no criminal intent on the part of the offender. The Act maintained this earlier position, that it was no offence to have sexual intercourse with a girl under twelve who 'freely consented', however ignorant.[32] 'Innocent' girls, of course, would not have so 'freely consented'. Carnal knowledge with a girl under ten years remained a felony under section 50. However, it was accepted that where girls under ten 'validly consented' to sexual intercourse, the charge should be reduced to 'attempted carnal knowledge', again shifting the emphasis away from the defendant's intent and making sweeping assumptions about young children's capacity to give informed consent to sex.[33]

The offence of indecent assault was equally problematic. It could be tried in magistrates' courts without a jury. It potentially covered a wide range of assaults, from slipping a hand up a skirt or blouse, to instrumental violation.

It carried a maximum of two years imprisonment but there was no guidance on sentencing. In 1867, the Home Office was forced to seek guidance from the law officers concerning the most appropriate charge where an indecent assault was committed but no great violence was used. Was it an aggravated assault carrying a sentence of six months? Were the magistrates bound to treat it as a common assault (maximum two months sentence)? Or should they indict for indecent assault? The Attorney General and Solicitor General advised that such assaults could properly be dealt with as aggravated assaults, presumably to avoid the necessary expense of a full jury trial.[34] But this failed to acknowledge the sexual context of such assaults. As already noted, a number of reported cases in *The Times* demonstrate that, though initially charged with indecent assault, the defendant was actually convicted for common assault, underlining contemporary ambiguity towards the issue and making it difficult to identify such cases in the historical record. Where the victim was very young, the maximum sentence could be expected: assaults in public places were a matter of respectable concern. But, by 1875, a fine of £5 and imprisonment until it was paid was not uncommon punishment. Similarly, where the victim was a servant, a more lenient approach was evident. As Conley observes, judicial officials were generally less concerned about the safety of young women 'once inside the master's home'.[35] In 1859, Thomas Jennings was sentenced to three months hard labour for indecently assaulting a fifteen-year-old servant, his defence being that he had been drinking and mistook her bedroom for his.[36] A particular *cause célèbre* involved peer of the realm, Lord St Leonards. On 23 May 1884, he pleaded not guilty at the Central Criminal Court to indecently assaulting servant Emma Cole during the absence of her employer. The evidence against him was overwhelming, the assault serious, and Emma reacted in stereotypically correct fashion – immediately complaining to another servant, and to her employer on his return. She also submitted herself to a medical examination the following day. Thus, despite considerable efforts on the part of the defence to discredit her, the jury swiftly found him guilty. Even so, St Leonards was discharged after having spent a mere seven weeks in custody.[37]

Sexual violence itself was no doubt a subject that the Victorian patriarchal establishment found difficult and disconcerting to debate. Any discussion was more likely to be conducted in the context of the broader moral dangers posed to society than concern for the personal wrongs perpetrated against individual women. The avoidance of any sex-specific language might also reflect society's contemporary denial, in the public domain at least, of any individual autonomy a woman might have over her personal sexuality, while clearly indicating a sexual dimension to the discourse.

Splintering the silence

There is little indication that the 1861 Act made any significant difference to convictions and sentencing practice, or impacted upon public attitudes about sexual violence. A trawl through *The Times* prior to the 1885 Criminal Law Amendment Act singularly fails to reveal any significant leading articles on the subject. This omission is repeated in the wide range of periodical literature of the time. Other social issues, such as the effects of alcohol on behaviour, or domestic violence, produced a wealth of debate. In a leading article on crimes of violence in the London Metropolitan area on 17 September 1875, *The Times* denounced inconsistencies in sentencing for wife assaults, but any sexual dimension to this was necessarily ignored, since husbands' sexual access to their wives was unlimited and uncontestable. Indeed, the 1870s saw considerable judicial concern about the apparent increase in domestic violence. By contrast, towards the end of the 1870s, a diminution in the publicly reported number of cases of sexual violence is evident. This is perhaps indicative of the collusive press–establishment relationship identified earlier, the former reinforcing the idealistic moral platitudes of the latter through 'responsible' reportage.

Nevertheless, from the late 1860s women began to vocalise their concerns about violence. As Lucy Bland states, the feminist-inspired campaign against the Contagious Diseases Acts started to break down the taboo of speaking about sex, but it was not until the social purity campaigns of the 1880s that the feminist agenda started to promote issues of sexuality and sexual violence.[38] Even then, women who were prepared to air such issues in feminist periodicals such as the *Englishwoman's Review*, were more circumspect when writing for the wider audience of the *Edinburgh Review, Contemporary Review* or *Westminster Review*. As Kent notes, the early pioneers of the feminist movement rarely spoke publicly about the sexual nature of their motives. Suffrage memoirs suggest that sexual issues were discussed privately, but only discreet hints appeared in the feminist press.[39] Both directly and indirectly, nineteenth-century feminist discourse reflected women's understanding of how they were treated by the law and the court process. Some, such as Millicent Fawcett, used issues relating to violence against women to support their arguments for granting women the franchise. But some opponents of women's suffrage, such as Margaret Oliphant and Eliza Lynn Linton, concentrated on the female need for protection and the necessity for invoking a male sense of chivalry as the only effective defence. Both sides of the debate emphasised the importance of maintaining existing high levels of female morality as a crucial factor in female safety. Such commentary and its impact on the public conscience certainly helped raise

the profile of violence against women. But it was other factors that precipitated the Criminal Law Amendment Act 1885, endorsing its philosophy
towards sexual violence.

'Moral dimensions'

The issue of female protection manifested itself at the start of the 1880s
more as a generalised moral panic than any concern about women as
victims of sexual violence. W. T. Stead's *Maiden Tribute* sought to rouse the
nation through his construction of sexual danger as a national, not a personal, issue.[40] Scandals surrounding the 'white slave trade', especially the
decoying of young women to Belgium, moved the government to set up a
Royal Commission.[41] Mr Thomas Snagge, a barrister appointed by the
Foreign Office to conduct inquiries in Belgium, found evidence of 'maybe
half a dozen' English girls in brothels in Brussels.[42] Despite this low figure,
the nation excited itself into a moral panic. An 1881 Select Committee of
the House of Lords 'investigated the matter at very considerable length and
made a most valuable Report'.[43] Its main recommendations prohibited the
procurement of females under twenty-one for the purposes of prostitution
overseas. However, the provisions only applied to innocent girls, not yet corrupted. Clearly, the moral dangers of debauching and exporting of 'innocent'
girls had a more powerful influence on the public conscience than the
regular sorts of violent outrages perpetrated by British sexual predators.

Both feminists and sexual purists entered the debate following *The Maiden
Tribute* but found it problematic to negotiate the dominant constructions of
'the moral' and their associations with women's sexuality. Fawcett argued
that, if women had been enfranchised, the 1885 Act would have been
passed without the necessity of forcing Parliament and the public to open
their eyes to the 'hideously perverted state of morals' running through
society.[44] The well-known philanthropist Ellice Hopkins highlighted the
existence of a 'conspiracy of silence', condemning both Church and state
for their failure to take the opportunity to 'save their own girls'.[45] From
her 'anxious work among the poor fallen women of London', Mary Jeune
advised that 'these women are invariably untruthful' and generally led
astray by men in 'their own position in life', warning that women hardened
in vice are 'unscrupulous' and that their statements should be treated with
great caution.[46]

The provisions of the preliminary Bills introduced between 1882 and
1885 generated considerable debate over the age of consent. The problem
(as in 1861) lay in differentiating between the sexually ingenious young

woman and the asexual (innocent) child. There was a consensus that severe penalties should be inflicted upon those who unambiguously defiled innocent girls of 'a very tender age', that is, under thirteen. The Bishop of Rochester, referring to an 'unfortunate superstition' of the advantages to be gained by violating young virgins, recommended the use of corporal punishment. Lord Salisbury agreed that, where proved, the offence was 'one of the most horrible that could be conceived, [and] the most defenceless class of the community was especially exposed to it'.[47] Ultimately, twenty-five lashes were deemed sufficient where the offender was less than sixteen years and a maximum of two years imprisonment for other cases.

Restraint over publicising indecent details was of greater concern than female vulnerability. Their Lordships were divided on Lord Milltown's proposal to remove the power of the magistrates to exclude the public from any court hearing, as the publication of such cases might be injurious to public morals or suggest to the minds of the uneducated offences they would never think of committing.[48] Only one contributor touched on the impact of publicity upon girls who might be deterred from coming forward to give evidence.[49] The issues that attracted the most heated debate, however, were those where men might be subjected to the malicious accusations of women, or to the likelihood of corrupt and immoral girls leading men astray. There was virtually no significant discussion in any of these debates of the problem caused by men sexually attacking women, only of the dangers of women being procured by men. Lord Shaftesbury highlighted the need to protect 'thousands of morally vulnerable women and girls returning home at all times of the night from factories, workshops and houses of business' from immoral male importunity, but the issue of their physical vulnerability was ignored.[50] Therefore, in seeking to understand why the 1885 Act was so persistently delayed and filibustered, it might be suggested that the real reasons lay in the susceptibility of perceived masculine vulnerabilities to largely mythological feminine predatory (ingenious) natures.

In 1885, a Private Member's Bill, broadly protective of masculine vulnerability to the hazards posed by women's sexual 'ingenuity' passed through Parliament. There was some debate on rape during the Committee Stage, but only in the context of the common law categorisations which vitiated consent. These were formulated into the three lesser provisions under section 3, procuring the defilement of a woman by threats, false representations and stupefaction. The statute also settled the law on defilement prohibiting sexual intercourse with a girl under thirteen (section 4). Carnal knowledge of a girl between thirteen and sixteen was also made unlawful – subject to a limited defence where the man was under twenty-four years of age (section 5), and of any female idiot or imbecile, provided the defendant was aware of her character. Nevertheless, as I have argued, these debates were informed less by an intention to provide women with effective legal remedies for the physical and other injuries caused by sexual violence and more by wider anxieties framed in a patriarchal moral discourse which defined women largely through their (problematic and unstable) sexualities. Bland comments that many feminists had high expectations of the Bill but later came to 'recognise that the Act's *application* was of no advantage to women' at all.[51] The 1885 Act was even largely ineffective in halting the white slave trade it set out to control, requiring further legislation in 1912.

Vague legal definitions and language combined with courtroom expectations that victims of sexual violence conformed to 'respectable' stereotypes rather than those that implied sexual 'ingenuity'. The power of the legal system to enforce patriarchal imperatives meant that cases were often decided in the light of these influences, rather than directly on their facts and circumstances. Overall, the treatment of women victims of sexual violence, both through the daily practical operation of the law and legislative discourse, suggests that Victorian society was not yet ready to acknowledge the real vulnerability of their position or to offer effective correction to male sexual predation.

Notes

1. *Times* 12 Oct. 1850.

2. Rob Sindall, *Street Violence in the Nineteenth Century: Media Panic or Real Danger?* (Leicester, 1990), p. 29.

3. Shani D'Cruze, *Crimes of Outrage, Sex, Violence and Victorian Working Women* (1998), p. 9.

4. 'Illustrated Interview: Sir Francis and Lady Jeune' *SM* 7 (1894), p. 584.

5. NRO/CA/374 Minute Book General Quarter Sessions, Nottingham.

6. J. Holt Schooling, 'Crime' *PMM* 15 (1898), p. 244.

7. V. A. C. Gatrell, Bruce Lenman and Geoffrey Parker, *Crime and the Law: The Social History of Crime in Western Europe since 1500* (1980), p. 289.

8. See PRO HO45/9547/59343(I)/263 and M. Elliot, *Criminal Procedure in England and Scotland* (1878), p. 2.

9. Reproduced in Schooling, 'Crime' p. 242.

10. *Ibid.*, p. 352.

11. J. Walkowitz, *City of Dreadful Delight: Narratives of Sexual Danger in Late-Victorian London* (Chicago, 1992).

12. D'Cruze, *Crimes of Outrage* p. 79.

13. N. Arnaud-Duc, 'The law's contradictions' in G. Fraisse and M. Perrot (eds.), *A History of Women in the West* (5 Vols, Harvard, 1993), 4, p. 81.

14. Amanda Vickery, 'Golden age to separate spheres? A review of the categories and chronology of English women's history' in Pamela Sharpe (ed.), *Women's Work* (1998), pp. 294–331; Lucia Zedner, *Women, Crime and Custody in Victorian England* (Oxford, 1991), Ch. 1.

15. Susan Kingsley Kent, *Sex and Suffrage in Britain, 1860–1914* (Princeton, N.J., 1987), p. 32.

16. Anna Clark, *Women's Silence Men's Violence* (1987), p. 5.

17. Ginger S. Frost, *Promises Broken: Courtship, Class and Gender in Victorian England* (Charlottesville, 1995), p. 108.

18. Carolyn A. Conley, *The Unwritten Law: Criminal Justice in Victorian Kent* (Oxford, 1991), pp. 93–95.

19. 'Illustrated Interview' p. 581.

20. *Times* 13 Jan. 1853.

21. Sir M. Hale, *The History of the Pleas of the Crown* (2 Vols, 1936), 1, p. 627.

22. *Times* 12 Oct. 1850.

23. *Ibid.*, 22, 24 Oct., 26 Nov. 1860.

24. *Ibid.*, 31 July 1876.

25. PRO Crim1/8/7.

26. *Times* 27 Oct. 1853; Sue Lees, *Carnal Knowledge: Rape on Trial* (1996) Ch. 4; K. Soothill *et al.*, 'Judges, the media and rape' *JL&S* 17 (1990), pp. 211–233.

27. Lucy Bland, *Banishing the Beast: English Feminism and Sexual Morality 1885–1914* (1995), p. 57.

28. Judith R. Walkowitz, 'Dangerous sexualities' in Fraisse and Perrot, *A History of Women in the West* p. 370.

29. Bland, *Banishing* pp. 250–251.

30. W. T. Stead, 'The maiden tribute of modern Babylon' *PMG* (1885) 4 July, 6–10 July; Walkowitz, *City*.

31. Per J. Coleridge, *R v. Hallett* 9 Car and P. 747 and see *R v. Fletcher* 1 C.C. 39.

32. 9 Georg II IV.

33. *R v. Beale* 1 C.C. 10.

34. PRO HO 119/18.

35. *Times* 27 May, 30 June 1875; Conley, *The Unwritten Law* p. 86.

36. *Times* 28 Jan. 1859.

37. *Ibid.*, 24 May, 7 July 1884.

38. Bland, *Banishing* pp. xiii, xvii.

39. Kent, *Sex and Suffrage* p. 158.

40. Walkowitz, *City* p. 84.

41. Charles Terrot, *The Maiden Tribute: A Study of the White Slave Traffic of the Nineteenth Century* (1959).

42. Hansard, HL Select Committee 1881 (448) ix 355.

43. Hansard, HC 1885 [299] 198 Report on the law relating to the protection of young girls.

44. Millicent Garrett Fawcett, 'Speech or Silence' *CR* 48 (1885), p. 327.

45. Ellice Hopkins, 'The apocalypse of evil' *CR* 48 (1885), p. 332.

46. Mary Jeune, 'Saving the innocents' *FtlyR* 38 (1885), p. 345.

47. Hansard, House of Lords, HL 1883 [280] 1385, 1386.

48. *Ibid.*, 1388.

49. HL 1883 [281] 404.

50. HL 1884 [288] 410–412.

51. Bland, *Banishing* p. 303.

CHAPTER SIX

'She resisted with all her might': sexual violence against women in late nineteenth-century Manchester and the local press

JOANNE JONES

From the mid-nineteenth century, the British popular press was engulfed by a public craving for sensation news, guaranteeing maximum exposure for cases of seduction, domestic abuse and murder. Taking their lead from the more lurid publications, the daily and weekly newspapers fed a voracious appetite for crime news, revelling in patterns of vice and villainy, both locally and nationally, as tales of abuse and violation became a lucrative business. Victims and defendants were paraded before eager audiences who, well versed in the nineteenth-century literary genres of sensation and melodrama, came to look upon crime news as a good read with the added spice of being grounded in reality. From a comfortable distance, readers were able to spy on the negotiated relationship between victim and defendant, be it familial, marital, one of courtship or between strangers. As commercial undertakings, the newspapers' sensational narratives enticed, entertained and informed readers, but they were not simply sources of vicarious pleasure for 'respectable' audiences who, unaccustomed to the daily grind of working-class districts, were enthralled by its colourful presentation. In choosing to report acts of everyday violence as news, in spite of their apparent statistical decline, the newspapers' narratives invoked wider concerns of perceived disorder within working-class neighbourhoods and, in doing so, spelt out the case for regulation and reform.

Falling under the umbrella of sensation news were acts of sexual violence against women, or more specifically rapes and indecent assaults. Though a sexual agenda may have underlain a number of physical assaults, both in motive and enactment, it was an agenda largely ignored by the popular press whose preferred focus for sexual violence was sexual crime. Such newspaper coverage of sexual murder, rape and indecent assault harnessed the narratives of sexual danger, which in many forms 'reverberated around courtrooms, drawing rooms, street corners and the correspondence columns of the daily press'. These narratives were diffused to embrace many aspects of the lives of working-class women, including their '. . . work, lifestyle, reproductive strategies, fashion and self display and non-familial attachments . . . '.[1] Anna Clark has identified the partial framing of social anxieties in understandings of female sexuality from the early nineteenth century. Problems of moral disorder could allegedly be solved by controlling female sexuality.[2] Crimes of sexual violence, therefore, provided a focus for fears of feminine disorder and sexual transgression. Judith Walkowitz has located nineteenth-century male sexual violence within these broader narratives of sexual danger through the infamous serial murders of Jack the Ripper in 1888.[3] Late nineteenth-century 'cultural dynamics and struggles' she insists, can be traced through the popular narratives of sexual danger personified by a murderer who Jane Caputi has identified as 'father to an age' and whose legacy to women was an ominous warning to behave. A range of different discourses – medical, legal and criminal – produced narratives around the Ripper murders, which linked dangerous female sexualities to the violence that followed.[4] Formative as the Ripper narratives were, newspaper representations of everyday sexual violence before and after these prolific crimes were teeming with fears of sexual irregularity and uncontrolled femininity. Newspaper reporting assessed the measure of the victim's culpability and the extent to which she was considered to have solicited the violence directed against her, drawing from and perpetuating the notion that women possessed the power to provoke sexual violence in men. In directing their censure to the behaviour of the victims, the newspapers' narratives framed female sexuality as a recurrent threat to respectable masculinity, a threat against which all men must be ever vigilant.

Using the narratives of sexual violence that were reported by the late nineteenth-century Manchester press as a case-study, this chapter considers how the accounts of sexual violence attempted to rationalise and organise that experience for the reader. Written largely by middle-class men for a profit, they operated within and moved between the paradigms of contested class, gender and sexuality relations occupied by not only the victim and defendant but also by the journalists themselves. As such, the narratives provided a commentary, specific to each case, which passed judgement on the behaviour of victims and defendants while acknowledging their working-class environment and thereby accommodated both class and gender expectations. These narratives did not promulgate formulaic, black and white representations of the victim, defendant and crime, rather, ones composed from shades of grey, as they sought to attribute degrees of responsibility for, and contributions to, moral and social disorder.

Manchester popular press

By the turn of the century, a mass reading public was firmly in place, bolstered by a series of legal, technical and marketing breakthroughs.[5] Circulation figures, though susceptible to exaggeration by eager editors, made impressive reading; the *Daily Telegraph* reaching 142,000 and *The Times* 65,000 as early as 1861.[6] Manchester, often referred to as the 'archetypal industrial city', was a prolific producer of newspapers and journals, particularly at this period. The *Manchester City News* claimed Manchester as the largest producer of newspapers outside London, publishing 23 titles.[7] The range of newspapers achieved significant readership. The circulation of the *Manchester Evening News* fluctuated between 130,000 and 170,000 daily in the final years of the nineteenth century, owing in part to its cheaper price. The more expensive *Manchester Guardian* sold fewer copies at 48,000.[8] More than 200 magazines and journals were also launched in Manchester between 1860 and 1900 and, although many were short-lived, the range of titles was striking.[9] Although credited with a broader readership, the daily and weekly, evening and morning Manchester newspapers were instructed and staffed largely by the middle classes and, as such, offered a convenient platform for the brand of middle-class reformism that predominated in the late nineteenth century. Filled with political and economic comment, literary news, sporting details, and club and society agendas, the newspaper pages espoused the ethics of self-improvement and education, whether through reports of charitable organisations and intellectual societies, or editorial questions asked and solutions offered to problems of perceived immorality.

Manchester was a large, industrial city with all its attendant social problems. It had flourishing commercial and retail sectors, but was also home to a large and diverse workforce, much of which was casual labour. Casual and cyclical employment reduced a significant section of the working class to perennial or recurrent poverty. In 1888, the Manchester Statistical Society recorded that 20.7 per cent of heads of families were in irregular employment and that over half the population of Ancoats was 'very poor' with a weekly income of less than four shillings per adult.[10] An increase in residential segregation by social class from the 1860s had separated the 'tree-lined suburbs'[11] largely inhabited by the Manchester middle classes from the cramped, insanitary quarters which generally housed working people. Specific districts such as Ancoats and Angel Meadow gained notoriety as dens of iniquity, housing the 'rowdy' and the habitual criminal, although in fact the segregation was not so simplistic. Both Kidd and Hewitt have argued that these conditions were not universal and even these poorest districts were home to a broad cross-section of the working class of diverse economic standing.[12]

Nevertheless, convinced that exclusively working-class districts were devoid of any refining cultural, social and moral influence, a middle-class campaign of redemption began in earnest. Social investigations and newspaper editorials created images of drunken savages lurking in dark alleyways, prostitutes trawling the streets for custom and habitual criminals preying on the respectable.[13] Large-scale, middle-class intervention in working-class behaviour and habits, exerting a 'civilising' influence perceived as absent, was framed as the redemption of the Manchester outcast. The Bishop of Manchester called in 1871 for 'something that would bridge over these prodigious chasms which separated the high from the low, the learned from the ignorant, the refined from the coarse and brutal'.[14] This attempt to counter a perceived threat of disorder was conducted with philanthropic and evangelical zeal, much publicised by the Manchester newspapers, although it was not necessarily accepted or unquestioned by its recipients. By juxtaposing a commentary on social respectability to a criticism of the disreputable, the Manchester newspapers clearly identified their intended audience as those readers who had already attained a respectable status and those who could aspire to it.

Sexual violence and the Manchester popular press

Newspaper coverage of sexual violence cannot be considered factual in its representations of the crime, victim or defendant. Deliberate journalistic selectivity was inevitable, owing to tight deadlines and predetermined column space. Journalists heard accounts of violence and retribution in the courtrooms one day and printed it for their readers the next, choosing pieces of information they considered most important – and, it should be remembered, most profitable – which fitted neatly within the confines of their columns. On another level, they were controlled by the evidence given in the courtroom and were thus susceptible to the selectivity of others. This was not restricted simply to the answers offered in response to specific questions but included the selective memories of victim, defendant and witness, which were framed within their subjective experience and by their own agendas. In this sense, the newspaper coverage of sexual violence could not reflect the actual experience of the crime, only a constructed version. Because of its wide-scale availability and its potential presence within the homes and lives of so many, this version and the representations it spawned is extremely powerful.

In their study of sexual murder, Cameron and Fraser implied that newspapers past and present consistently asked the question, 'what do women do to get themselves murdered?'[15] When confronted with a bruised, beaten, raped or murdered woman, the late nineteenth-century Manchester newspapers asked similar questions by continually placing the victim's behaviour against the violence she suffered. The focus of the reports oscillated between the violent event and the femininity of the woman subjected to it. The newspapers sought to explain the crimes through the actions and the behaviour of the victim and not the attacker, defining his violence not in the context of her experience but in that of her behaviour.[16] As a result, the narratives relied heavily on displays of feminine respectability and conformity in their discussions of sexual violence. These were provided through the victim's social background as well as her actions before, during and following the crime, and were used as the benchmarks for the victim's respectable status. In 1876, the *Manchester Evening Mail* recounted the attempted rape of Elizabeth Dale by James Goodwin and applauded her respectable conduct and demeanour in the face of such violence.[17] The newspaper report described the victim as 'the daughter of a well-to-do farmer, 18 years of age and of remarkable prepossessing appearance', choosing to refer to her as 'Miss Dale'. It told its readers that the attempted rape was perpetrated as the victim took a message from her mother to some labourers in a nearby field. It specified that 'the hayfield is distant about half a mile from the house and as she left having fulfilled her commission, to return to the house, the prisoner who had been employed on the farm during the hay harvest followed her. As soon as she saw he was coming behind her she quickened her steps.' The newspaper report qualified the victim's movements by stating that she was fulfilling a task for her mother and, therefore, had a valid reason for being away from the domestic space, although by specifying that the distance was only half a mile the report suggested she had not strayed far. This was affirmed by her attempt to return immediately to the safety of the house once her duty was fulfilled. By quickening her steps once she sensed the defendant was following her, the victim demonstrated vigilance together with an awareness of the potential dangers that awaited her outside her designated space.

Feminine respectability and sexual conformity were also judged according to the victims' behaviour during and following the sexual violence, drawing from discourses of sexual consent and of sexual violation.[18] Elements of struggle, physical injury, emotional distress and witness presence were woven into the newspapers' narratives of sexual crimes as supportive evidence of the victim's accusation. In the case of Elizabeth Dale, the attempted rape was grounded in the victim's resistance. When the defendant asked her for a kiss she had indignantly refused and it was on meeting this refusal that James Goodwin subsequently 'seized her, threw her down and attempted to outrage her'. The newspaper in almost glowing terms described the victim's reaction:

> She resisted with all her might and after a struggle lasting ten minutes in which she succeeded in so severely scratching his face that it bore evident marks of her resistance even on Saturday, the prisoner became frightened and raised her, still however tightly clutching her by her arms. Two labourers named Saunders and Sawnbell had been attracted to the spot by Miss Dale's cries and they compelled the prisoner to release her. Her cuffs, hat and collar were covered in blood, her dress was torn in several places and she was much bruised about the body.

The ferocity with which the victim had struggled was striking – not just resisting but struggling with 'all her might', using all her physical strength to fend off her assailant and inflicting physical injury. Her scratch marks were almost admired and paraded as a trophy, exposing the contradiction between expected feminine passivity and justifiable aggression.[19] The newspaper represented the victim as fighting as though her life depended upon it, guarding her feminine virtue as though it were her life and, thereby, identifying the symbiotic relationship between the two.[20] Evidence of her exhaustive physical struggle was provided and invested with symbols of pollution. The bruises on her body, the scratches on the defendant's face and her rumpled and torn clothing were interpreted as signs of disorder.[21] The articles of clothing in themselves were evocative of respectability and their dishevelled state symbolised an assault on that respectability. Two male witnesses were drawn to the site after hearing her cries and, significantly, it is their presence rather than her own agency that assured her eventual release. The content and tone of this narrative depicted a scene of successful female resistance to an attempted rape, thereby evoking the eternal myth that women would not be raped if they struggled vigorously enough. However, it did not grant the woman control over her own sexuality as her struggle did not divert the imminent danger but only delayed it long enough until patriarchal protection could be restored.[22]

As Anna Clark has argued, the routine association of sexual violence with movement within and between public spaces sounded a clear warning to all women.[23] By straying from designated feminine spaces, a woman not only risked sexual violation and injury but almost solicited it, as it was her presence in a particular place that invited the violence. If she was removed from such space, then the defendant's tendency to rape or abuse would be eliminated. The newspapers' narratives endorsed this message. Elizabeth Dale was sexually assaulted by a man she met while outside her domestic environment. If she had not been walking in that place, no matter how warranted, James Goodwin could not have attempted the rape. From this perspective, the roles of victim and defendant were essentially reversed since the defendant was represented as responding to an environment constructed by the woman herself. This implied not only the intrinsic danger of female sexuality but also the susceptibility of masculinity to the alleged temptations of Eve. Even the exemplary narrative of the attempted rape of Elizabeth Dale suggested that the presence of a young woman of 'prepossessing appearance' walking in open space inflamed the 'unguarded passions' of men. The consideration, therefore, for the newspapers was how the woman responded to her role as potential provocateur and whether or not she successfully preserved her respectability, even when she aroused, and was confronted by, these 'unguarded passions'. Fortunately for Elizabeth Dale, she had taken the necessary steps to safeguard her respectable status, which the newspaper's narrative duly confirmed.

Living on a farm and the daughter of a wealthy farmer, Elizabeth Dale's ventures into open space were perhaps limited, but for a large proportion of working-class women daily utilisation of such space was simply unavoidable. The majority of indecent assaults and rapes reported by the Manchester press were perpetrated as the woman occupied public areas and tangential spaces, such as alleyways or other adjoining areas. Women became victims of sexual violence whether they walked alone or accompanied, or travelled on foot or by train. Margaret Conley, a young factory operative, was repeatedly raped by ten men she had come across in a public house.[24] Mary Tinker was raped by a man who engaged her in conversation while she was sitting on a doorstep,[25] and both Mary Ellen Hill and Elizabeth Rooney were sexually assaulted as they travelled on trains.[26] The routine and legitimate occupation of public space by a significant proportion of women was acknowledged in the the reports by the Manchester press. Nevertheless, close parallels were drawn between a victim's occupation of non-domestic space, particularly tangential space, and women who traditionally had walked the thoroughfares and alleyways in search of custom. The streetwalkers' patrol of the public thoroughfares, public houses and music halls in the poorer districts of Manchester, particularly Ancoats, Angel Meadow and Deansgate, was both a common and disturbing sight. Prostitutes were at once perceived as 'miserable creatures, ill fed, ill clothed and uncared for', and symbols of vulgarity and social degeneration.[27]

Prostitutes' uncontrolled movement within designated space served to characterise it and the people, or specifically the women, within it. This guilt by association was illustrated in the case of Ann Green who was raped by John Benson, a stranger to her, as she walked home late one Friday night after visiting her sister. Benson claimed to have recognised her as a woman called Sarah and began following her down the street. He repeatedly asked her to have a glass of wine with him but she vehemently refused and tried to hurry home, walking up a nearby passageway. It was while in the passageway that her assailant dragged her into an entry leading from it and tried to put two sovereigns and some silver in her hand. The offer of money suggests he believed her to be a prostitute. This might have been a case of mistaken identity but though she pushed his money away and screamed in protest, he still committed the rape. In its coverage of the crime, the newspaper eventually acknowledged her reputable status but implied that her presence in a public thoroughfare after dark had called into question her femininity. Regardless of her correct behaviour, her presence there had effectively labelled her as disreputable.

The narrative inextricably linked the violence suffered by Ann Green to her occupation of public space, thereby issuing a mandatory warning to women, but whilst there was an underlying criticism of the victim's movements it was not dismissive of her status as a victim. Newspaper narratives of sexual violence that occurred in non-domestic space were governed more specifically by the victim's behaviour within that space. Margaret Conley may have been in a public house prior to her rape but the report was still headlined by the *Manchester City News* as a 'brutal case of violation'. During the course of the coverage, her movements were qualified and imbued with a degree of respectability:

> On Saturday night last about half past eleven she went into the Bull's Head in Woodward Street along with a friend of hers and saw the prisoners sitting there with five other men. Two of the men asked her to have some drink but she refused. After sitting there for a short time they began to be very rough with her and her friend upon which she went out and was making her way home when two of the men overtook her and asked her to walk with them. She refused and they threatened to ill-use her if she did not. She told them to go home and mind their own business . . .

The report recalled how she was not alone in the public house but accompanied by a friend and how she stayed only a short time owing to the rough behaviour of the defendants. She repeatedly refused the defendants' company and sexual advances, even in the face of violent threats. The entire report was sympathetic to the victim and outraged at the conduct of the men, only five of whom had been apprehended, dwelling on the violence she suffered. Similar treatment was afforded to Ellen Hazelwood by the *Manchester Evening Mail* which again conveyed its sentiment in the headline, 'brutal outrage on a woman'.[28] The report anchored the rape within the broader framework of the victim's daytime drinking in a public house but stated that on leaving she had 'asked a girl to accompany her to the station'. Further indications were given of the victim's respectability by references to her shawl and bonnet, which had been removed during the course of the attack and were found on the riverbank the next day. Prostitutes were partially identified by certain types of clothing and a dress code; 'bonnetless, without shawls, they presented themselves "in their figure" to passers by'.[29] By drawing attention to Ellen's dress and its subsequent removal, the coverage not only affirmed her outwardly visible respectability but also suggested that the rape had involved its removal both literally and figuratively.

The movements of Ann Green, Margaret Conley and Ellen Hazelwood prior to their attacks were not exceptional. It was while going about their daily routines that these women were confronted with sexual danger. The newspapers' narratives implied that sexual violence was lying below the surface of the everyday, working-class environment. By being in places and acting in ways which men might misconstrue as akin to prostitution, these women scratched that surface and were capable of rousing men to such violence. It was the women's presence and actions in public places which were offered up as the catalysts for sexual violence, prompting the outburst of a predatory masculine sexuality which civilised society inhibited. In these three cases, the newspapers' reports drew attention to the women's attempts to diffuse their inflammatory personas, which included respectable dress, walking with chaperones, and verbally and physically rebuking sexual advances. In all these cases the women's customary presence in the public space was reconciled with their watchful behaviour.

Such supportive narratives can be contrasted sharply with the description of other victims who seemingly wandered around the streets without due care and attention, unaware of the potential dangers they faced or, it was argued, even created. The *Manchester City News* provided a derisory description of Mary Tinker in its account of her rape by two men. Mary was described by the report as 'a widow of middle age at present an inmate of the workhouse but [who] was at the time of this offence residing with her sister in Hanover Street in the city'. No reason was given for her change of address but her lack of permanent residence immediately suggested social instability, which was further supported by the description of her employment. Whereas Margaret Conley had been described as a factory operative and Ellen Hazelwood as a tailoress, Mary Tinker was reported only as 'obtaining a living by charring'. The coverage then framed her rape within the context of her drunken behaviour, explaining that on the night of the rape 'she had been out drinking and on that account remained in the streets, being too afraid to go home drunk'. The undercurrent of disgust at her drunken condition was exacerbated by her inability to remember where she was, offering only that she 'sat down on a doorstep somewhere in Ancoats'. It was then that two men approached her and engaged her in conversation. The powerful image of Mary in a drunken and disorientated state sitting on a doorstep in one of the notorious districts of Manchester and engaging strange men in conversation again drew immediate parallels with prostitution. This was perpetuated by her agreement to their proposal to 'treat her', rather than refusing their advances, as Margaret Conley had done. The newspaper admitted that Mary had assumed that the offered 'treat' was more drink and believed she was going to a public house, noting her subsequent alarm when the second prisoner came up and she was forcibly carried to a nearby stable. However, the newspaper's narrative was sceptical of her accusations and her denial of consent, reflected by its use of the phrase, 'according to her version of the affair, each of them successively violated her', a strategy which was not employed in the Margaret Conley case. The content and tone of the coverage drew heavily from the suggestion that Mary had solicited the violence and aligned its sympathy with the defendants, despite their eventual guilty conviction. Their actions were framed within her behaviour and ultimately responsibility lay with the victim. This was reiterated by the concluding references to the defendants as being respectable family men and the distress at 'the unenviable position in which they were placed, [Thomas] Jones occasionally shedding tears during the trial'.

The newspapers repeatedly provided accounts of struggle and resistance, which were not overtly stated as the criteria of validity and femininity but implied as such through their routine inclusion. In 1876, the *Manchester Weekly Post* recalled the attempted rape of a lady's maid by John Mason. It stated during the course of its coverage that the victim 'did her utmost to get away from her assailant who to prevent her screams being heard put his hand over her mouth and threatened to murder her. The struggle between them lasted half an hour and was only terminated by the appearance of Miss Surtess's coachman.' Again, evidence of her struggle was afforded by her exhausted state and her disordered appearance as, 'her clothes were almost torn off, her face disfigured and she is much bruised about the body'.[30] The resistance of other victims was in vain but it was repeatedly suggested that the women were overcome by several men or excessive physical violence, and usually were unconscious at the time of the rape. A policeman found Dorothy Marsden unconscious after hearing her screams but, unfortunately, the rape had already taken place. However, the newspaper still attributed a degree of respectability to the victim by implying her spirited resistance, stating how her clothes were 'almost torn away and the remnants covered in blood'. Although she was an elderly woman, the report told its readers she had 'struggled vigorously and screamed loudly.

She had rolled over and over with the prisoner and was eventually rendered unconscious. During the time she was unconscious she was feloniously assaulted.'[31] There were no other witnesses to this scene but the newspaper evoked her strenuous resistance to great effect, especially given her age and fragility. It demonstrated a refusal to submit, even to the point of unconsciousness and near death.

To return to the case of Mary Tinker, the coverage questioned the resistance she offered during her rape. The report had earlier cast doubt over the woman's character in light of her behaviour and this was continued throughout its description of the rape. Unlike the earlier cases in which the women were portrayed as fighting tenaciously against their attackers, Mary Tinker was described in more neutral terms. The report stated that she 'screamed out murder and made what resistance she could but it being midnight she failed to alarm anyone except a policeman who came up and found one of the men with her. She informed him what had happened and he took him into custody.' No reference was made to any physical injuries sustained and there was even a faint accusation of failure as her screams only attracted a policeman, although Dorothy Marsden's screams had not been any more successful. Again, her discovery was described in more muted terms than in the earlier cases, simply stating the policeman 'found one of the men with her'. No reference was made to a dishevelled or distressed state, and there was no description of her having 'struggled vigorously' or 'rolled over and over' with her attacker. The policeman was not reported as rushing to her assistance and preventing a further assault but simply 'came up and found one of the men with her'. The phrase 'with her' did not immediately signify a rape was taking place at all, compared to the Margaret Conley case where the defendant was 'in the process of repeating his brutal design'.

The rape of Elizabeth Jones by John Brittain was recorded on the same page as Mary Tinker's charge and identified a complementary set of criteria being used.[32] The newspaper report called into question the validity of Elizabeth's claim, owing to her disreputable behaviour before the assault and because of her reaction afterwards. Elizabeth Jones was an elderly woman about sixty years of age who claimed she had been accosted by the defendant in 'an apparently friendly manner' as she made her way to the local workhouse. Promising her a cup of tea and a new dress, Brittain induced the woman to accompany him home but as he was doing so he led her down a by-lane where he raped her. The report stated that the rape was committed in mid-afternoon 'in spite of her screams of resistance', but did comment that 'the place was somewhat secluded'. This would suggest that the woman's screams were not likely to have been heard but also implied she was at fault in accompanying him there. Ann Grundy, however, did hear the victim's screams and went to her door. Seeing the prisoner with Elizabeth, she threw some dirt at him but 'with no effect'. In throwing dirt at John Brittain, the witness might have simply grabbed at the first thing that came to hand but it was a clear indication of her contempt for him and his actions, and was also symbolic of the accompanying pollution. The prisoner was apprehended four hours later but positively denied the charge, claiming it was 'all gammon'.

The narrative then implied the victim's sexual consent. This began with its accusation that 'it would seem she did not make a very indignant complaint to Mrs Grundy and that she afterwards went to a public house where she got a pennyworth of beer and said nothing about the affair there'. She did not report the rape until the evening. The newspaper reproduced the lengthy defence commenting on 'the improbability of the old woman's story', reducing Elizabeth from victim to 'old woman'.[33] It then repeated another version of the affair given through the eyes of two male witnesses, Seth Owen and Isaac Ogden, who claimed to have seen the victim earlier the same day drinking with the defendant. Ogden claimed she had told the prisoner of her distress and her intention to travel to Liverpool where she had a daughter, but also claimed that she drank out of his glass and took some money from him. He said she had then left the public house but was followed by the prisoner. Ogden claimed that 'she was not then sober' and in doing so introduced drunkenness as another mitigating factor against the accused. The testimony of this witness suggested that a drunken woman had taken money from the defendant and had invited the assault. This connection was substantiated by the testimony of Seth Owen who claimed to have seen the victim in a pub later that evening. After engaging her in conversation, she told him Brittain had ill-used her but added, 'Oh he has done me no harm and if he had given me 5s. I should have said nothing about it.' This was denied by the victim but had irretrievably anchored the rape in the framework of prostitution. Whether or not the victim would have consented to sex with the defendant for 5s. was unrelated to her rape, but unfortunately it implied that the victim's sexual consent was cheaply obtained and cheaply regarded, and complemented the newspaper's narrative.[34]

Set against the backdrop of anxieties over the perceived disorder in working-class neighbourhoods, the newspaper coverage of sexual violence embodied wider concerns of working-class lifestyles. Woven around the newspaper reports of sexual murder, rape and indecent assault were moral tales of female and male conduct. The narratives invoked deeply entrenched cultural anxieties about the intrinsic danger of female sexuality and the threat it posed to civilised masculinity. Although the routine movement of working-class women within and between public spaces was duly acknowledged, their presence, no matter how legitimate, was framed as a temptation to men, which both men and women must guard against. Nevertheless, case by case the newspapers passed judgement on the inflammatory character and behaviour of each victim. The underlying conviction of the newspapers was clear; working-class women were confronted with sexual danger in their everyday lives but they were expected to safeguard against it and to ensure their respectability remained intact at all times. This moral commentary not only provided guidelines on respectability to working-class women but also warned middle-class women of the dangers of public urban space. It provided working-class men with lessons on restraint but also provided neutralisations to all men for potential lapses in terms of the provocative nature of female sexuality. In no small measure, of course, this commentary was classed as well as gendered. It concealed middle-class sexual violence by focusing so closely on working-class conduct. Thus, it also legitimated the regulation of middle-class gender relations within the constructed private sphere.

Notes

1. J. Walkowitz, *City of Dreadful Delight: Narratives of Sexual Danger in Late-Victorian London* (Chicago, 1992), p. 6; see also M. Beetham, *A Magazine of her Own: Domesticity and Desire in the Woman's Magazine, 1800–1914* (1996), pp. 115–130.

2. A. Clark, *Women's Silence, Men's Violence: Sexual Assault in England, 1770–1845* (1987), p. 12.

3. Walkowitz, *City* p. 2, Chs 3–4.

4. J. Caputi, *The Age of Sex Crime* (1987), p. 4.

5. These included the abolition of advertisement tax (1853) and stamp duty (1855). J. Knelman, *Twisting in the Wind: The Murderess and the English Press* (Toronto, 1998), p. 25.

6. L. Brown, *Victorian News and Newspapers* (Oxford, 1985), p. 52.

7. *MCN* 21 March 1891.

8. J. Nicholson, 'Popular imperialism and the provincial press: Manchester evening and weekly papers 1895–1902' *VPR* 13 (1980), p. 96.

9. M. Beetham, '"Healthy reading": periodical press in late Victorian Manchester' in A. J. Kidd and K. W. Roberts (eds.), *City, Class and Culture* (Manchester, 1985), p. 172.

10. C. Chinn, *Poverty Amidst Prosperity: The Urban Poor in England, 1834–1914* (Manchester, 1995), pp. 26, 46; Kidd and Roberts (eds.), *City, Class and Culture* p. 51.

11. *Ibid.*, p. 49.

12. M. Hewitt, *The Emergence of Stability in the Industrial City: Manchester 1832–1867* (Aldershot, 1996), p. 58; Kidd and Roberts (eds.), *City, Class and Culture* p. 50; N. Kirk, *The Growth of Working-Class Reformism in Mid Victorian England* (1985), pp. 174–240.

13. Newspaper headlines include: 'The great unpaid' *Comus* 13 Dec. 1877 p. 5; 'Suppression of vice' *Comus* 20 Dec. 1877 p. 3; 'Evils of prostitution' *MC* 9 Feb. 1883 p. 6.

14. Hewitt, *The Emergence of Stability* p. 24.

15. D. Cameron and E. Fraser, *The Lust To Kill: A Feminist Investigation of Sexual Murder* (Oxford, 1987), p. 31.

16. E. A. Stanko, *Intimate Intrusions: Women's Experience of Male Violence* (1985), pp. 34–47.

17. *MEM* 25 July 1876.

18. A. Clark, *Women's Silence, Men's Violence*, pp. 128–134. For twentieth-century perspectives see S. Edwards, *Female Sexuality and the Law: A Study of Constructs of Female Sexuality as they Inform Statute and Legal Procedure* (Oxford, 1981), pp. 101–114; Stanko, *Intimate Intrusions*, pp. 34–47.

19. Compare Stanko, *Intimate Intrusions*, p. 35.

20. A. Clark, *Women's Silence, Men's Violence* p. 128.

21. S. D'Cruze, *Crimes of Outrage: Sex, Violence and Victorian Working Women* (1998), p. 43.

22. See also *MCN* 1 Dec. 1892.

23. A. Clark, *Women's Silence, Men's Violence*.

24. *MCN* 26 June 1865.

25. *Ibid.*, 5 Aug. 1865.

26. *Ibid.*, 10 April 1873.

27. J. Walkowitz, *Prostitution and Victorian Society: Women, Class and the State* (Cambridge, 1980), p. 26.

28. *MEM* 24 July 1876.

29. Walkowitz, *Prostitution* p. 26.

30. *MWP* 20 April 1878.

31. *MCN* 3 Dec. 1892.

32. *Ibid.*, 5 Aug. 1865.

33. For the pejorative use of images of older women see D. Spender, *Man-made Language* (1990).

34. Compare Stanko, *Intimate Intrusions* pp. 42–44.

CHAPTER SEVEN

Women professionals and the regulation of violence in interwar Britain

LOUISE A. JACKSON

Edwardian feminists and child welfare groups had been united in their criticism of criminal justice in Britain as a system run exclusively by men. If a young woman of fifteen alleged assault by a man, she would face medical examination by a male surgeon, questioning by a male policeman and, if the case went to trial, she would find herself surrounded by male lawyers, judges and jurors. In cases involving 'indecency', female spectators would be asked to leave the court to preserve their 'modesty'; the young woman herself would be left to give evidence of an intimate and personal character to a room of male professionals. The National Society for the Prevention of Cruelty to Children (NSPCC) protested in 1913 that 'she should always be accompanied by a woman, one who has had a wide experience of human nature and is possessed of much human sympathy'.[1] The Women's Freedom League (WFL), a suffrage organisation, ran a vociferous campaign in the pages of The Vote, calling for women magistrates, women jurors and women police.[2]

The Women Police Volunteers, set up in 1914 by Margaret Damer Dawson, Mary Allen and Nina Boyle of the WFL, aimed to provide a body of female officials to question women and child victims, attend to their welfare and escort them in court. Parliamentary committees throughout the 1920s recommended that women police should play an invaluable role in the investigation of cases of indecent assault upon women and children. Women doctors, too, demonstrated their concerns about issues of violence. Throughout the 1920s, '30s and '40s, the Medical Women's Federation campaigned for the systematic employment of female police surgeons to examine victims of sexual assault. Nesta Wells, for many years the only female police surgeon in Britain, was appointed in 1927 by the Manchester constabulary to treat women police and to examine cases of sexual and common assault, concealed abortion and abandonment of babies, abduction or suicide in women.

Focusing on the campaigns and interventions of women police and doctors, this chapter will consider the ways in which the overlapping concepts of class, gender, age, race and space shaped professional strategies towards violence from 1918 to 1939. Did women professionals behave differently from their male counterparts? How were attitudes towards clients, victims or offenders bound up with notions of personal identity? What types of violence and abuse did they target and why? How was violence explained, described and dealt with?

Most studies of the women police have tended to provide narrative accounts that detail the long struggle for their appointment,[3] and, indeed, similar histories could be written of the battle for women police surgeons. The appointment of women police was piecemeal and their duties varied across the country. In Metropolitan London, Gloucestershire and Bristol, women were employed as attested officers. In Liverpool, however, women were given grants by the Watch Committee to patrol parks and open spaces as a private concern; they were refused powers of arrest and were not permitted to take statements. Despite differences in origins and work tasks, there were similarities of scope, intent and outlook.

Organised thematically rather than chronologically, this chapter is based on the premise that professional strategies must be understood within wider cultural and political contexts. A discussion of women's perceptions of their roles and identities will lead on to an evaluation of their relationships with female victims. A shift in their focus of concern – from adult woman to child victim – will be linked to the politics of gender and class. It will also be argued that a renewed emphasis on women's domestic role, and on the family as a social bedrock, directed attentions away from the private sphere as a locus of violence.

Notions of gender affected both the work women did and women's attitude to work. The duties of women police and police surgeons were earmarked early on as those concerning the welfare of women and children; duties deemed more appropriate for women than for men by virtue of their sex. Although their involvement in official police work was new, the association of women with 'welfare' was a long one. During the nineteenth century, the welfare of victims of violence and neglect had been the domain of a wide range of voluntary and philanthropic societies, a product of the evangelical impulse to missionise and civilise the poor.[4] Middle-class women had expanded their role beyond the private, domestic sphere by venturing into this voluntary sector.[5] Public welfare work was justified in terms of feminine vocation: caring for the less-well-off was an extension of the nurturing role associated with the ideal Victorian wife and mother. Women's emotional and practical skills were deemed to suit them for their involvement in 'social' work, which was denoted as a specifically feminine activity. Arguably, this compartmentalisation itself reinforced the association of middle-class masculinity with the 'political'.[6]

This division between male and female roles did not remain unchallenged. Late nineteenth-century feminism developed a sustained critique of gender stereotypes and the suffragist movement fought for women's recognition in the political sphere. Yet, the interwar years saw a re-intensification of the division between feminine and masculine spheres as women were increasingly delineated in terms of biological traits and characteristics.[7] This chapter will seek to examine how notions of separate spheres influenced the work of women police and surgeons.

Social class also shaped and constructed personal identities and professional relationships. Given the cost of attending medical school, it was inevitable that women doctors should be drawn from the middle classes. Although police work is not generally considered professional, early women police generally came from a higher social strata than their male contemporaries. Lilian Wyles, employed by the Metropolitan Police CID from 1922 onwards, compared her occupation to a doctor's, arguing that it required similar levels of professional duty and vocational dedication.[8] Only one-fifth of early women recruits came from a working-class background.[9] Metropolitan Police Commissioner Sir Nevil Macready made it clear in 1920 that he preferred a 'refined and educated woman'.[10]

The systematic expansion of social work as a result of professionalisation often involved the increased regulation of the family by a new cohort of lower-middle class 'experts'. The doctor, the NSPCC inspector, the health visitor and the policewoman all participated in the surveillance of street and home; particularly the streets and homes of the poor.[11] Mothers were continually targeted, first by voluntary and then by professional welfare agencies intent on educating them on matters of health, nutrition and hygiene.[12] If children were the future of the nation, then mothers had to be indoctrinated in the skills of 'proper parenting'. However, the surveillance was far from total. Specific issues became 'social problems' at different moments of time, whilst others were neglected. Explanations for their rise and eclipse must be linked to wider political agendas. Furthermore, it should not be assumed that mothers were either complicitous with the efforts of social workers or passively victimised by strategies of social control. Organisations like the police and the NSPCC were viewed with ambiguity. In some situations they were an unwanted intrusion; in others, mothers used them to prosecute abusive or violent husbands.

Types of violence are defined and given meaning through language. The physical act or injury can never be forgotten, but it is in the form of words that their traces are left to historians, whether the 'official' words of reports compiled by police, Parliament or other institutions, or the individual and not necessarily representative voices of personal memoirs. Oral history has deliberately not been used here as the processes of recollection may themselves obscure the particularities of the language that was used to describe and define violence between the wars. Furthermore, it was through words that police and doctors labelled victims and assailants, a process that could have a profound effect on their subsequent treatment. It is important to draw attention to the shift from the euphemistic evangelical language of the Victorian and Edwardian period, which described sexual abuse in terms of the 'white slave traffic', 'moral corruption' and 'moral outrage', to a medicalised language which made reference to eugenics, national degeneration and mental deficiency.

Women's sphere?

The suggestion that there was a demise in feminism during the 1920s and '30s is always likely to evoke the riposte 'there has always been a women's movement this century'.[13] Interwar feminist campaigners tended to focus on single issues (such as the appointment of women police and police surgeons) rather than wider lobbies for equality. Nevertheless, a series of single-issue campaigns can effect immediate practical changes in women's daily lives. The single-issue strategy can be read in terms of pragmatism rather than dilution. It is clear, however, that the 1920s saw a splitting of feminist ideologies. 'Old' feminists such as Margaret Rhondda and Winifred Holtby advocated equal rights and opportunities for men and women, believing that gender difference should be eradicated.[14] A 'new' feminist approach, associated with Eleanor Rathbone, emphasised gender difference rather than equality, arguing that women should be valued for their special feminine role.

These two positions were reflected in the campaigns for the employment of women police and continued to shape discussions about their role. Edith Tancred argued that 'there is a special sphere of usefulness for policewomen in preventing girls from getting into trouble in the streets and in detecting and bringing to justice the vile and cowardly class of criminal who prey on women and girls'.[15] Given the defensive reflexes of male police constables intent on preserving their own jobs, the 'difference' argument that 'social welfare' work with women and children was most appropriately women's sphere was more likely to be acceptable to men. Indeed, some male police officers welcomed the opportunity to divest themselves of the task of taking evidence from women and children. In 1920 Lady Nott-Bower described the reactions of police officers at Richmond Police Station when the magistrate had asked her to assist in taking a statement from a female rape victim: '[They said] "If you only knew how glad we should be to have women to deal with these cases! They are cases we hate". They said more than that. The older men said how afraid they were of these cases as charges might be made against them.'[16] Rape cases put men in an embarrassing and compromising position. Moreover, rape victims were seen as a potential threat who might make 'false' allegations of harassment against 'innocent' officers.

The question of whether women working with assault victims should be appointed with an official police capacity proved more controversial. London police magistrate Frederick Mead argued vociferously that the taking of statements should be the work of welfare volunteers since women were incapable of performing the duties of detection and investigation.[17] Eilladh Macdougall, employed by the Metropolitan Police Force as just such a 'lady assistant' from 1907 onwards, did not see her work as police work. Her background was in evangelical rescue work with the Southwark Diocesan Association for the Care of Friendless Girls and she clearly saw her vocation in relation to an older philanthropic tradition. She was involved in setting up a home in Lambeth for the victims of 'the white slave traffic' in 1908.[18] Clearly a woman of independent means, she continued as a volunteer 'lady assistant' until her retirement in 1932. Her alleged refusal to have any dealings with the new women police in the 1920s suggests that she viewed career women with disdain.[19] Female matrons were appointed as statement-takers in Liverpool and Richmond without being attested as police.

Not all officers were as grateful as the Richmond men. Policewomen often had to battle to gain acceptance from colleagues. WPC Rosa Rouse of Gloucestershire Constabulary had to endure peers who snubbed her and refused to give her work. At Staple Hill Police Station she regularly took statements in cases of incest during the early 1930s but, on moving to Cheltenham in 1936, found herself treated as an errand girl. She has described how she was expected to watch as male colleagues interviewed a young female servant accused of concealment of birth:

While she was telling her story, she was contradicted and told she was telling a lot of lies . . . I was so angry I called the officer aside and told him not to betray his ignorance and inexperience any further. The girl had burst into tears and was terribly upset, insisting that she was telling the truth. She had said that when the baby was born, there was no-one to cut the cord and she waited for the afterbirth to come away, still attached to the baby. This was said by the interviewer to be absolutely impossible. From previous experience, I knew that not only was it possible but probable.[20]

Her comments provide an insight on the bullying tactics used by some male police in their questioning of women. It also seems that, in this case, they were pushing for an admittance of infanticide.

Women police stressed that they were more likely to get an accurate account of events because of their ability to gain the trust of women and children. This was not necessarily an essentialist argument; rather, a recognition of children's awareness of gender stereotypes and an acknowledgement that women's social experience was different from men's. Highly developed interpersonal skills needed to be combined with detailed background knowledge of law, medicine and nursing, as well as considerable patience. Emily Miller, investigating officer with the City of Glagow Police, drew attention to the considerable expertise involved:

One New Year's morning I went to [see] one [child] aged two years and nine months. I was 25 minutes with that little girl before she would speak to me, and before I could mention the case at all I had to 'make friends' with her. I got her on her granny's knee and asked her about who had hurt her. That is where the strain comes in all the time – to get at the child's point of view'.[21]

Lilian Wyles suggested that women's empathy resulted in the production of witness statements that more accurately reflected children's speech patterns (though she herself rarely produced verbatim accounts): 'I remember reading a statement taken by a detective-sergeant from a little boy of six, which ran, "I reside with my parents and infant sister in a spacious house situated in . . .". Could anyone believe such wording came from the mouth of a small boy?'[22]

Campaigning rhetoric should be read with care if we are to distinguish 'spin' from personal belief. It is likely that, in many cases, the deployment of the 'difference' argument was a strategic move, which recognised its persuasive powers amongst a broad, non-feminist audience. Indeed, some campaigners made reference to both 'equality' and 'difference' in their attempt to gain support. Throughout the 1930s, women's groups in Oldham lobbied the Watch Committee for additional women police officers to work with WPC Clara Walkden, who had been appointed in 1921. The local representative of the National Union of Women Teachers argued that women police 'should act just the same as men in the detection of crime and all the other duties of the police'.[23] She also fell back on the argument about welfare work, suggesting that women police would be useful in curbing 'the number of men "hanging about school playgrounds" and of the molesting of children'. It was the argument about difference that won the day. The Chief Constable said that policewomen's work was limited but important in its scope as social work. Two additional women police constables were finally appointed since, 'in view of the danger to women and children from molestation by men, it was considered it would be money well spent'.[24]

The category of 'woman'

Despite 'equal rights' support for the Oldham campaign of 1937, Clara Walkden herself argued that women had been admitted to the police on the clear understanding that they were 'more qualified by nature' to attend to women and children in distress.[25] Women, she said, have 'a natural sympathy and understanding', which was an ability that would be 'claimed by any true woman'. Walkden was alarmed that the Policewomen's Regulations of 1933 might be used to expand policewomen's role beyond welfare work.[26] She saw patrolling, plain clothes duty and detective work as outside women's separate and different sphere: 'the individual right of every woman is as a woman', she wrote; 'she must have the quality of her sex, otherwise she cannot inspire the confidance [sic] necessary in such service.' A police officer should not be required to 'forget her status as a woman'.[27]

If 'woman' is indeed a shifting category whose meaning is subject to continual re-articulation, Walkden was participating in a very specific construction.[28] For Walkden, the identity of 'woman' was tied up with essentialist notions of virtue, based on moral purity and sexual respectability, which equipped her to act as a moral guide. These special qualities, which Walkden suggests are innate or inborn, required protection. Hence patrol work, which might lead her to mingle with prostitutes was 'detrimental to the reputation of woman' and likely to 'degrade'. Intervention to suppress physical violence would also be 'in opposition to womanly characteristics', suggesting that aggression was unfeminine. Frequenting packed parties and public houses in plain clothes would cause her to 'lose caste'. Walkden considered that women were useful as police officers by virtue of their sex, which gained them a particular type of confidence. If they lost their reputation, status and, therefore, identity as 'woman', they would lose the respect and trust of the public.

For some women doctors the logical conclusion of the 'equality' argument would come to mean the total rejection of 'woman' as a meaningful category, either essentialist or experiential. Nesta Wells continued to believe

in a special role for women throughout her career: 'I feel strongly that
. . . sexual assault cases should be examined by and will be better done by
a woman doctor.' By 1967, however, when to some the battle seemed to
be won, Rochdale police surgeon, Lois Blair, would argue that: 'Attitudes
have changed. Whether it be a man or a woman doctor who examines a
girl does not really matter. What does matter is the empathy not the sex of
the doctor.' For Blair, 'equality' meant no distinction between men and
women's work, and no special role for women.[29]

Women, welfare and domesticity

Nineteenth-century feminist campaigners drew attention to wife-beating
as a brutal result of gender inequality. Yet, as Jan Lambertz has argued,
concerns about violence against women had been replaced by the interwar
period, with a welfare agenda that focused on the child.[30] The nineteenth-
century Societies for the Protection of Women and Children had linked
their needs together, but they gradually disbanded with the development
of the NSPCC. Although the NSPCC sometimes helped both mothers
and children who were the objects of paternal brutality and neglect,[31]
it concentrated its attentions on the needs of children. While organisations
such as the Women's Co-operative Guild continued to represent the interests and experiences of ordinary women, women professionals tended to
cast young children – rather than adult women – as innocent victims
deserving their assistance and protection. In 1919 the Liverpool Women
Police Patrols stressed that 'the children and youth of the nation are our
greatest concern'.[32]

The end of the First World War led to a reassertion of the ideals of
domestic femininity, and a stress on the importance of family duties and
responsibilities.[33] While rejecting or postponing the domestic role themselves (the Policewomen's Regulations of 1933 stipulated that women must
leave the force on marriage), women police nevertheless reinforced familial
ideology in their involvement in domestic disputes. Lucy Bland has noted
that the Women Police Service often assisted battered women in prosecuting or securing separation orders during the First World War.[34] Yet the
reports of the Liverpool Women Police Patrols indicate that, unless there
was extreme brutality involved, they preferred where possible to return
errant wives to their husbands. Patrol reports recorded, with approval and
satisfaction, cases where husbands and wives were reunited after instances
of violence.[35] The central office of the Liverpool Women Police Patrols
offered advice on separation orders and affiliation cases, but this advice was

tinged with a moralistic approach to marriage guidance that stressed the importance of family cohesion as the basis for national stability.

Sexual assault

In high-profile campaigns of 1938 and 1942 (the latter also involving the Business and Professional Women's Club), the Medical Women's Federation (MWF) argued that the appointment of women police surgeons was a specific necessity to encourage reporting of child sexual abuse.[36] An extremely high percentage of reported cases of sexual assault (including rape) involved child victims. Of the 2000 cases of sexual assault examined by Manchester's woman police surgeon Nesta Wells between 1927 and 1954, 83 per cent of victims were under sixteen years of age.[37] These statistics for reported crime do not bear any necessary correlation to 'real' patterns of abuse. Given the sympathy accorded the child victim, it is likely that the figures conceal the incidence of sexual violence against adult women. Rape within marriage was not outlawed until 1991.

Some women constables, like male contemporaries, demonstrated considerable reluctance to believe the words of women victims. Lilian Wyles felt that: 'Taken as a whole there are not a large number of cases of genuine rape, though there are many spurious and doubtful complaints alleging that offence.'[38] When she first began taking statements, she used to carry a 'little red book' which listed 'the salient points to be brought out' in interview. These points were based on cases she had heard in court and on her reading of standard legal works. Relying on texts of jurisprudence and court practice developed by men, Wyles simply duplicated traditional 'masculinist' approaches. Wyles's cynical view is perhaps also a product of a class prejudice that associated immorality with working women (those most likely to bring cases to the police) and virtue with middle-class femininity. Nesta Wells began to develop a more nuanced understanding of consent and resistance:

> The rape cases were always difficult. How far were the signs consistent with resistence [sic]? At what stage did resistance start? I felt sure that in some cases women with slow reactions did not mind or perhaps not appreciate the full meaning of the initial approaches by the man, but resisted strongly when he tried to penetrate, at which stage he could more easily overcome her by force.[39]

Wells began to question prevalent assumptions about rape, outlining the possibility of what we might now call date-rape and, indeed, recognising that women had a right to refuse intercourse at any stage. Other document-ary sources suggest a more conservative approach. The 'sexual difference' argument had implied that women were more sympathetic to the plight of women and child victims. Yet women police had to demonstrate their ability to work within the parameters of conventional legal custom and practice. Some felt frustrated by this; others, like Wyles, embraced it. It is all too easy to criticise Wyles and to assume that 'woman' should be 'the bearer of alternative values' in relation to police work. To do so, however, reinforces the essentialist stereotyping of women as 'caring' and, further-more, privileges sex over other categories such as class or race in the shaping of social attitudes.

Gender, age and sexual danger

For female victims of assault, age was a crucial factor in determining treat-ment within the legal process as a whole and, more pertinently, by women police. The categories of childhood, adolescence and adulthood were inter-preted in relation to a wider series of understandings about class, gender, sexual reputation and social space. In 1931 the following impressionistic description was given of the day-to-day work and typical clientele of a woman police patrol in Liverpool: 'the flighty, noisy girl, who is obviously trying to attract attention for excitement and romance; the older woman with determined and evil designs on half-drunken young seamen; the tactful enquiry when she comes upon a tearful girl apparently aimlessly wandering about; small children begging; a careful watch for men trying to attract young girls or children.'[40] This report perpetuated and reinforced common stereotypes of the vulnerable child, the precocious adolescent and the vicious adult whore. Small children were more likely to be construed as victims, whilst older women were often depicted as predatory on men.

This extract from a patrol's journal drew attention to the problem of the older woman:

Two women frequenters of . . . public house left it with two youths (about 19 and 23) who were the worse for drink. Elder woman put her arm through younger man's and both women pressed close to him. Later . . . I inter-vened . . . and found they were seamen. I was suggesting they should go back to their ship when the elder woman fell down directly in front of the younger man. I picked her up and told her to leave the youths alone. She went away quickly. Younger one said he had been trying to get away from her, but couldn't . . . .[41]

Judith Walkowitz and Anna Clark have both shown how Victorian 'narratives of sexual danger' – including newspaper reports of rape trials and the Jack the Ripper murders of 1888 – had served to exclude women from evening streets.[42] In the reports of the Liverpool Police Patrols, we can detect a reconfiguration of gender, space and sexual danger in relation to the conceptualisation of age and life-cycle. Female children are at the perils of predatory older men, but young men require protection from the evil designs of older women. Street life contaminated any natural moral status associated with femininity. The Liverpool Police Patrols did not, like Clara Walkden, feel they were themselves 'degraded' through their contact with prostitutes; rather, they retained an inherent notion of moral superiority as 'woman', based on their class position and official capacity. It was argued that 'their own womanhood makes its silent appeal to men and girls alike'.[43] They did, however, make very clear moral judgements about lower-class women who had been 'corrupted' by the streets and, like Walkden, located woman's moral reputation as central to her identity.

Adolescent females formed an intermediate or transitional category that was subject to very careful moral assessment. In their descriptions of sample cases, the Liverpool patrols continually labelled young women as 'respectable' or 'of bad character'; as 'immoral' or 'weak-willed'. Those judged immoral were disregarded and depicted as a threat, while the 'moral' received assistance.[44] The patrols made it very clear that their hostel in Knotty Ash was not designed for 'prostitutes'. It was to take young women of respectable character who could be trained as reliable domestic servants. Lilian Wyles described girls in the thirteen to sixteen age group as 'young "madams" more often than not', who exaggerated and twisted their evidence in court 'to make themselves sensational'.[45] In contrast, she used the emotive terms 'little children' and 'tender age' to refer to those in the younger, non-precocious age bracket.

Did the presence of women police make the streets safer for women? The Liverpool Police Patrols argued that their active profile was a deterrent which prevented 'indecent offences against young people, gutter crawling by men in cars, persistent picking up of, or by, young girls'.[46] They believed that 'danger is averted where often a man would have to adopt methods which might rouse opposition or even defiance'.[47] The patrols aimed, ultimately, to clear the streets altogether; those lingering there were all, potentially, either victims or threats. Once the streets were cleared, however, it became even harder to reclaim them for women.

The emphasis placed on public space as the terrain of sexual danger served to obscure the presence of abuse within the home. Given the stress on the domestic idyll during the 1920s and '30s, such a delineation also drew attention away from the family as a site of abuse or violence. Police contact with victims took place when they had run away from home, were reported missing or found wandering and begging in the streets. Young children were likely to be referred to the NSPCC,[48] whilst adolescent girls might be housed in one of the patrol hostels.[49] Mechanisms were clearly available to help victims of physical cruelty in the home. Where incest was involved, however, it is likely that most incidents were swept under the carpet. Wells commented that cases of incest were rare, but this does not tie up with recent studies which suggest that the majority of victims of sexual assault are known and even related to their assailants.[50] The figure of the 'park pervert' evoked considerable anxiety in the interwar period. The Liverpool patrols supervised parks and playgrounds during school holidays: to attend to injuries but 'above all watch was kept for suspicious characters loitering in the vicinity of the children's playgrounds'.[51] Women doctors suggested a range of preventive measures including instructions from parents against 'receiving gifts from strange men' and the patrolling of children's parks by policewomen.[52] The 'park pervert' was a loner, a stranger who terrorised public space, rather than someone's father or brother who abused within the private sphere.

Cruelty, class and mental deficiency

Linda Gordon's study of social work agencies in Boston, Massachusetts, has shown that the growing interest in psychology in the interwar period led to a redefining of the causes of abuse and family violence, with a resultant shift in blame.[53] According to Gordon, adolescent girls were increasingly labelled as delinquent while male offenders were pathologised and located within psychological categories of sexual perversion. It is important to stress that, in England, girls as young as nine had, throughout the nineteenth century, been interrogated in court for signs of moral delinquency and precocity. There was no sudden shift from victim to threat. Rather, girls in the transitional age band continued to be questioned about their sexual reputation.

What was new in the interwar period was the development of an argument that both offenders and victims tended to be psychologically retarded or 'mentally deficient' (prior to the assault). This trend, which Gordon has identified in the American records, was also apparent to some extent in the publicity material produced by British welfare agencies. The NSPCC increasingly identified 'mental deficiency' as a general cause of cruelty to children, which it linked to arguments about eugenics (controlled breeding) and national degeneration. The NSPCC 1933 *Annual Report*, for example, publicised in the Liverpool press, suggested that cruelty to children was more likely to occur within 'large feeble-minded families'.[54] Poverty and brutality were both hereditary; a result of the interbreeding of the lowest classes. Throughout the nineteenth century, the accounts of social investigators such as Henry Mayhew and Charles Booth had constructed the poor as a brutalised 'other' in opposition to the 'respectable' middle classes; now this line of argument was re-established on a new quasi-scientific basis. It was an argument which drew attention away from the 'professional' or 'artisan' family as a site of abuse, serving to bolster class prejudices: it was the 'poor' who were the child abusers. It also served to define violence in terms of the psychological deviancy of the individual, avoiding any critique of the 'social', of the power dynamics of class and gender relations, or wider economic structures.

The analysis of violence, neglect and abuse as a product of the mental deficiency of the lower classes was also apparent in the reports of women police and doctors. Reflecting back on her work as police surgeon in Manchester, Nesta Wells suggested that 'incest cases were not very numerous, perhaps two or three each year, but tended to involve the mentally slow . . . the men also tended to be of low mentality'. She noticed that 'a fair proportion of sex offenders were of poor mentality; some suffered from perversions, some were old and/or ineffective unstable personalities'.[55] According to Lilian Wyles incest cases were few and far between and explanations should be left 'to the psychiatrist and psychologist'.[56] Representatives of the MWF who gave evidence to the Select Committee in 1924 delineated two 'classes of offenders': wayward youths perhaps induced by drink or the overcrowded living conditions associated with the urban poor and 'men who are morally and mentally deficient due to actual disease'.[57]

With the loss of male life during the First World War and the retrenchment of domestic ideology, the blame for sexual abuse was clearly fixed on the marginal: the psychologically damaged. Normative male sexuality, scrutinised by Josephine Butler in the 1870s and by the suffragettes at the turn of the century, was not an area of concern for interwar women professionals. In 1943 the Liverpool Police Patrols produced a full list of stereotypes to describe the adolescent girls they found wandering on the streets: 'the careless', 'the wanderer', 'the mentally deficient', 'the morally deficient', 'the runaway', 'the physically unfit', 'the workshy' and 'the absconder'.[58] Each category placed the blame on the girl herself and defined her as delinquent. Where nineteenth-century feminist campaigners might have asked questions about the circumstances of her past and blamed brutal fathers or employers for homelessness, the patrols found fault in the victim herself.

While Gordon's arguments about victim-blaming explain the treatment of adolescents in the legal–welfare system, they cannot be applied to younger children in the British context, who were still viewed with considerable sympathy in medical discourse. It has often been argued that psychoanalytic theory of the 1920s and '30s emphasised sexual 'phantasy' and ignored children's 'real' experiences of sexual abuse.[59] Nevertheless, the papers of the MWF indicate a continued interest in the psychological effects of sexual abuse.[60] Reflecting on earlier work, Dr Elspeth Macleod of the Institute of Child Psychology wrote in 1942 that: 'in cases of children seen by me at clinics or privately, after some form of abnormal sexual experience there has always been a marked emotional disorder. In some cases the experience has been so terrifying that the child has repressed the memories of it entirely, so that even to his own unconscious mind, he denies that it has happened.'[61] Macleod, like other members of the MWF, argued that local authorities should set up psychological clinics to provide psychotherapy for infant victims.[62] The theory of repressed memory had not disappeared from the medical agenda. The extent of its influence is clearly an area for further research.

Thus, categories of age played a crucial role in the evaluation and understanding of violence and its victims. Women police and doctors increasingly shifted their attention to children as the main objects of concern, failing to acknowledge the presence and needs of adult women victims. The new discussions of 'mental deficiency' operated to survey and regulate the behaviour of male offenders and adolescent 'delinquents' in terms of a model of normality/deviancy. Rather than hinting at wider issues of exploitation (as had the feminist use of the 'white slave trade' model), the 'disease' model drew attention away from issues of power or control and focused instead on the individual. To this extent, perhaps, women police officers' development of their professional status undermined their feminist potential when they confronted the issue of male violence.

Notes

1. *CG* March 1913, p. 27.

2. S. Jeffreys, *The Spinster and Her Enemies: Feminism and Sexuality 1880–1930* (1985), pp. 60–63.

3. J. Carrier, *The Campaign for the Employment of Women as Police Officers* (Aldershot, 1988); J. Lock, *The British Policewoman* (1979).

4. K. Heasman, *Evangelicals in Action: An Appraisal of their Social Work in the Victorian Era* (1962).

5. F. Prochaska, *Women and Philanthropy in Nineteenth-Century England* (Oxford, 1980).

6. D. Riley, *Am I that Name? Feminism and the Category of 'Women' in History* (1988), pp. 47–51.

7. S. Kingsley Kent, *Making Peace. The Reconstruction of Gender in Interwar Britain* (Princeton, 1993).

8. L. Wyles, *A Woman at Scotland Yard* (1952), p. 123.

9. 'Minutes of Evidence of the Committee on the Employment of Women in Police Duties' PP xxii (1920), 1087, Q. 1010.

10. *Ibid.*, Q. 179.

11. D. Armstrong, *Political Anatomy of the Body. Medical Knowledge in Britain in the Twentieth Century* (Cambridge, 1983); J. Donzelot, *The Policing of Families* (1980).

12. J. Lewis, *The Politics of Motherhood: Child and Maternal Welfare in England 1900–1939* (1980); A. Davin, 'Imperialism and motherhood' *HWJ* 5 (1978), pp. 9–65.

13. D. Beddoe, *Back to Home and Duty: Women Between the Wars 1918–1939* (1989), p. 136; D. Spender, *There's Always Been a Woman's Movement This Century* (1983).

14. J. Alberti, *Beyond Suffrage. Feminists in War and Peace 1914–28* (Basingstoke, 1989).

15. *Standard* 15 Oct. 1937.

16. PP xxii (1920), 1087, Q. 1421.

17. *Ibid.*, Qs. 2621–2623.

18. PRO, MEPO 2/5562, Metropolitan Police Home for Women and Children.

19. Wyles, *Woman at Scotland Yard* p. 119.

20. R. M. Ashby (neé Rouse), 'A policewoman's history' *PR* 21 Sept. 1984, p. 1830.

21. PP xxii (1920), 1087, Q. 2055.

22. Wyles, *Woman at Scotland Yard* p. 136.

23. *OWC* 25 Feb. 1939.

24. *Ibid.*

25. GMPM, papers of Clara Walkden, handwritten notes for report on the First Provincial Policewomen's Conference, 1937.

26. Statutory Rules and Orders, 1933, no. 722.

27. See note 25 above.

28. Riley, *Am I that Name?*

29. GMRO, M. L. Blair, 'Police surgeon 1967' *JMWF* (1967), cutting in scrapbook collected by Dr Mabel Lindsay of the Medical Women's Federation, p. 235.

30. J. Lambertz, 'Feminists and the politics of wife-beating' in H. Smith, (ed.), *British Feminism in the Twentieth Century* (Aldershot, 1980), pp. 25–46.

31. *LC* 24 July 1922.

32. LWPP, *Report of the Care and Training School for Women* (Liverpool, 1919), p. 16.

33. Kent, *Making Peace*.

34. L. Bland, 'In the name of protection: the policing of women in the First World War' in J. Brophy and C. Smart (eds.), *Women in Law. Explorations in Law, Family and Sexuality* (1985), pp. 23–49.

35. LWPP, *Annual Report* 1933, p. 9.

36. Contemporary Medical Archives Centre, Wellcome Institute for the History of Medicine: MWF, SA/MWF/D.15, Police court examinations 1938–39 and SA/MWF/D.18, Women police surgeons 1942–43.

37. GMRO, N. Wells, 'The need for women police surgeons' *JMWF* (1967), MWF scrapbook, p. 235; see also N. Wells, 'Medical women and the police force' *MPC* 22 Oct. 1941, pp. 317–319.

38. Wyles, *Woman at Scotland Yard* p. 121.

39. Wells, 'The need for women police surgeons'.

40. LWPP, *AR* (1931), p. 6.

41. LWPP, *AR* (1928), p. 7.

42. J. Walkowitz, *City of Dreadful Delight: Narratives of Sexual Danger in Late-Victorian London* (Chicago, 1992); A. Clark, *Women's Silence, Men's Violence: Sexual Assault in England 1770–1845* (1987).

43. LWPP, *AR* (1923), p. 5.

44. LWPP, *AR* (1921), p. 12, and *AR* (1929), p. 3.

45. Wyles, *Woman at Scotland Yard* p. 157.

46. LWPP, *AR* (1929), p. 5.

47. LWPP, *AR* (1923), p. 5.

48. PP xxii (1920), 1087, Q. 2078, evidence of Dundee policewoman Jean Forsythe Wright.

49. LWPP, *Report of the Care and Training School for Women at Knotty Ash* (1925), p. 3.

50. J. Plotnikoff and M. Woolfson, *Prosecuting Child Abuse* (1995).

51. LWPP, *AR* (1933), p. 6.

52. SA/MWF/D.7, Home Office Committee to Enquire into Sexual Offences Against Young Persons, 1924–26, notes submitted by Mabel Ramsay to MWF, 11 Feb. 1925.

53. L. Gordon, *Heroes of their Own Lives: The Politics and History of Family Violence: Boston 1880–1960* (1989).

54. 'Cruelty to children. The indirect causes. Mental deficiency in parents, large feeble-minded families' *LDP* 23 Dec. 1933.

55. Wells, 'The need for women police surgeons'.

56. Wyles, *Woman at Scotland Yard* p. 204.

57. SA/MWF/D.7, prepared notes for representatives, 3 Apr. 1924.

58. LWPP, *AR* (1943), pp. 6–7.

59. L. De Salvo, *Virginia Woolf: The Impact of Childhood Sexual Abuse on Her Life and Work* (1989); J. M. Masson, *The Assault on Truth. Freud's Suppression of the Seduction Theory* (1985).

60. SA/MWF/D.7, notes of Dr Evie Evans, 2 March 1925; 'Minutes of Evidence of the Joint Select Committee on the Criminal Law Amendment and Sexual Offences Bill' PP vi (1920), 851, Q. 455.

61. SA/MWF/D. 18 Aug. 1942.

62. See *ibid.*, letter from Dr Mabel Lindsay to Dame Janet Campbell, 31 Aug. 1942, and letter from Miss Rew to Dr Lindsay, 30 Oct. 1942.

CHAPTER EIGHT

Exposing 'the inner life': the Women's Co-operative Guild's attitude to 'cruelty'

JACKY BURNETT

The Royal Commission on Divorce and Matrimonial Causes which sat between 1909 and 1912 represents a pivotal point in our understanding of divorce, being the moment at which the shift from a judicial to an administrative procedure began.[1] Both Hammerton and Bland stress the importance of the evidence of the Women's Co-operative Guild (WCG) to the divorce law commission. Its testimony of marital difficulties amongst 'the better-off working class and lower middle class represented by the Guild . . . makes it impossible to speak of any steady decline in domestic violence by the Edwardian years'.[2] Recent historical scholarship has addressed the tensions between class and gender surrounding the private marital problems of working-class women.[3] Ayers and Lambertz argue that 'the quality of marital relationships is crucial to an assessment of the history of working-class urban culture and gender relations'. Their study of interwar, working-class Liverpool explores the link between economic roles within the family and the potential for domestic violence.[4] Hammerton also sees domestic violence as rooted in '. . . disputes over routine measures of persecution, over finances and differing views of authority . . .'.[5] Hammerton echos Ellen Ross in emphasising that for the most part 'marital discord mostly remained private and secluded from the public eye . . .'.[6] Elizabeth Roberts argues that the majority of women in abusive marriages were '. . . compliant, dutiful, silent, uncomplaining'.[7] Lucy Bland emphasises women's increasing politicisation through the women's movement and their attempts to challenge male sexuality, and as Joanne Jones's and Catherine Euler's chapters in this volume demonstrate, domestic violence was a concern of both feminist and conservative opinion. However, for the nineteenth century at least, the majority of working-class women in unhappy or abusive marriages were effectively denied an avenue to directly voice their discontent.[8]

Many social surveys and much legislation of the late nineteenth and early twentieth centuries addressed home, marriage and sexual relations; subjecting private areas of life to 'unprecedented public scrutiny and regulation'.[9] Such surveillance could be resisted by working-class women who confronted well-meaning social workers with 'provoking diffidence'.[10] This use of reticence as a defensive strategy was a powerful component of working women's respectability but made it difficult not only for them to use the courts to end their own unsuccessful marriages but also to supply the evidence the Royal Commission needed to bring about divorce reform.[11] 'Strangers – what do they know of the inner life, and come to that, what do friends and neighbours know?'[12] However, the Women's Co-operative Guild became an effective avenue for working-class women to articulate their thoughts and opinions on divorce law reform. The Guild's organisation enabled a cloak of anonymity to fall over the women who presented evidence:

> The Guild had canvassed their members' opinions on the divorce question widely, and were most explicit on the hidden cruelty that these women would not recount to a magistrate, and for which there was no redress, that is sexual cruelty, including marital rape, infection with venereal disease, and infliction of unwanted pregnancies followed by violent attempts to bring on a miscarriage.[13]

Through the exposure of such cruelty and in their analysis of their experiences, the Guild arguably made the most radical call for reform presented to the Commission.

The Women's Co-operative Guild

Formed in 1883, the Women's Co-operative Guild complemented the existing co-operative movement. It specifically attempted to provide an educational forum for women co-operators and increasingly emphasised a goal of 'full and real citizenship' for women which stressed equality with men.[14] The Guild can be identified with the broader late nineteenth-century women's movement, but also represented a significant step in organising women previously excluded from political activity.[15] Crucially, the Guild structure provided a forum in which the voices of working-class women could be heard. From its initial membership of seven in April 1883, the Guild grew to 12,000 members in 1899 with 250 branches nationally. By 1912 it boasted 525 branches comprising 27,000 members. Membership peaked at over

87,246 with 1805 branches in 1939.[16] Guild members were '. . . almost entirely married women belonging to the artisan class, and [were] associated, through their husbands and relatives, with all the prevailing trades of the localities in which the Guild branches are situated'.[17]

The aim of the Guild was that of self-education, to demonstrate that women were 'not just consumers', yet at the same time acknowledging the potential power women had as managers of the household budget.[18] The Guild constructed working women's household responsibilities as a basis for public and political action as citizens. It was far from conservative: it was a radical, campaigning organisation within the labour movement. Women's economic independence and equality through wielding the power of enfranchisement were both common Guild themes. The WCG campaigned for women to hold the Co-operative shares in their own names, even though, 'Guild members are very loath to deprive their husbands of rights, however much they may desire to exercise their own.'[19] The named share was economically and politically important. It provided married women with income of their own, through dividends, and gave them voting rights at the quarterly meetings of their society. The share gave Guildswomen a certain level of personal autonomy within the family.[20] Guild philosophy and methods are demonstrated in its reaction to a County Court judgment of 1907 regarding married women's savings in the Co-operative Society. The Court ruled that 'a wife's savings, made out of money given her for household purposes, belonged to her husband'.[21] Mindful of the impact this could have on the quarterly dividend, the Guild responded with a flurry of activity:

> Inquiries were made and a great many cases were collected in which the amount allowed to the wife for carrying on the home was seen to be painfully insufficient. The matter was discussed at all sectional conferences, and questions for legal opinion were submitted through the Co-operative Union. As a result, Co-operative Societies were advised to refuse to pay out a wife's shares to the husband unless an order from a court of law was produced, as required, before a husband can legally claim them.[22]

This is indicative of the strong organisational, democratic, and consultative nature of the Guild. If the money, secured by a thrifty wife, belonged to the husband, the wife was a dependent, fulfilling a subservient role which negated the notion of equality within marriage. Wives' economic status and marital equality were two key Guild notions. The Guild linked private marital relations to public citizenship through the issue of suffrage: 'so that the law shall recognise perfect equality between man and wife, and that no longer shall a married woman be considered the mere agent or chattel of her husband.'[23] It spoke from the perspective of married *working* women and effectively reformulated dominant ideologies to justify its campaigns:

> We acknowledge proudly and willingly that home *is* the women's sphere, but at the same time we know that home does not mean house, for the Guild has taught us that for the building of a home woman must not always stay in the house.[24]

A home required 'happiness, healthiness and freedom', which gave women a legitimate interest in industrial, civic and state questions.[25] The Guild linked knowledge to responsibility. It discussed education, health, children, women's legal position, marriage and divorce. Members' concerns as mothers extended to education for children and school clinics. Their position as workers led them to redefine 'work', and to agitate for a minimum wage for employed women. They repeatedly emphasised the natural extension of home to both local government and demands for the suffrage.[26] For the Guild, the private and personal was public and political. Thus, by 1910 the Guild was a representative, democratic organisation of working-class women which had demonstrated its ability to collect and debate information relating to women's lives and which was able to articulate demands that provided solutions. It was an ideal organisation to provide evidence when the Royal Commission on Divorce and Matrimonial Causes began to determine whether working-class women wanted divorce law reform.

Divorce law reform

The 1857 Matrimonial Causes Act had enabled couples to divorce without a private Act of Parliament. Divorce was not possible without prior adultery, clearly acknowledging marriage as a sexual contract. The penalty for adultery was more severe on women than men. A man could divorce his wife for adultery alone, while the woman needed to prove adultery with an 'additional aggravation' of either desertion, cruelty, incest, rape, sodomy or bestiality.[27] The sexual double standard, enshrined in the statute book, was underpinned by patriarchal ideology that considered a wife's adultery to be worse than her husband's. Arguably, an adulterous wife violated both private and public laws. A man's ownership of children, property and lineage, including control of his wife's sexuality through exclusive access to her body, was located in the private sphere. However, these matters entered the public domain through civil law in property claims, divorce and separation, and custody of children.[28] The state intervened in matters that were both private *and* the 'collective interests of society'; a patriarchal society but one that, by the turn of the century, was seeing considerable social change. Although the 1857 Divorce Act had resulted in more accessible divorce, the costs of at least £40 and the requirement to sue for divorce in London, could prove prohibitive to working women.[29] In 1906, 546 divorces were granted compared to the 7007 separation and maintenance orders awarded in 1907.[30] These figures imply a far larger scale of marital breakdown than the divorce statistics suggest. The limited redress available through Separation and Maintenance Orders after 1878 was dependent on a husband's violence being proven in court, and there was also no guarantee that separated husbands would pay the maintenance awarded by the magistrates' court.[31]

Successive legislation passed during the second half of the nineteenth century demonstrates the increasing willingness of the state to intervene in marriage, and its concern with the physical and financial vulnerability of women. By the Edwardian period, divorce law reform was firmly on the agenda.[32] However, in other countries divorce was more equitable and easier to obtain. Emigration to the colonies and America provided errant husbands with the chance to abandon wife and family, and renege on maintenance orders where they existed.[33] The 1909–1912 Royal Commission focused on three basic questions: was there a need to increase the number of divorce courts; should grounds for divorce be extended, particularly for desertion and incurable insanity; and would easier divorce lead to greater immorality?

Women and the Royal Commission

Feminist agitation prior to 1909 had helped to change other aspects of family law. Courts had normally awarded custody of children on divorce and separation to the father. By arguing that the mothering role was necessary, distinctive and female, women campaigners were able to claim rights as mothers, wives and equals. The legislative outcome was the Infants Custody Acts of 1873 and 1886 which gave custody of young children to mothers where parents divorced. The Married Women's Property Acts of 1870 and 1882 gave married women greater control of their individual property. However, married women were still seen by feminists as disadvantaged compared to single women.[34]

Middle-class feminist calls for the gender equalisation of *existing* laws ignored the additional disadvantages that working women experienced through class inequalities. An extension of the late Victorian franchise on the grounds of gender alone would give only middle-class women the vote, inheritance laws only affected those with property and divorce remained the province of the better-off. However, it should not be assumed that working-class women were uninterested in such developments; certainly by 1898 the WCG in Manchester were discussing equalisation of divorce.[35] The evidence of the WCG to the Commission proved that working-class women both understood and supported issues of women's rights, equality, and autonomy, in public and private. These issues were not simply restricted to middle-class discourse; working-class women (particularly in the WCG) drawing upon their own experiences were more than capable of framing their own agenda.

The Royal Commission on Divorce and Matrimonial Causes (1909–1912) not only had women commissioners, but also ensured that the views of women's organisations were represented.[36] Women's organisations demanded that only women could speak for women, that as mothers they should be consulted in matters affecting children and, by extension, envisaged a role for themselves as custodians of the 'race'.[37] With the exception of the Mothers' Union, all the women's organisations consulted were in favour of divorce reform. They challenged the patriarchal structures that were underpinned by the sexual double standard. The ability to protest, even if covertly, is evident in women's testimony. Discourse surrounding 'sex antagonism' thus shifted between the political demand of the suffrage and the personal demand of private dignity, and the two were particularly interconnected by the Women's Co-operative Guild.

Evidence of the Women's Co-operative Guild

A woman told me the other day that she never told anyone about her husband's neglect and cruelty, because no one really believed her. He was so soft-spoken in front of other people, and they always said he only wanted a little managing. 'Good heavens!' she said, 'I wish they could have him to manage for one month. I have been married to him 18 years, and these last three nights I have slept on the floor rather than in the same bed.' Yet I don't think enquirers would learn any reason for a divorce, unless they took the woman's single word for it. Even her own children do not know.[38]

The Guild's testimony sought to present the 'inner life' that was largely closed to social investigators. It directly engaged with the covert nature of much wife abuse. It made public that which was private; gave credence to that which was not believed by strangers, family or neighbours, or hidden from children. It spoke of neglect and cruelty, and hinted at potential sexual abuse. The Guild's credibility was intensified by the class and respectability of its members, its democratic structure, the scope of its evidence and its determined call for noticeably wider reform than that suggested by much middle-class feminist input to the Commission.[39]

The Guild was determined to be seen as the authentic voice of working-class women, and to establish their evidence as more valid than that of the much larger, but anti-divorce law reform, Mothers' Union. Because Guild members were already involved in its educational programme on 'industrial, social and political questions affecting working women', they claimed to approach such contentious issues with objectivity. Such objectivity was gender constructed, framed as it was by Guildswomen's 'experience of life'; experience galvanised through their roles as 'wives, mothers, and housewives'. Guildswomen displayed 'a balanced practical judgement'.[40] The Guild's evidence took the form of individual and branch responses, presenting both personal and collective opinions. The evidence was compiled through a questionnaire sent to 520 branches (of which 431 responded), with an additional questionnaire distributed to 124 individual members of the Guild. The individual Guildswomen approached were all past or present elected officials – their elected status implies that these women enjoyed the confidence of their branches, districts or sections, and according to Llewellyn Davies 'they were merely selected on account of their intelligence . . . and with no regard to their views on the subject, which were unknown in every case'.[41] Some Guild respondents were opposed to divorce, though over both individual and branch responses, their number did not exceed 10 per cent.[42] The Guild stressed that as 'married working women', they represented 'the largest class of women', and that 'all this evidence is absolutely that of working-class women'. The Guild's class identification was an important dimension, as was their reiteration of respectability unencumbered by religious and moral censure.[43]

Guildswomen's evidence described the dismal marriages and prolonged suffering of members, their relatives, friends and neighbours based on 'manuscript letters – often many pages long, laboriously written after thought and consultation'.[44] They claimed 'a close knowledge of the sufferings and needs of others'. They represented themselves as the type who inspired confidences, individual narratives being disclosed 'in a way no district visitor or such person, however kindly disposed, hears them'.[45] Guildswomen actively mobilised their social networks and their personal social standing as a research method. The evidence included 131 specific cases in which women were ill-treated, deserted, and made miserable through marriages which were either virtually non-existent or a continual endurance test devoid of affection. Although 131 cases represented a tiny fraction of actual separations, the insight they provide into working-class married life was a considerable achievement. The Guild demonstrated the pathos, strength, courage and resilience of working women. Their call for reform, articulated through experience, was a powerful and very persuasive force. It conveyed the distress and anger that the existing laws provoked amongst Guildswomen. Their evidence established that divorce was an option that working women wished to exercise and clearly demonstrated how the existing divorce, maintenance and separation laws resulted in misery. As one Guildswoman emphasised, 'I am personally looking forward with hope that divorce will be brought within the reach of the people, and I shall be one of the first to try for that relief.'[46]

The Guild concluded that;

> The general attitude of the women towards divorce is very definite. They look upon it as a much needed method of release in cases where the marriage tie involves a life of degradation and suffering, most often to women and children. No woman could inflict on a man the amount of degradation that a man may force on a woman. The desire for reform does not proceed from any light wish for a life of pleasure, or for the loosening of home ties.[47]

The Guild argued that 'owing to the state of the law and the fear of hostile public opinion, this suffering is so often borne unseen that the extent and character of it is not realised'.[48] Thus, the Guild attempted to steer the debate away from the purported immorality of separation and the stigma of divorce:

> To speak of degradation and suffering under the term of 'hardships,' and to advocate and admire a compulsory 'patient endurance' of them is placing strange values on moral conduct. It is the power of choice, which is the essence of renunciation, and alone gives it its value. If divorce is considered a sin, and the patient endurance of degradation and compulsion a virtue, a most serious moral confusion is created. It means that women's self-respect and happiness are sacrificed, and adultery on the part of men condoned.[49]

However, Guildswomen were keen to stress that the majority of them were happily married. They linked a demand for divorce when marriage involved 'degradation' and 'suffering' to an idealistic vision of marriage based on companionship, respect, love and equality. Thus, the Guild attempted to harness the language of morality for their own purposes; 'moral' became linked to 'happy' and was synonymous with 'civilised'. They linked morality explicitly to motherhood, yet still managed to challenge the existing patriarchal structure of marriage and the family. Guildswomen achieved this through criticism of the sexual double standard, the abuse of conjugal rights, the wife's economic dependency particularly as a result of motherhood, and guardianship of children.[50] In doing so, they began to produce a critique of degradation and suffering that represented an attempt to redefine notions of cruelty to include physical, sexual, verbal, psychological and economic abuse.

Cruelty

The existing maintenance and separation laws accepted physical cruelty as grounds for separation, but these the Guild saw as inadequate, particularly as husbands were aware of the clause. One woman decried a drunken, adulterous and work-shy husband, complaining of his 'fits of ungovernable rage . . . cursing and swearing, using the most filthy language it is possible to imagine and holding a knife over me, but never touching me, because then, and only then, could I get a separation. He never lost himself enough to forget that.' This Guildswoman identified verbal and psychological abuse and also spoke of her shame in being seen in public with her husband because of his womanising.[51] Guildswomen demonstrated that women's concerns for their own respectability prevented their seeking support or redress from a law which did not recognise their experience.

> I was not accustomed to talk to my neighbours. Shame held me silent. This he knew. When we reached home, he pushed me in the passage and locked the door. Then to terrify me he beat a chair into small pieces against the wall, and also threw the burning lamp to the ground; . . . he threw me also to the floor and held me there, until the floor cloth became alight. He then laughed at my fright . . . . He knew only too well shame of his conduct would seal my lips. I would not defend myself. This is the cruelty that stabs the heart though the body may be free from the marks of brutality.[52]

This physical coercion and emotional terrorism would not in themselves satisfy a magistrate. But the Guild argued, '[s]ome of us women consider moral cruelty worse to bear with than physical cruelty. There are many ways in which a husband can be cruel without breaking the law as it stands at present.'[53] The rules needed to be rewritten. Guildswomen presented cases, including their own, where husbands, heedful of existing legislation, delighted in humiliating, shaming and silencing their wives, and nowhere was this more obviously so than in the sexual arena.

The sexual double standard and challenges to male sexuality

The Guild was clear that; 'There should not be two codes of honour. If a man expects to mate with a virtuous woman, it should be her right to expect the same from him.'[54] Guildswomen were virtually unanimous in demanding sexual equality. The sexual double standard was justified by other witnesses through women's reproductive role. The Guild directly confronted this argument: 'A witness said an offence on the part of the wife involved "confusion of progeny", and was therefore criminal. I fail to see where the difference lies. In the man's case, it must involve "confusion of progeny" in the woman with whom he has committed adultery, just as much as in the wife's case.'[55] Only a wife's adultery was considered to corrupt the home, whereas the Guild argued that adulterous men sent '. . . the trouble to someone else's home'.[56]

The Guild argued that 'unfaithfulness . . . [was] the most refined cruelty of all' and was effectively sanctioned by existing laws, which some husbands deliberately exploited. 'He would not ill treat me although carrying on with other women, because he knows if he did, I should apply for separation or divorce.'[57] The Guild cited cases where husbands '. . . brought another woman . . . [into the matrimonial home] . . . and demanded she should live with them. The house was in his name, so . . . [the wife] . . . had either to submit or leave him: in which case she would have had no claim for maintenance and there were four children to be kept, so she lived through it.'[58] This was a damning indictment of the way husbands could flaunt their economic power. Not even the separation and maintenance laws could provide relief, unless there was sufficient evidence of physical violence.

One Guildswoman poignantly expressed the humiliation of living with an adulterous husband: 'I felt so degraded. I had not the same privilege as the beasts of the field. No one can possibly imagine what it is unless you go through it, to feel you are simply a convenience to a man. I used to feel I was much more degraded than the poor unfortunate women who make a living by it . . . .'[59] The Guild's evidence made public this 'inner life' and allowed married, working-class women to present their experiences in a way that not only criticised the existing divorce laws, but the institution of marriage itself. It also pointed out the 'cruelty' inflicted by an adulterous husband infecting his wife with sexually transmitted diseases. One

Guildswoman commented, 'This I can speak on with a personal knowledge of, being a victim to it myself, which has meant years of misery for me . . . .'[60] Other evidence pointed out the dreadful consequences where syphilis was passed to unborn children.[61]

For the Guild, cruelty included both mental and sexual violence. The psychological impact of adultery was underlined. The evidence effectively challenged male sexual dominance and the Guild's demands demonstrated a desire to curtail male sexual appetite some two years before this argument was famously taken up in Christabel Pankhurst's *The Great Scourge*.[62] The Guild's extended definition of cruelty also included excessive childbirth, enforced abortion and husbands forcing their sexual demands upon wives too soon after childbirth:

> The tenth day after the baby was born he came home drunk and compelled me to submit to him. Of course, I had no strength and was at his mercy . . . . Babies came rather fast. Then I got told I was like a rabbit for breeding and drugs was obtained, as he did not want children, although I was compelled to submit . . . . I was so badly treated that when I knew my condition for the fourth time, I took something which nearly ended my existence. It poisoned me . . . .'[63]

The Guild highlighted the detrimental effect such demands had on women's health, both physical and mental. They challenged the notion of conjugal rights and, though wrapped in the language of submission, highlighted the existence of marital rape: 'When I had been threatened by . . . [my husband] . . . legally insisting on conjugal rights, the thought of publicity has made me submit . . . . Because I had vowed by the marriage law, there was no help but to submit as a duty.'[64]

By challenging male sexuality, women were arguably attempting to determine their own. The aim was control over reproduction by limiting male desire. Recreational sex was presented as the excess of male sexuality, with wives forced to abort foetuses, creating a situation akin to prostitution.[65] The Guild overtly criticised marital inequality based on the husband's sexual power. Husbands, not wives, posed the biggest threat to 'morality' and divorce was presented as a way of restraining the abuses the prevailing system endorsed. The Guild argued that not only should men learn some self-restraint, but that women should cultivate greater self-respect. Self-respect was constantly linked to the attainment of equality, and, for such equality to flourish, women first had to realise that they were autonomous individuals with the right to control their own bodies. 'I feel sure that if women had equal chances with men in this respect [marriage laws], they would respect themselves more and really look upon their bodies as their own property, and not so soon give in to the brutal desires of lazy, selfish men.'[66]

Solutions

The Guild's evidence highlighted the way in which, under the existing laws, working-class women were already seeking their own individual solutions to marital breakdown. None of the women mentioned were divorced, though some had obtained separation and maintenance orders. The rest had devised makeshift solutions from family support, to cohabitation or bigamy. Some passed themselves off as widows and took paid employment. A minority sought solace in drink, or escape through suicide.[67] These strategies often compromised respectability and all excluded the option of legal remarriage. The Guild demanded specific reforms to the existing divorce laws, which encompassed equalisation, extension and availability.

Central to the Guild's demands was the notion of personal autonomy, the element of 'choice' which was essential for self-respect: 'We want to get rid of the idea that a man owns his wife just as he does a piece of furniture . . . . There is much harm done by a woman regarding herself as a man's personal property.'[68] The Guild saw marriage as both a sexual and economic contract, but one which needed to be modified to protect women from abuse – physical, mental, financial and sexual. It sought to limit men's power as husbands and fathers through essentially feminist proposals.[69] However, the Guild aimed not to overthrow the 'family', but to inject a greater degree of equality into marriage. It required not only that men modify their behaviour, but also that women elevate their own position. Companionate marriage, embracing an equal and complementary partnership, was the Guild's underlying philosophy.[70]

For Guildswomen, divorce was not just an escape from hardship; if equal, affordable and extended they believed that divorce would strengthen marriage.[71] Guildswomen rejected the pessimism which viewed divorce as the destruction of the home: instead divorce would become a device to ensure the happiness and stability of family life. The Guild called for an extension of grounds for divorce to include desertion for over two years or where a separation order had lasted three years, also for serious incompatibility, or mutual consent. Divorce on the grounds of insanity (with restrictions) or cruelty emphasised the physical and mental health of women, particularly through the Guild's redefinition of cruelty that moved beyond the physical, to the sexual and psychological. The Guild also argued that, for separated or divorced wives, maintenance should be collected through the courts, severing the social and emotional link between husband and family, reducing it to an economic responsibility that should involve the state. The Guild called for cheaper divorce and also proposed 'where necessary, the payment by the state of the whole costs'.[72]

Under the existing laws, married women only had guardianship of children under seven and, if they left an abusive husband, could risk losing their older children. The Guild saw children as an emotional support that enabled women to endure painful marriages, as well as financial contributors whose income could enable women to leave abusive marriages. The Guild specifically called for the 'general suitability of the parent for bringing up children to be the ground on which the guardianship should be decided'.[73] A sizeable minority of Guild respondents overtly favoured the mother. 'I would lean to the mother if she is not too depraved. I think a mother is more likely to do right to her children than a man, because a man may provide for them, but he cannot look after them.'[74] The Guild opposed other witnesses' emphasis on reconciliation. In rejecting the possible intercession of officials, Guild respondents displayed their distrust of the reconciliators' prying eyes. They were only prepared to expose so much of the 'inner life'. Respondents actively constructed a distance between themselves and the 'poorer classes' whose families were most likely to be subject to philanthropic or professional interventions.[75] The Guild's self-image was aligned quite explicitly to notions of respectability. The majority of Guildswomen wanted divorce to be tried behind closed doors: 'the desire that no details should be published is also nearly unanimous.'[76] The Guild's stance led it to a wider criticism of the legal system. It called for 'women to be given some part in the administration of the law'; more specifically, the Guild believed that women should serve on juries.[77]

Conclusion

The success of the Guild's evidence on divorce law reform embraced a 'style of social investigation and practice of politics based on self-representation'[78] and prepared the ground for the highly influential survey and publication *Maternity: Letters from Working Women* in 1915.[79] *Maternity* further exposed the impact on working women's health of continuous pregnancies and lack of maternity care. It implicitly took up the criticisms begun by the divorce law reform evidence on sexual cruelty and saw the Guild's first demands for birth control information. The Guild later became the first working-class organisation, and the first women's organisation, to adopt a resolution calling for birth control information to be made available in maternity and child welfare centres (1923).[80] Large families and low wages were linked to 'the unearthly struggle to live respectably'[81] and, just as the Guild tried to influence maternity policies, so they endorsed the 'endowment of motherhood' through proposing a universal 'state bonus' in 1919.[82]

Despite the publication of the Royal Commission's Majority Report in 1912, there was no immediate reform. None of the recommendations were implemented until 1923, when equalisation of the divorce law was finally written into the statute book.[83] It then took until 1937 for an extension in grounds beyond adultery.[84] However, the experience of contributing to the commission had a galvanising effect on the Guild. Eileen Yeo asserts that the WCG came to represent an 'exemplary' form of empowering social motherhood, 'by giving [Guildswomen] skills for public citizenship and by ratifying their capacity to manage their own family and domestic affairs'.[85] Certainly, this merging of the public and private came of age in the testimony presented to the Royal Commission on Divorce and Matrimonial Causes. The wide scope of their demands for reform exposed a specific female agenda, with a strong feminist slant rooted in the Guild's knowledge of and commitment to the experience of respectable working women.[86]

Notes

1. A. James Hammerton, *Cruelty and Companionship: Conflict in Nineteenth-Century Married Life* (1992), p. 1.

2. *Ibid.*, pp. 1–2; Lucy Bland, *Banishing the Beast: English Feminism and Sexual Morality 1885–1914* (1995), p. 184.

3. Ellen Ross, ' "Fierce questions and taunts": married life in working-class London, 1870–1914' *FS* 8 (1982), pp. 575–602.

4. Pat Ayers and Jan Lambertz, 'Marriage relations, money, and domestic violence in working-class Liverpool, 1919–39' in Jane Lewis (ed.), *Labour and Love: Women's Experience of Home and Family, 1850–1940* (Oxford, 1986), pp. 194–219.

5. Hammerton, *Cruelty* p. 3.

6. Hammerton, *Cruelty* p. 3; Ross, 'Fierce questions' p. 18.

7. Elizabeth Roberts, *A Woman's Place: An Oral History of Working-Class Women, 1890–1940* (Oxford, 1995), pp. 120–121.

8. Bland, *Banishing*.

9. Hammerton, *Cruelty* pp. 1–2.

10. Ellen Ross, *Love and Toil: Motherhood in Outcast London, 1870–1918* (Oxford, 1993), p. 18.

11. Hammerton, *Cruelty* p. 51.

12. Margaret Llewellyn Davies, RCDMC Vol. iii (1912), p. 160, case 56. (PP, 1912–1913, vol. xx.)

13. Hammerton, *Cruelty* p. 50.

14. Margaret Llewellyn Davies, *The Women's Co-operative Guild: 1883–1904* (Kirkby Lonsdale, 1904), p. 161.

15. Ellen Mappen's introduction to Clementina Black, *Married Women's Work* (1983); Jean Gaffin and David Thorns, *Caring and Sharing: A Centenary of the Co-operative Women's Guild* (1983).

16. *MSCH* Aug. 1899 and Aug. 1912; Gaffin and Thomas, *Caring and Sharing* p. 117.

17. Llewellyn Davies, *Women's Co-operative Guild* p. 148. The Guild was open to women over seventeen.

18. Women's Co-operative Guild, *The Women's Co-operative Guild: Notes on its History, Organization and Work* (Manchester, 1932), p. 2.

19. Llewellyn Davies, *Women's Co-operative Guild* p. 99.

20. In 1895 Manchester and Salford Equitable Society's membership totalled 11,782, of whom 800 were women. *MSCH* Feb. 1896 and Nov. 1896; Margaret Llewellyn Davies (ed.), *Life As We Have Known It* (1977), p. 91.

21. Catherine Webb, *The Woman with the Basket* (Manchester, 1927), p. 99.

22. *Ibid.*, p. 100.

23. Mrs Gasson, *Wives' Savings* (Kirkby Lonsdale, 1907), p. 8.

24. Anna Blair, *Education in the Guild Room* (1912), p. 4.

25. *Ibid.*

26. *MSCH* Aug. 1912.

27. Geoffrey Best, *Mid-Victorian Britain* (1985), p. 303.

28. Ursula Vogel, 'Whose property? the double standard of adultery in nineteenth-century law' in Carol Smart (ed.), *Regulating Womanhood: Historical Essays on Marriage, Motherhood and Sexuality* (1992), pp. 147–165.

29. Sir William Cobbett, RCDMC Vol. i, p. 402.

30. Divorce figures from Lawrence Stone, *The Road to Divorce: England 1530–1987* (1992), p. 435; separation and maintenance figures from RCDMC Vol. ii, p. 458.

31. Best, *Mid-Victorian Britain* pp. 303–304. Magistrates could also grant separation orders for desertion after 1886.

32. Stone, *Road To Divorce* p. 392; Best, *Mid-Victorian Britain* p. 303.

33. Margaret Llewellyn Davies, RCDMC Vol. iii, cases 10 and 99. For a wife who deserted, see Herbert Greenwood Wrigley (Manchester), RCDMC Vol. ii, p. 79, case D2.

34. Bland, *Banishing* p. 124.

35. Eleanor Barton, RCDMC Vol. iii, p. 38. Lady Alice Maude Bamford-Slack (Women's Liberal Federation), *ibid.*; *MSCH* March 1898.

36. Two of the fourteen Commissioners were women: Mrs May Edith Tennant and Lady Frances Balfour. Evidence was presented by the Women's Industrial Council, the Women's Liberal Federation, and the Mothers' Union as well as by the WCG.

37. *CC* 29 July 1909, p. 1.

38. Margaret Llewellyn Davies, RCDMC Vol. iii, p. 160, case 56.

39. *Ibid.*, p. 149.

40. *Ibid.*

41. *Ibid.*

42. *Ibid.*, pp. 149–171.

43. *Ibid.*, p. 149.

44. *Ibid.*

45. *Ibid.*, p. 150.

46. *Ibid.*, p. 167, case 115.

47. *Ibid.*, p. 151

48. *Ibid.*, p. 150.

49. *Ibid.*, p. 162.

50. *Ibid.*, p. 151.

51. *Ibid.*, p. 168, case 117.

52. *Ibid.*, p. 167, case 114.

53. *Ibid.*, p. 156.

54. *Ibid.*, p. 153.

55. *Ibid.*

56. *Ibid.*

57. *Ibid.*, pp. 152, 151, 153.

58. *Ibid.*, case 5. See also case 3.

59. *Ibid.*, p. 167, case 113.

60. *Ibid.*, p. 156, case 36.

61. *Ibid.*, p. 156, case 34.

62. Sheila Jeffreys, *The Spinster and Her Enemies: Feminism and Sexuality 1880–1930* (1985), p. 49.

63. Margaret Llewellyn Davies, RCDMC Vol. iii, p. 166, case 113.

64. *Ibid.*, p. 167, case 115.

65. *Ibid.*, p. 156, case 29.

66. *Ibid.*, p. 151.

67. *Ibid.*, p. 160, case 67.

68. *Ibid.*, p. 151.

69. Bland, *Banishing* p. 184.

70. Margaret Llewellyn Davies, RCDMC Vol. iii, p. 151.

71. *Ibid.*

72. *Ibid.*, p. 153.

73. *Ibid.*, pp. 158–159.

74. *Ibid.*

75. *Ibid.*, pp. 159–160, 170.

76. *Ibid.*, p. 159.

77. *Ibid.*

78. Eileen Yeo, 'Some contradictions of social motherhood' in Eileen Yeo (ed.), *Mary Wollstonecraft and 200 Years of Feminisms* (1997), p. 131.

79. Margaret Llewellyn Davies (ed.), *Maternity: Letters from Working Women* (1978).

80. Gillian Scott, *Feminism and the Politics of Working Women: The Women's Co-operative Guild, 1880s to the Second World War* (1998), p. 170.

81. Llewellyn Davies (ed.), *Maternity* p. 89.

82. Scott, *Feminism and the Politics of Working Women* p. 166.

83. Bland, *Banishing* p. 185.

84. Hammerton, *Cruelty* p. 119.

85. Eileen Yeo, 'Some contradictions of social motherhood' p. 131; Naomi Black, *Social Feminism* (Ithaca, N.Y., 1989), p. 109.

86. Gillian Scott, 'Working-class feminism? The Women's Co-operative Guild, 1880s–1914' in Yeo (ed.), *Mary Wollstonecraft* p. 139.

PART III

The representation of violence

CHAPTER NINE

'Only when drunk': the stereotyping of violence in England, c. 1850–1900

JUDITH ROWBOTHAM

In Gilbert and Sullivan's *Trial by Jury*, Edwin, defendant in the breach of prom- ise case providing the central plot, argues that, being 'always in liquor', if he married Angelina, the plaintiff, he would beat her. This provides the excuse for the judge to suggest that, since Edwin claims when drunk, 'he would thrash and kick her', 'let's make him tipsy, gentlemen, and try'. Angelina objects: Edwin enthusiastically does not![1] The Victorian comic opera takes this no further, but the libretto's humorous linkage of drink and violence provides a provocative clue to the elaborate, often contradictory, codes that encircled the stereotyping of Victorian violence. Such expres- sions of popular facetiousness have considerable implications for compre- hension of the scale of everyday violence and its practical dimensions. For example, they indicate the extent to which external factors, including alcohol, were held to contribute to the practice of violence and the ways in which, in some circumstances, types of physical force were unlikely to be severely condemned. This raises the question of the contributions made to the codes surrounding expressions of violence by factors of class, age, race and, above all, gender (though race, as a factor, cannot be fairly dealt with here for reasons of space, and consequently the focus is entirely on the 'British', not including the Irish). In relation to these, specified levels of violence were 'acceptable': other levels or types, especially when perpet- rators were identified by gender, were not. And there were certain victims (notably animals, though this aspect of Victorian violence also will not be considered here) where respectable society increasingly positioned itself against any expressions of violence outside the increasingly formalised and organised rituals of sport, with their links to British masculinities. In terms of violence against human targets, only incidents involving excessive levels or 'unacceptable' types of violence were likely to involve the courts, and these cases never represented more than a proportion of the everyday violence present in communities.

Understanding the nature of violence requires that both acceptable and unacceptable aspects of violence are considered, including attempts to establish the broad outlines of stereotypes used to construct the nature of Victorian violence. This perspective emphasises the problematic nature of the inclusion of physical force in patterns of Victorian daily life. For example, alcohol played a part, as reason, if not justification, for some violence. But, generally, it was the alcohol, not the violence, that was identified as both causal factor and real social problem. That violence was an actual part of Victorian family, as well as community, relationships was accepted. Vic Gatrell has commented, 'Violence in the nineteenth century was ubiquitous.'[2] However, representations in popular writing underline the complexity of this acceptance in a society where certain expressions of violence were not so categorised, being regarded instead as useful assets to the operations of both the nation and the community. The term 'violence' was generally reserved for physical actions that, if unchecked, attracted the attention of the law.

Incidents of physical violence identified as too minor to warrant legal intervention or community disapproval were everyday occurrences. But, for reasons that included its useful potential, and the domestic segregation or practical ghettoisation in geographical terms of many of its more threatening forms, physical violence was not categorised as a major threat to national social stability. Rather, violence was classified as one of several manifestations of other underlying social evils, including insufficient moral education among the masses. Though the prime focus here, physical violence was not the only issue: verbal violence was another dimension, either accompanying or substituting for physical violence. But while forms of mental abuse were recognised as a problem, they were often not dissociated from physical forms and were overall less a matter of popular concern.

Examination of popularly consumed sources and commentaries indicates that violence was believed to become susceptible to management when part of a process of categorisation; which serves to emphasise the gender dimensions. The conviction that violence was in some way manageable is underlined by Victorian pride in statistics showing declines in convictions for violent crime.[3] An associated set of intricate societal codes evolved, intended for national consumption, relating types of violence to human characteristics. These rules categorised violent incidents as acceptable or unacceptable in accordance with presumptions about the class, age or gender of both practitioners and victims of violence. According to the intended audience, different descriptors were employed to interpret the realities of violence. Consequently, the impact, individually or communally, of violence and the context of its perpetration formed the core of an essentially moral interpretation of what did, or did not, constitute violence.

Most work done on violence has relied primarily on the various forms of legal record and related 'serious' comment. But, despite the numbers who encountered the legal process, most Victorians learned about violence in its broader parameters through popular writing – fiction, newspaper reporting and articles in popular periodicals. It was certainly through these that most learned how to interpret violence. Many favourite authors were inspired by criminal cases, finding them a rich source which, given popular fascination with 'crime', endowed their works with both readership appeal and moral clout. Mrs Henry Wood, along others like Silas Hocking, based tales on close reading of press reports. But, like most popular authors, their writings juxtaposed those extremes of violence alongside more everyday examples of violence in their depictions of Victorian society, as part of a 'realistic' didactic exercise in advising readers how to navigate social perils safely and morally.[4]

Examination of these sources provides wide-ranging representations of the violence experienced in daily life and of contemporary perceptions thereof, broadening and deepening impressions gained through court records, with their frequent imagery of hardened and/or drunken brutes or viragos. Violence dealt with in the courts may often have been of a domestic variety, but the scale on which it was practised made it more than everyday in impact. In seeking to understand Victorian constructions of acceptable and unacceptable forms of violence, two associated perspectives emerge. First, contemporary community acceptance that giving a wife a black eye or a child a series of bruises was deplorable but not automatically criminal. Second, endorsement of this by the legal process: significant numbers of cases of alleged domestic violence, especially involving male defendants, were dismissed by courts as either overreaction on the part of overzealous neighbours or police, or resulting from malicious and revengeful accusations by a wife or child.[5]

It could not be claimed that these popular representations initiated categorisation, or the rules of management, of violence. But, intended for immediate consumption, they demonstrate sufficient uniformity on the part of the producers towards violence and its practitioners for it to be argued that these writings perpetuate and disseminated a widespread comprehension of the stereotypes and their workings. Thus, they not only provide useful clues to the inevitably ambiguous boundaries between acceptable and unacceptable levels of violence. They also reflect changes, or continuities, in attitudes towards everyday violence at a time when several significant Acts covering unacceptable aspects of physical assault (for instance, the 1861 Offences Against the Person Act; the 1878 Matrimonial Causes Act; the

1885 Criminal Law Amendment Act) were established in statute law. As the noted legal figure Sir James Stephen commented: 'you cannot punish anything which public opinion, as expressed in the common practice of society, does not strenuously and unequivocally condemn.' He added: 'both law and public opinion do, in many cases, exercise a powerful coercive influence on morals.'[6]

Mention of such Acts in popular sources not only introduced their provisions to popular consciousness but also helped to reaffirm associated practical codes of societal behaviour relating to violence. This was part of the process of construction of individual and communal identities, emphasising that the Victorian period saw little real modification in attitudes towards the practice of violence in relation to class, race, gender and age considerations, even where changes to the law might seem to indicate shifts. Such were essentially superficial, relating to popular panics or scandals, rather than alterations in fundamental attitudes towards violence and its categorisation.[7] And while there was an apparent shift in the analyses of the reasons for criminality, including violent criminality, during this period – from the moral perspectives of Mayhew, say, to the psychological perspectives of Havelock Ellis – the cultural attitudes underpinning both remained constant.

There is always, of course, a problem with relating the images in popular writing to what may be termed reality, or with official policy. However, authors like Hocking explicitly stated their writings were rooted in fact, often identifying their sources, which in itself helped to create a certain respectable reality.[8] Also, government officials often took serious account of writing of this nature in their various minutes and comments on social crises and moral panics, since 'legislation ought in all cases to be graduated to the existing level of morals in the time and country in which it is employed'.[9] Indeed, it can be argued that aspects of these categorisations of violence became something of a self-fulfilling prophecy, once their parameters were established in the substantive terms of the law. While there was room for discretion in certain areas of law and judgments, this discretion rarely operated for offences that were identified as issues of moral outrage. Defendants convicted of violent crime were often found guilty primarily for what, in Victorian perceptions, constituted transgression against society, rather than against the actual victims. Offenders were, thus, liable to punishment and judicial comment predicated on social stereotyping (especially class and gender conventions) and on associated fears of resultant damage to society from perpetration of the offence, not assessment of damage done to the victims.

This resulted from the reality that physical violence, or the potential for it, was an important part of individual male identity and a key element in the Victorian sense of communal national identity. Thus, some aptitude for violence was desirable among boys – indeed 'proper boys' had to show a willingness to engage in a variety of physical exertions, including 'fighting', whatever their social class. Reginald Dalmain was 'no novice with his fists – what public schoolboy ever is?'[10] Hocking's slum-dwelling, ill-educated Joe Bradley was Dalmain's echo since, provoked by 'meanness and treachery', Joe could demonstrate an ability to 'pound' another boy 'to a jelly'.[11] Possessed of instinctive aggression, part of the ideal process of maturation into a 'manly' Briton, of whatever social class, was the development of appropriate 'right' feeling that would ensure any expression of physical force was not misdirected. So through appropriate, rule-driven sports like cricket, aggression was controlled and channelled. Newbolt's poem, *Vitae Lampada* is typical in its explicit links drawn between games, the Briton's characteristic fighting instinct, the safety of the realm and maintenance of Empire. More informally, but still in the interests of maintaining community morality and healthy masculinity, there were always times when the honest brown fist of a Briton – worker or gentleman – was the only remedy a less honest man could understand. Having whipped the well-born cad that had slandered the fair name of a woman, Viscount Vale was asked: '"I thought I heard a dog howl?" "You did", he replied.' The 'only language' the cowardly and deceitful agent, Richardson, could understand was a 'deserved good thrashing', administered by an upright Tom Battle.[12] Both law and popular writing reflected this attitude. The fictional magistrates' benches, hearing the grounds for the complaints of assault against Viscount Vale and Tom Battle, laughed the cases out of court, echoing the newspaper reporting of similar cases.[13]

There was a well-established expectation that working-class adult males constituted the category most prone to outbursts of physical violence, including domestic ones. It has been argued that middle-class masculinity, including its protectiveness towards women, was 'compromised' by 'the unruly men of the working class'.[14] But contemporary respectable reactions to disorder were complex. The least ambiguous forms of 'unruliness' were incidents involving several men from the same broad social category. Where no real damage was done to property or person, and there was no serious disturbance of the peace, especially affecting those of a 'better' social category, such occurrences were regarded relatively indulgently: as the outcome of untrained and untamed passions which were still, in their origins, generally honest and natural impulses. Nor, despite any unfortunate individual results, could they safely be stifled, given the national importance of the British fighting instinct. Improvements would come through education, teaching the individual working-class man to control, rather than to erase, his natural aggressive impulses.

Physical violence directed against wives and children was more problematic, though still not comprehensively condemned. Where the working-class abuser was also depicted as having good traits, being hard-working or fond of his children, his violent outbursts were often depicted as not being *intentionally* brutal but simply predictable, if unfortunate, expressions of the temper and instinctive good standards that made him properly 'British'. Untidy and slovenly wives who did not provide supper on time could provide a reasonable excuse for impatience resulting in a black eye, and the descriptive rhetoric would also imply that, if the provoking circumstances were amended, the marital violence would cease. Though Mrs Cross in *Mrs Halliburton's Troubles* was a habitual recipient of her husband's fist, Cross was depicted as the real victim because of his wife's slatternly ways; a perspective regularly echoed in court reports.[15] Even commentators discussing more extreme forms of masculine abuse of women focused on the issue of female incitement to violence as an exculpatory factor, distancing primary responsibility from the perpetrator. The *Daily Telegraph*, commenting on a celebrated scandal, agreed that George Hall had been harshly treated when sentenced to twenty years for shooting a wife who 'would have druv any chap mad'. Six months would have been fair, 'given the provocation'. Had he confined himself to 'thrashing her', he could have been let off entirely.[16]

However, only a brute would beat a good wife without provocation. Authors used incidents as signals to indicate a nasty character, though even here not automatically irreclaimably so. Philanthropy took this perspective seriously. Sister Alice in *Idylls of the Poor*, a work of advertised 'faction', could recount for serious consideration the tale of the reformed husband who rejected wife-beating (she irritated him by her meekness) once he realised his wife was dying.[17] While Francis Power Cobbe may have rejected the reality of the stereotype in her summary of wife-beaters, its continued expression in popular writing and reporting indicates that Cobbe's measured words had little contemporary effect.[18] For one thing, it impinged too much on the favoured Victorian stereotype of long-suffering, self-sacrificing womanhood. Even legal comment helped to perpetuate this construct: 'one of the most puzzling attributes of the female character is her sometimes invincible, unreasoning and self-sacrificing devotion to a most brutal ruffian of a man.' And 'a woman whose face has been beaten almost to a jelly by her burly brute of a husband in the dock, will plead ardently to the magistrate not to be "hard on him", because "he has always been a very good husband"'.[19]

Hitting a child was another complex commonplace. 'Correction' was a necessary part of paternal responsibilities, and overcorrection was generally depicted more as unfortunate than wrong, since it could be considered to spring from positive, even moral, instincts. But there was a gender dimension, suggesting that paternal chastisement was more profitable for boys than girls, unless a girl had already 'gone to the bad', when a severe fatherly beating might be useful to the victim as well as relieving the feelings of the justifiably outraged parent.[20] As part of the general construction of working-class identities, it was expected that there would be little male verbal violence not linked to a more readily measurable physical cruelty. A good man was one who never, unprovoked, raised fist, foot or voice against his children (or wife). Shouting at them was not identified as a separate problem. But *regular*, sober brutality against children was given as an indication of an irredeemably bad nature. Her father 'raised his strong arm' to fell the hymn-singing child heroine of *Madeline's Temptation*. It was realisation of the deliberation behind the action that forced her comment, 'It is all over now, and I shall never, never win him for God.'[21]

As with so much other crime, violence was, almost by definition, categorised as a working, rather than a middle-class, characteristic. Middle and upper-class males were accepted as having the same innate capacity for aggression, but, as a result of their training, were presumed to be able to control and, certainly when it came to inter-male violence, to channel it profitably – into sport, for instance. Depictions of middle or upper-class violence, consequently, tended to identify its expressions positively, rather than as social or legal problems. Accused of manslaughter, Erskine Peveril was 'charming – handsome, high-spirited, a splendid horseman and excellent at every kind of sport. He had gusts of passion sometimes; but so have most young men.' This comprised a list of qualities and a degree of self-control that indicated it was virtually impossible he could be guilty. It was finally revealed that all Erskine had applied to the unfortunate victim was 'condign chastisement', meaning that it was not unacceptable criminal assault but justifiable reprimand for a bad servant. The jealous gamekeeper had struck the fatal blow, when the victim was lying stunned on the ground – an innately *lower*-class action.[22]

As part of the expectation linked to middle-class male control over aggressive instincts, the luxury accorded to the working-class man of occasionally indulging in physical cruelty towards family members was not available. Consequently, and despite the reality that commentators such as James Hammerton have revealed, physical wife-abuse made virtually no appearance in popular writing and was similarly absent from contemporary categorisations of likely male violence. This may help to explain its delayed identification by modern scholars as a middle-class, Victorian social problem. The issue of mental or verbal violence towards women *was*, though, acknowledged as a potential middle-class attribute, and so, like the more physical expressions of brutality lower down the social scale, became an element of undesirable middle-class behaviour. Authors of advice texts identified it mournfully: fictional heroines, like Margaret Arbuthnot in *A Wilful*

Ward, were warned to be on their guard against it.[23] Yet, except in the rarest of cases, when youth linked to parental pressure could be some excuse, women linking their lives to 'bullies' were perceived as being largely to blame for their own misery. Womanly moral instinct should warn against a brute.[24] Yet, there was little associated expectation of encounters with physical violence. True, certain authors of sensational novels, like Mary Braddon or Ouida, did depict aristocratic verbal and physical violence against women – but this was essentially an aspect of the continuing respectable ambiguity over aristocratic moral standards. But, however encountered, the issue of female responsibility was central to considerations of the origins of both verbal and physical violence:

> There is something more spiritual in the case of the man who is driven by jealousy and misery to a temporary madness of violence . . . none of us is capable of saying how he might act if his affections and his self-respect were suddenly and cruelly outraged. Even when we endorse the verdict, it is still possible to feel some shred of pity for the criminal. His offence has not been the result of a self-interested and cold-blooded plotting, but the consequence – however monstrous and disproportionate – of a cause for which others were responsible.[25]

The middle or upper-class man driven to physical expression of his misery by female misconduct was still a victim, even though behavioural expectations were higher than for working-class males.

Conduct towards children was central to assessments of the role of physical violence in everyday middle and upper-class life. Verbal bullying was frowned on as unnecessary, but its occurrence was acknowledged as a characteristic of unfortunately natured fathers.[26] Paternal physical correction of prepubescent children was acceptable, so long as undertaken in a spirit of morally inspired didacticism. Corporal punishment of older boys, by fathers or their substitutes, was a positively character-forming exercise:

> 'James Harrington, have you ever had a caning?'
> 'No, sir, never.'
> 'Hold out your hand.'
> Jim holds it out at once, and receives one smart blow. He winks . . . but still holds out his hand bravely.
> 'There, my boy', says Mr Allen kindly, patting his head, 'that will do. It will teach you to remember my rules, which must be obeyed.'
> Jim retires, feeling rather proud . . . he has come out of it all with honours.[27]

Male or female, authors of boys' school stories endorsed the importance of physical chastisement – though there was an increasing unease in medical literature about the potentially undesirable effects of beating the older boyish bottom. But the link between sex and violence was not widely discussed as being dangerous to either their moral integrity or physical instincts. But, especially when adolescent, daughters were less readily regarded as suitable subjects for paternal physical correction. One, largely unarticulated, reason was fear that such punishments might actually awaken a less innocent girl to her sexual nature. Medical texts and pornography shared the view that experience of physical violence, including whipping the adolescent female fundament, could awaken undesirable passions.[28]

The powerful gender dimension to the stereotyping of violence was at its most explicit when categorising feminine expressions of violence. Women were expected to be the main victims of violence, as well as its incitors, if not always directly culpable in either of these capacities. Working-class women could be excused, to some extent, for the poor management that led to male wrath by respectable comment referring to their inadequate training.[29] But, since no advantage was perceived as resulting from any aspect of female violence, women could not be, acceptably, its perpetrators. Consequently, little real complexity or subtlety was displayed in assessments thereof. Instead, there were a range of sweeping generalisations: 'one of the most staggering and repugnant attributes to man exhibited by bad women is their perfectly fiendish cruelty.'[30] Physically violent women of any class were widely condemned as abnormal: 'Tenderness is a feminine virtue . . . a woman devoid of tenderness is an abomination, and a perversion of nature.'[31] The broader social implications ensured violent women were classified by the law as they encountered it, and by popular writing, as either beings so bad as to be sub-human or effectively insane. Certainly they were deemed social outcasts, for female violence would not only ensure their own lasting degradation but also that of the immediate family and even neighbours.

For most women, then, nothing that could be depicted as a genuine expression of physical violence was acceptable, regardless of social background or circumstantial excuses for unhappiness. The latitude accorded to males was not extended to their feminine counterparts. There might be (especially for lower-class and so ill-trained girls) an indulgence for youthful pushing, slapping or hair pulling. But the very rhetoric used underlined the expectations of the minimal force and relative weakness of the participants and the emotions involved. There was even an unease in advice manuals about depicting mothers physically correcting their children. It became usual to advise that the maternal role involved verbal scolding (ideally involving tones of gentle, moral sorrow for sins committed), with fathers undertaking physical chastisement. While it was admitted that emotional, overworked, working-class mothers might more excusably hit their children in a heated moment, there was unequivocal condemnation for any excessive use of force.[32] There was scant sympathy for the pressures that might drive women into fights. Women could not legitimately sort out grievances in such ways. Lacking the potential, moral dimension associated with inter-male violence, incidents of female physical aggression were more likely to end up exposed to the operations of the law. So while 'women made up a fifth of the total convictions' for assault, it was the greater gravity with which they were regarded by society, rather than the actual scale of female assaults that resulted in this prominence.[33] Non-physical violence – especially abusive language – was also condemned as unacceptable. Frances Power Cobbe commented of the termagant female that she was 'the tyrant of her husband, nay, of the whole court or lane in which she lives'. This disapproval took little account of the lack of practical alternative expressions for many women. Wives driven to verbal aggression by husbandly neglect or improvidence were criticised by the sanction that assumed that good women did not have any *natural* aggressive instincts. A good woman's tendencies were presumed to be towards gentleness and yielding to masculine dominance.

Since it was a challenge to the divinely ordered system of human relations for women to react to stress or unhappiness aggressively, bellicose women were, unlike violent men, particularly vulnerable to both social and legal sanction. This is emphasised by physical descriptions of perpetrators. Only unmitigatedly brutal men were likely to be depicted as 'more fiend than man'.[34] But aggressive women were, almost universally, portrayed in ways that demonised them, partly by stressing their lack of physical feminine attributes. In some adult writing there was even an implication that allied to their capacity for violence were predatory sexual instincts. References to 'dark' looks or 'sensual' aspects possessed by such women provided coded warnings. No good woman displayed such characteristics. This could also hint that violent women were on the verge of insanity, since an excessive sexual appetite and consequent blunting of the maternal instinct was stereotypically one indication of female madness.[35] This was further underlined by apparent acceptance that while for men education was the way to control violence, there was rarely any hope that genuinely violent women could be so 'trained' into normal, respectable and relatively submissive characters.[36]

It might be expected that drink would complicate the stereotyping of types of violence and the perpetrators. However, while it was generally accepted that drink was the single greatest stimulus to violence, alcohol was regarded more as the catalyst than the creator of violence, only bringing out latent characteristics in individuals. The closer the person was to brute nature, the more likely that drink would stimulate violent conduct of some kind.[37] There was a powerful class as well as gender dimension to alcoholism. The working-class drunkard had to become teetotal in order to recover: but alcoholics from the upper orders could, like Lord Temple, announce after a period of abstinence that 'a glass of wine' no longer posed any danger.[38] Thus, indulgence in alcohol by such men could be regarded with disapproval, as 'wasteful' and 'uncivilised', but was not seen by most commentators as a stimulus to violence. Middle and upper-class temperance was advocated more for the good example it provided for the lower orders than as a matter of necessity.[39] Expectations about the essentially more primitive masculine nature at the 'lower' ends of society meant that drinking, especially of spirits, was identified as a real problem; one likely to promote a loss of control resulting in violence. A central element in many temperance campaigns was the belief that violence between working men could be effectively controlled if drunkenness was largely eradicated.[40] Yet, among many commentators there was a certain sympathy for the concept that, for working men, moderate imbibing was a natural taste that should not be stigmatised. From this perspective, a minor brawl or striking your wife or child in the aftermath of an occasional drunken evening was a predictable, if regrettable, commonplace that did not threaten social stability. There could be sympathy, even from the legal system, for the overworked father without sufficient wifely support who, in a drunken instant, killed his child, especially if he turned teetotal thereafter: 'It is all the work of an instant. He raises his unsteady arm . . . . A startled, half-reproachful cry of "Dada", which penetrates even his besotted brain.'[41]

However, it was never acceptable for a woman, whatever her class, to indulge freely in drink; the debauching impact of alcoholic excess on the female frame and mind was depicted as horrific. Women were accepted as being more susceptible to alcohol's negative effects – including the stimulus to violence resulting from a lack of self-control. The temptation to indulge was not expected to be a serious problem for the more instinctively refined middle or upper-class woman, unless she was insane. The widowed Mrs St John, in *St Martin's Eve* had her latent madness developed by her late husband's fine champagne, and so murdered her stepson in an expression of child abuse that was seen as typical of deranged women.[42] A mere taste for alcohol by a woman of respectable background was cited by many as being in itself a mental disease – dipsomania – as with Carey's Aline Lyndhurst. This theme was much discussed in periodical literature of all types, as series such as 'Stories from the Diary of a Doctor' or 'Adventures of a Man of Science' in *The Strand Magazine* indicate.[43]

Many working-class women faced regular temptation in the shape of easy access to alcohol, as well as the example of husbands and sons who drank. This temptation was admitted, but was not a sufficient excuse to justify these women in intemperance, even given presumptions about their lesser capacity for self-restraint, for various reasons. A drunken woman was a temptation to crime, particularly sexual crime. She was not in a state to defend herself or to arouse the protective instinct natural to all good Britons. Comment on incidents where drunken women were sexually assaulted emphasised this perspective. Mr Justice Willes, in 1856, remarked that there was 'some doubt entertained whether the offence of rape could be committed upon the person of a woman who had rendered herself perfectly insensible by drink', making the woman the culpable factor.[44] Then again, drink was stereotypically presumed to be the stimulus to women to act 'out of normal female character'. The majority of domestically violent working women were represented as being also drunkards. Husband abuse was, to some extent, a matter of comic humour – generally depending upon a depiction of a physical inbalance in the respective sizes of husband and wife.[45] After all, men were expected to be able to look after themselves physically and so were culpable if they failed. Only weak or debauched characters were likely to find themselves at the physical mercy of a drunkenly violent woman.[46]

The deeply ingrained belief in the existence of natural maternal instincts, even among working-class women, ensured that child abuse stimulated by drink was always unforgivable. It was in such direct contradiction of beliefs about the nature of mother-love that arguments for the redemption of drunkenly abusive women, literary or real, were generally held to be unconvincing. Hesba Stretton wrote her best-seller, *Jessica's First Prayer*, with Jessica victimised by her cruel, drunken mother. She wrote a sequel, *Jessica's Mother*, but despite her reputation and the huge popularity of the original, the sequel did not succeed: contemporaries would not accept the reality of the mother's reformation.[47] 'Only when drunk' as an excuse for female violence was not available: drunkenness was merely a demonstration of the depths to which a woman had sunk. While female drunks were undoubtedly a regular feature of popular writing they were 'realistically' depicted as beyond help. Women had 'less will power than men and therefore less self-control', meaning 'few, if any female dipsomaniacs are ever thoroughly cured'. *Male* drunkards, however, could cure *themselves* with sufficient will power.[48] It cannot be claimed that such representations reflected daily reality, certainly for working-class women. In practice, working-class communities at least maintained attitudes that were relatively tolerant to female imbibing and any resultant minor violence. Reports from domestic mission societies indicated that drink was a regular problem encountered when dealing with such women, identified largely by bruises displayed by children and husbands. But the reports also indicated a lack of community condemnation unless extremes of violence occurred.[49]

Yet, popular representations of violence and its causations indicate the difficulties that women, working-class in particular, faced if forced in some way to submit their actions to establishment or legal scrutiny. Certain levels or categories of male violence could be surrounded with justifications that, except in extreme cases, would evoke some sympathy. That option was rarely available to women. Even campaigners and institutions sympathetic to women's plight and seeking to remedy women's powerlessness, such as suffragists, were generally circumspect in their expressions of sympathy for women 'guilty' of violence. Stephen argued that in 'acts of violence against women', the law should act – but could only be 'as severe as it can be made without defeating itself'.[50] As this implied, women reacting violently to circumstance or masculine provocation were liable to loose both public and legal sympathy for any grievances, and also claims to respectable status. Any substantiated accusation of drunkenness automatically placed the woman in the wrong.

It would be impossible in a short chapter to cover all the nuances of the categorisations of violence and associated gender stereotypes. However, the outlines covered here are in line with attitudes towards issues not discussed, such as violence towards 'defenceless' animals. Victorians could find humour in the vision of a drunken Edwin beating an Angelina, but not in the vision of a drunken woman abusing a worthy husband. It was only where the relative powerlessness of verbal nagging was contrasted with physical male strength that Victorians could be amused by any form of female-initiated violence. Such gendered stereotypings of violence, and the linkages made therein with drink, effectively and significantly constrained women's liberty of action in daily life but had far less negative impacts on male behaviour.

Notes

1. W. S. Gilbert, *Trial by Jury* (1875).

2. V. A. C. Gatrell, 'Crime, authority and the policeman-state' in F. M. L. Thompson, (ed.), *The Cambridge Social History of Britain, 1750–1950* Vol. 3, *Social Agencies and Institutions* (1990), p. 296.

3. J. Holt Schooling, 'Crime' *PMM* 15 (1888); Lucia Zedner, *Women, Crime and Custody in Victorian England* (Oxford, 1991), pp. 33–40.

4. Judith Rowbotham, *Good Girls Make Good Wives. Guidance for Girls in Victorian Fiction* (Oxford, 1989), Introduction.

5. See, for example, reports from the Middlesex Sessions, *Times* 23 Nov. 1860, 9d.

6. James F. Stephen, *Liberty, Equality, Fraternity* (1907), pp. 172–173.

7. Kim Stevenson in this volume (Ch. 5); *Hansard* 3rd series, 279, col. 1294 (31 May 1883); 280, col. 767 (18 June 1883).

8. Silas Hocking, *Our Benny* (1879), in Preface citing as sources his pastoral work in Liverpool and the Liverpool local press.

9. Stephen, *Liberty* p. 173.

10. Evelyn Everett Green, *Battledown Boys, or, An Enemy Overcome* (1892), p. 30.

11. Silas Hocking, *Our Joe* (1884), pp. 50, 54.

12. Evelyn Everett Green, *The Guardianship of Gabrielle* (1903), p. 330; Green, *Battledown Boys* p. 235.

13. Green, *Gabrielle* p. 380; Green, *Battledown Boys* p. 245; *Times* 30 March 1878, 11e; *SDT* 28 Oct. 1865.

14. A. James Hammerton, *Cruelty and Companionship: Conflict in Nineteenth-Century Married Life* (1992), p. 61.

15. Mrs Henry Wood, *Mrs Halliburton's Troubles* (1862), pp. 243–244; *Times* 23 Nov. 1860, 9d.

16. *DT* 6 March 1884.

17. Mabel King, *Idylls of the Poor* (1898), pp. 68–69.

18. Frances Power Cobbe, 'Wife torture in England' *CR* 32 (1878), pp. 55–87.

19. Hargrave Adam, *Woman and Crime* (1907), p. 4.

20. Wood, *Mrs Halliburton* p. 215.

21. A. Fitzgerald, *Madeline's Temptation* (1893), p. 12.

22. Evelyn Everett Green, *Madam of Clyst Peveril* (1905 edn, 1st pub 1899), pp. 24, 281.

23. Sarah Tytler, *Papers for Thoughtful Girls* (1862) Ruth Lamb, *A Wilful Ward* (1895).

24. *Ibid.*, pp. 90–93.

25. 'Strange studies from life: 2 – The love affair of George Vincent Parker' *SM* 21 (1901), p. 363.

26. See, for example, Rosa Nouchette Carey, *Aunt Diana* (1888), pp. 102–103.

27. Ismay Thorn, *Geoff and Jim* (1890), pp. 36–37.

28. Anonymous, *Romance of Lust* (1879); Anonymous, *First Training* (1867, republished 1995); Stephen Marcus, *The Other Victorians: A Study of Sexuality and Pornography in Mid-Victorian England* (1966), pp. 255–256.

29. M. M. Brewster, *Sunbeams in the Cottage, or What Women May Do. A Narrative Chiefly Addressed to the Working Classes* (Edinburgh, 1854).

30. Adam, *Woman and Crime* p. 17.

31. Antony Guest, 'The state of the law courts: 4: The criminal courts' *SM* 2 (1891), p. 89.

32. Charlotte Yonge, *Womankind* (1877).

33. Lucia Zedner, *Women, Crime and Custody in Victorian England* (Oxford, 1991) p. 35.

34. L. T. Meade and Robert Halifax M. D., 'Stories from the diary of a doctor: the small house on Steven's Heath' *SM* 10 (1895), p. 517.

35. Adam, *Woman and Crime* p. 301.

36. *Ibid.*

37. Sarah Tooley, 'Lady Henry Somerset at Duxhurst' *SS* 4 (1901), p. 25.

38. Mrs Henry Wood, *Danesbury House* (1859), p. 265.

39. Laura Platt, *Plucked from the Burning* (n.d., *c.* 1865), pp. 27–28.

40. *Ibid.*

41. M. E. L., *Dr. Ted* (1893) p. 2.

42. Mrs Henry Wood, *St Martin's Eve* (1864).

43. Rosa Nouchette Carey, *Basil Lyndhurst* (1888); L. T. Meade and Robert Halifax M. D., 'Stories', *SM* (1891–1894); L. T. Meade and Grant Allen, 'Adventures of a man of science' *SM* (1894–1897).

44. *Times*, 6 Dec. 1856, 12c.

45. D. Jerrold, *Mrs Caudle's Curtain Lectures* (Norwich, 1855), for example.

46. Rosa Nouchette Carey *Aunt Diana* (1888), *Mary St. John* (1891) Chs. 14, 15.

47. Hesba Stretton, *Jessica's First Prayer* (1882); Hesba Stretton, *Jessica's Mother* (1891).

48. Adam, *Woman and Crime* p. 16.

49. *Annual Reports* (1875–1889), Liverpool Mission.

50. Stephen, *Liberty* p. 235.

CHAPTER TEN

Keeping ourselves to ourselves: violence in the Edwardian suburb

JULIE ENGLISH EARLY

On 15 July 1910 the front page of every major London daily featured the grisly discovery of a filleted human torso buried in the coal cellar of a North London suburban home. The remains were presumed to be those of Cora Crippen, last seen at the end of January. After she disappeared, her husband, Dr Hawley Harvey Crippen, had earlier notified her friends, first, that she had been called to the United States on family business, then, that she had been taken ill, and finally, that she had died in California shortly before Easter. However, inconsistencies in Crippen's stories raised suspicions which only escalated when Crippen's typist, Ethel Le Neve, began to accompany him to social events – wearing Cora's jewellery – and soon moved into the Crippen home at 39 Hilldrop Crescent. Cora's friends went to Scotland Yard. When Chief Inspector Walter Dew interviewed Crippen, Crippen admitted that he had lied. His wife had left him for another man, he said, and he had made up the story to avoid the embarrassment of scandal. Dew was largely satisfied, but shortly returned to clarify a few small points. He found, first, that Crippen and Le Neve had fled, and second, the decomposing human remains in the coal cellar.[1]

For the next five months, the Crippen case was front-page news. It began with international bulletins for apprehending the pair – with some surprises. Scotland Yard's Wanted poster announced that Crippen was also known as Franckel; and the victim, his wife Cora, 'otherwise Belle Elmore, Kunegunde Mackamotzki, Marsangar, and Turner'. Ethel Clara Le Neve ('alias Mrs Crippen') had changed her name from the more prosaic Neave,[2] and as a final fillip was, it seems, cross-dressed as a young man for their escape. In short, the suburban doctor, his wife, and his lover might not have been quite what they seemed. In Belgium, Crippen hastily booked passage to Montreal, but once the *Montrose* was under weigh, her captain, catching up on recent newspapers, began taking a closer look at the rather odd father and son, John Philo Robinson and Master Robinson, among the passengers. Captain Kendall blocked out Le Neve's hair from newspaper photographs and chalked out Crippen's moustache. Encouraged by his detective work, he sent a Marconigram to Scotland Yard. Scotland Yard sent Dew by a faster ship to apprehend them when the *Montrose* arrived in Canada.

For a week, newspapers on both sides of the Atlantic carried stories charting the progress of the chase with accounts of life on board. Captain Kendall sent wireless reports of what Crippen and Le Neve had eaten, what books they had taken from the ship's library, how often they strolled the deck. With the couple oblivious to the world's surveillance, newspapers were also free to release details of the planned capture when the ship arrived. At home, interviews with anyone who had had the least brush with Crippen, Le Neve, or Cora provided fresh copy, as did transcripts of the coroner's inquest, exhaustive investigations into each of the principals' lives for any new angle, and the progress of the extradition proceedings. Crippen's and Le Neve's return to London in August was nearly a public circus, followed by more transcripts from the Bow Street hearing committing them for trial, their separate trials, Le Neve's release, and Crippen's execution on 22 November 1910.

Fundamentally a classic love triangle gone wrong, the case might have commanded little attention had it not tapped so unerringly an array of up-to-the-minute circumstances surrounding the principals. The case had everything: transatlantic escape, cross-dressing, the first capture by wireless, an office romance (women clerical workers were still a new and, to some, disturbing phenomenon), Crippen's rather murky business affairs as a patent medicine entrepreneur, and Cora Crippen's tangential connection to the world of the music halls. Curiously, however, as reporting continued over the life of the case, rather than heightening its sensational elements, accounts tended to normalise them. Both in contemporary reporting and retrospective accounts, fascination with the Crippen case has centered on its elements of ordinariness. Simply, the case offered the lure of formulating 'timeless truths of the human heart' by unveiling the hopes, desires and failings of lives lived behind suburban doors.

In this, the shaping of the Crippen case to a fixed narrative is particularly instructive. Its gradual consensus in characterising the principals and deriving the case's meaning reflects two impulses: first, to create a timeless story of thwarted true love among the suburban 'little people', with murder rendered a 'regrettable' incident sanitised of its violence; and second, to subsume spousal murder to an effect of a larger, more significant cultural commentary. In this unfortunate version, the murder of a woman was (or is) not really 'about' women after all. Seen as insignificant in itself, it instead becomes symptomatic of a cultural crisis made to matter in a way that violence against women too often does not. Simply, the narrative of the Crippen case that has come down to us offers a model of the erasure of gender to frame an issue of class that quickly escalates to an issue of culture.

Crippen was convicted of poisoning his wife with hyoscine, then mutilating her body: beheading it, dismembering it, removing her sexual organs, and burying the filleted torso in the coal cellar. He never confessed, never explained, and in this silence became a blank slate to be written on. Remarkably, by the close of months of newspaper attention and his conviction, the image of a cold, methodical murderer and mutilator failed to take hold. In its place was the image of a principled, honourable and beleaguered little man whose necessary execution was met with rueful regret. Against all odds, the case was shaped to a strangely moral tale of the sad little man pushed to the point where he might discover his own deep wells of character to become, in one memoirist's view, 'a martyr and a hero of romance'.[3]

To see how this happens, we must restore the cultural context that the timeless story would erase. No matter how sensational or singular, or alternatively how archetypal the Crippen case may seem, the responses to it and the understanding of its cast of characters were deeply embedded in what was perceived as an Edwardian urban crisis centred on the changing character of London. London's geographical sprawl, the changed composition and sheer size of its workforce, and the new technologies transforming business life, domestic life and leisure produced what many perceived as a hyperactive and increasingly unknowable city with too many opportunities and too many comforts available to too many people. Persistent throughout the discourse on the city is widespread nervousness about a poorly-defined lower middle class, growing at a startling rate, filling suburb after suburb, as they approached critical mass with the potential to debase the national character. Edwardian concerns about the city and its suburbs appear directly in public debate on the condition of England and the national character, in urban fiction, and always as a significant backdrop, in the reporting on the Crippen case.

In the first days of reporting the 'North London cellar murder', newspapers faced the challenge of fixing for their readers just what sorts of people the Crippens might be. Crippen identified himself as a doctor, but doctors were scattered up and down the social scale. More reliable perhaps would be the sort of neighbourhood in which he lived, yet that proved even less precise. In the first stories, his street, Hilldrop Crescent, was variously identified in Kentish Town, Camden Town, Islington, Holloway, and Tufnell Park – designations that were, if not correct, almost correct (Hilldrop Crescent was in Lower Holloway), but each with varying nuances of general, if inexact, class association.

Crippen's suburb was certainly convenient to business in the City, but the 'walking suburbs' had long lost any social cachet that they may have had when they were developed largely in the 1850s, '60s, and '70s. Conventional wisdom described the movement over time of the 'better classes' outward in concentric rings to more distant suburbs, leaving behind the new arrivals, especially the growing lower middle class. This rough scheme, appealing in its easy categories, was, however, wholly unreliable: individual suburbs had never had class homogeneity, nor did they evolve it.[4] Updated frequently, suburban house-hunters' guidebooks precisely detailed the quality of individual streets. A *Cornhill* magazine series in 1901 on how Londoners lived at varying incomes pointed to fine but certain distinctions. 'Thousands of snug little suburban homes can be had at 10 to 12s. 6d. a week', the writer observed; but 'the twelve-and-sixpenny house' will be 'in a very different road from the road of ten-shilling houses'.[5]

What house hunters vaguely knew gained investigative precision with the publication in 1902 of Charles Booth's seventeen-volume analysis presented to the Royal Statistical Society, *Life and Labour of the People in London*. His street-by-street survey with maps colour coding each by class documented the highly mixed character of virtually every district of greater London. Even within a neighbourhood, Booth commented, 'we are told that contingents from different streets would never mix'.[6] Two decades before Booth, an 1881 residential guide to Holloway indicated that 'such houses as those in Hilldrop Crescent may be accounted of the superior, and those in Torriano Grove and Road a fair sample of the convenient smaller, class'.[7] By the time of the Crippen murder in 1910, Holloway was certainly unfashionable, its location in the inner ring by then marking it for many as a 'clerks' suburb', yet Booth's map, only a few years earlier, showed that the street had retained its middle-class stability. With solid, semi-detached rather than terraced houses (for the most part still single-family occupied), Booth coded it 'well-to-do'. In 1910, photographs of 39 Hilldrop Crescent accompanied every story on the discovery in the cellar; with a solid, even somewhat imposing, façade framed with mature trees, it looked like every other semi-detached of the same vintage. For newspaper readers, the photograph of the site gave up virtually nothing about Crippen even as the prominent use of the image vainly suggested that it should.

The very detailed effort by the guidebooks or the *Cornhill* to read the suburbs only underscored their unreadability. Thus the newspapers' concern to 'place' Crippen, and their confusion in attempting to do so, were only symptomatic of a widespread and anxious discussion about an imprecise and increasingly unknowable proportion of the population, which was swelling, many felt, at an alarming rate. Commentators would find that identifying measures, long serviceable to a reasonably crisp, three-tiered class system (where one lived, how one lived, occupation, income) simply did not work. Even on Booth's maps the coding for 'mixed class' was pervasive. Many skilled labourers earned more than clerks, or lived more comfortably without the expenses of clerkly respectability for travel and dress. Less successful doctors and solicitors or small businessmen might themselves have only clerkly incomes. Growing occupations loosely included in the lower middle class – teachers, engineers, municipal workers, journalists, policemen – varied considerably in education and training. If the lower reaches of the middle class seemed amorphously defined yet insistently a factor in Edwardian commentary on the state of the culture, they were handily conceptualised by identification with a more readily named scourge of urban life – the suburbs.

Edwardian London was, in fact, a bewildering sprawl of suburbs. Unique among European cities, London was predominately a city of houses, not flats. The pattern, a foreign observer had said, accorded with the English character that valued independence and privacy above all else.[8] Yet paradoxically, English critics were considerably less sanguine about the effects of this privacy and independence – with great reservations about those to whom it should be extended. It had long been a commonplace (well back to the mid-Victorians)[9] to deplore the aesthetic blight of the suburbs: they were, the critics said, dreary, monotonous and shoddy. However, throughout the Edwardian decade, critiques of the suburbs took a more ominous turn.

In fiction and in public discourse around the turn of the century, the suburbs became an anxious locus, a naggingly worrisome *terra incognita*, vast and unknowable. In 1909, H. G. Wells's 'condition of England' novel, *Tono-Bungay*, provides the provincial narrator's first impressions of London. He is stunned to see, not a glittering capital, but 'this boundless world of dingy people' living in 'endless streets of undistinguished houses'. They are, he muses, 'inexplicable people who, in a once fashionable phrase, do not "exist"'.[10] But exist they did, and everywhere: 'south of this central London, south-east, south-west, far west, north-west, all round the northern hills . . . disproportionate growths.' And they are hardly benign. To Wells's narrator they represent 'the unorganised, abundant substance of some tumorous growth-process, which indeed bursts all the outlines of the affected carcass and protrudes such masses as ignoble Croyden [*sic*]'.[11]

While those populating these cancerous growths represented a broad spectrum (professionals, businessmen, managers, office-workers, and, some worried, who knew what else), they were increasingly difficult to distinguish, producing an anxiety that, like the cancer of their suburbs, the indistinct lower middle class had reached critical mass. Each day enormous numbers, the new white-collar workers, descended on the City, like their 'betters' dressed for business. The morning swarm across London Bridge, long a staple photographic representation, had earlier been read as the sign of vital force, the paperwork energy that managed nation and Empire. In the new century, one journalist interpreted a darker vision: to him, the top-hatted swarm of men 'going to business' was a precisely clocked and classed engine producing streets 'seething with men'. 'In thousands . . . they come and come.' They are 'shadowy legions', 'swarming masses' that 'fuse into one monstrous organism . . . one mammoth breathing thing'.[12] In truth, they are clerks, but in business uniform, largely indistinguishable from their employers. And at night, they disappear into their monotonous, unremarkable (and most vexing), impenetrable suburbs.

In the suburbs, life was not lived in the street, but behind the twitch of the window curtain. And apart from those few evening hours with the returned *paterfamilias*, it was perceived as a world managed by women to represent the status and character of the family. While promotional material for suburban developments touted the virtues of *rus in urbe*, the great promise of the suburbs was privacy accompanied by small, easily managed public markers asserting respectability. Each family's autonomy, reinforced by neighbourhood design with separation by high walls and hedges, fostered isolation, but paradoxically, intense pressures for public conformity as well. The architectural uniformity of long rows of terraced or semi-detached units presented a sober public face with fixed gestures of propriety. Polished doorknobs and proper window treatments offered reassuring formulas for those unsure of the mysteries of class and taste, and such measures contributed to a strict, unspoken, and competitive code that disapproved of public eccentricity in a climate of reserve, suspicion, and fear of social self-betrayal. In Shan Bullock's *Robert Thorne*, his fictional clerk describes their house near Denmark Hill: 'You will see that we were making the best show we could. The brass knocker, the bay window, the dining and drawing room, establish the fact; whilst the Study gives evidence that already we had in view the great suburban ideal of being superior to the people next door.'[13] One woman remembered her mother's philosophy: 'She would say, I must have the windows right because more people pass by than come in.' Another remembers his suburban Edwardian childhood dominated by the principle of 'keeping yourself to yourself'. Visitors, he recalls, were 'few and infrequent'.[14] Yet the public show was to Max Beerbohm 'a tragic symbol' of stunted, anxious lives. He was amazed to see a bust of Minerva positioned in a front window – facing out. 'Minerva's back had been turned upon the inmates of the room, not in Divine discourtesy, but by the very inmates. Imagine the back view of a bust!'[15]

Like Beerbohm, most commentators had only the view from the street for assessing the denizens of Wells's 'tumorous growths'. Indeed 'more would pass by than come in'. The more revealing home interior was rarely seen.

Unlike the East End, where residents, constituted as a 'problem', could not prevent entry by social workers, school representatives, or health officials, the suburbs were not subject to such intrusions. Yet the expanse of empty streets – and twitching curtains – were irresistible challenges to the imagination. In one of many popular representations, Sherlock Holmes, for example, indulges a curious reverie on penetrating domestic privacy: if one could 'gently remove the roofs, and peep in at the queer things that are going on . . . it would make all fiction . . . most stale and unprofitable'.[16] The figure is taken up by George Sims, prolific journalist and playwright, who also edited a curious collection of vignettes on hidden corners of London life. In the collection, the dramas behind seemingly benign façades only want the fourth wall lifted. The sketch 'In London's Shadowland' imagines private and potentially explosive drama: hard-won respectability is about to crumble. In 'a pretty little villa in the North of London', a young clerk despairs of telling his wife that his share speculations with company funds will shortly mean their bankruptcy and disgrace.[17]

In most English writers' imaginations the privacy and independence that might have suited the suburban ideal to the English character was more often a distinct source of anxiety about what might be concealed once privacy and independence were extended to a class which was, they suspected, ill-equipped to handle either. In this view, the pressures of aspiring to poorly understood middle-class values at its best created the comic pathos of Minerva's bust facing outward to impress the neighbours. This version, ripe for the condescending humour on human foibles with which *Punch* often veiled class hostility, was famously rendered in the Grossmiths' *The Diary of a Nobody*. In *The Diary*, Mr Pooter naïvely chronicles the small hopes, pretensions, insecurities, and embarrassments of 'the little people,' all those like Pooter, living in their own version of The Laurels in Brickfield Terrace. For a more secure middle-class audience, Pooter's sincere embrace of their values prompts warm affection only in proportion to his comic ineptitude.[18]

At best, the lower middle-class suburban inhabitant was comically pathetic, consumed by little worries, little hopes, little dreams, all suited to 'little people'. At worst, the controlled gestures of respectability were seen as inevitably layered over innate vulgarity and undisciplined character that were bound to erupt in violence. In the Conan Doyle story, 'A Case of Identity', in which Holmes speculates on 'the queer goings on' that would make 'all fiction most stale and unprofitable', the tale begins with a peculiar newspaper report of a separation case in which the man of the house 'had drifted into the habit of winding up every meal by taking out his false teeth and hurling them at his wife'.[19]

Commentators content either with prurient imaginings of secretive, perhaps desperate suburban lives or alternatively with generic distaste and dismissal of a 'boundless world of dingy people' were baffled by the fine distinctions well known to those they attempted (vaguely) to imagine. Charles Masterman, a prominent Edwardian voice in debates on the city, was reported to have expressed incredulity at the absurdity of characters in a play debating the relative social merits of Clapham and Herne Hill.[20] Writers who comprehended such felt distinctions were a distinct minority, in some respects comparable to the more numerous social explorers of the East End. George Gissing's patient anatomy of Camberwell in his 1895 novel *In the Year of Jubilee* sought to depict paper-thin layers of status, well known to the denizens of this mystifying new world, but baffling to commentators. The *Spectator* reviewer, however, found only broad strokes necessary for defining Gissing's subject – a world, he presumed, unknown to his readers. The novel, he explains, centres on 'that vaguely outlined middle section of society which, in matters of physical comfort, approximates to the caste above it, and in its lack of the delicate requirements of life has something in common with the caste below it'.[21]

In 1905, T. W. H. Crosland found that this new species demanded explaining, even though he begins his book, *The Suburbans*, with a truism: 'All the world knows that the suburbans are a people to themselves. Persons of culture . . . have for a generation or so made a point of speaking of the suburbans with hushed voices and a certain contempt.'[22] Crosland's purpose, however, is not to disavow his readers of this view, nor to defuse it with the avuncular condescension of the Grossmiths, but patiently and precisely to detail the ways in which Edwardian suburbanites do, indeed, warrant contempt. Suburbia, he concludes, 'is a force against which honest people must struggle'.[23] Insofar as the dwindling 'soul of Suburbia' might be saved, it is in the national interest to halt the encroachment of suburban values that are 'as hard and as metallic and as unemotional as solid brass'.[24] Like many commentators, Crosland targets vulgarity, poor taste and pathetic pretensions, but at the heart of his diatribe is the deterioration of the family resulting from the inadequacies of the suburban wife:

> In nine cases out of ten your suburban woman is an utter shrew, termagent, and scold. She 'begins as she means to go on', on the advice of fat and puffy matrons who invariably gather round her in her early wifehood, and she goes on with something of a vengeance all the rest of her life. The married life of the suburb may appear to be tranquil and peaceful and undisturbed; really it is nothing of the kind. An armed neutrality, a cold resignation, is the best that can be said of it.[25]

Like Crosland, Gissing imagined domestic life as a hollow, if not vicious, fraud concealed behind seemingly respectable doors. And like Crosland's book, Gissing's *In the Year of Jubilee* assigns responsibility to women for what he views as the appalling values of suburban domesticity that, in one character's view, will inevitably lead to cultural disintegration: 'Before long, there'll be no such thing as a home', Mr Lord direly predicts.[26]

In the Year of Jubilee begins with a domestic scene in Camberwell. The Peachys, Ada and her husband, are Gissing's object lesson of the potential debasement of the national character that must result from the social mobility which suburban pretensions and values seemed to create. Gissing assumes that understanding the character of suburbanites requires imaginatively entering their homes to see what the markers of respectability might mask. The view from the street will tell nothing, nor will glimpsing suburbanites away from their homes (like viewing the swarm of men 'going to business') reveal the truth. Ada Peachy, for example, is in public fashionable, even elegant. Only in the home can we see that she is really 'one of these trashy, flashy girls . . . calling themselves "ladies"'.[27]

Mr Peachy, a clerk in a small disinfectant manufactory, invested a small bequest in his employer's company and was in one stroke elevated to partner. The Peachys immediately move from 'a modest home' to another Camberwell street of greater pretensions. Ada has filled the house with new furniture, but 'already slovenly housekeeping had dulled the brightness of every surface'. Her taste is showy, unnatural: there are no fresh flowers, but only 'pretentious ornaments' with 'a strange medley of pictures' including 'hideous oleographs framed in ponderous gilding'.[28] In the drawing-room are 'half-a-dozen novels of the meaner kind . . . [and] a multitude of papers . . . [with] serial stories, paragraphs relating to fashion, sport, the theatre, answers to correspondents (wherein she especially delighted), columns of facetiae, and gossip about notorious people'.[29]

Ada is greedy, shallow, frivolous, and lazy. She sleeps late; her servants are insolent and undisciplined; at twenty-seven, she looks thirty, her complexion dimmed by habitual use of 'paints and powders'. Her thin nasal voice rises readily to shrillness. She neglects all household duties preferring instead to fill her days with cheap, sensational reading. She has no taste, but is guided only by what advertising tells her is the latest fashion. In short, she has no values, no ethics. In Mr Lord's view, it is the greedy ways of women like Ada that force husbands to financial fiddles rather than what would seem a more appropriate crime: 'It is astounding to me that they don't get their necks wrung.'[30] That such women brought deserved violence on themselves is a view shared by Ada's less frivolous sister. '"If I were your husband"', she tells her, '"I should long since have turned you into the street – if I hadn't broken your neck first."'[31]

Gissing – and Crosland – were not alone in creating an indulged suburban housewife as the root cause of the nation's decline. In 1913, journalist Philip Gibbs tried his hand at a 'condition of England' tract, publishing *The*

New Man. On the eve of the Great War, Gibbs's anxious purpose was not simply to deplore the suburbs, but to call for a stiffening of the national character for the likely conflict ahead. Regrettably, the New Man, he argued, was in fact Suburban Man, a pathetic creature who had evolved in the last twenty-five years, and who would be woefully inadequate to the task soon at hand. Gibbs carefully distinguished the Old Suburbia, a Victorian enclave of middle-class virtues, from the New Suburbia that had extended privilege to an undeserving lower middle class who poorly understood and inevitably debased those values. The New Man was a spineless weakling, but he was also a victim, emasculated by that feminised seat of power, the suburb, where his shallow, selfish, and greedy suburban wife had systematically unmanned him. Like Gissing's characters who wax nostalgic for the disciplinary virtues of violence, Gibbs too regrets the apparent passing of an age in which the image of John Bull shaped the Briton's domestic arrangements as well as the face he presented to the world:

> The man was the master. He had the whip-hand. He demanded and expected obedience. But, apart from a touch of brutality now and then, inevitable in a man of strong character, he desired to use his power tenderly, and to cherish the woman who was his helpmeet. That at any rate was the ideal, and though some men, perhaps many men, fell far short of it, they believed in the ideal.[32]

Without that 'ideal' of domestic 'brutality now and then, inevitable to a man of strong character', the New Man had lost his character, which is to say, his manliness. As lamentable as this deterioration was for the individual man, and for the proper ordering of the family, it signalled, in Gibbs's view, a national crisis when potential combat would call on the will to manliness that he feared was now an atrophied moral muscle.

As a matter of scale, the domestic failings of his household that suburban man – at the cost of his manhood – has shirked from correcting, seem bizarrely disproportionate to the stakes Gibbs imagines. Yet the failings are contingent upon supposing the hidden cancer of disorderly lives in domestic disarray behind suburban doors. And its sign, if only one were to see it? Their houses, the commentators were all certain, must be untidy. If it seems extreme to imagine the future of the nation at risk because of slut's wool behind the door, it is useful to revisit end-of-the-century literature diagnosing the inadequacies of the East End working class.

In a 1910 comparative study of German and English working-class life, investigators judged the German working-class housewife's skill, ability, and commitment to a clean and tidy home far superior to her English counterpart. Poverty and overcrowding were neither excuses nor issues. The issue, the study maintained, was character.[33] A model, working-class wife would rise early, maintain vigilant cleanliness, no matter the challenge of her surroundings, and exercise self-denying prudence to make unremittingly wise choices for feeding her family while regularly eschewing all indulgences. Those who did not were slatterns. Indeed, readily identified in the working class, women's lack of character was the ineffable 'something' that the *Spectator* reviewer found retained in the lower middle class, the 'something' it held 'in common with the caste below it'.

Simply, the suburbs were perceived as a problem. In their sprawling mass, they signalled a distinct shift in the weight of the class structure, yet their 'ethnography' remained mysteriously unknowable to the cultural critics who would both imagine and pathologise them. Commentators were baffled by how to read the suburbs. When the descriptive tools of addresses, income and occupation no longer seemed coherent or reliable measures to 'know' a burgeoning portion of the urban population, they increasingly found a measure, aggressively imagined, in the suburban woman and transformed her from symptom to cause. Pervasive in the discourse on the crisis of the city – even the national character – the failings of the new suburban, lower middle-class woman were a given in interpreting the murder of Cora Crippen.

In the many months of reporting the Crippen case, and in nearly a century of retelling it, the fixed point of certainty has been the character of the victim, Cora Crippen. In his introduction to the edited trial transcript in the Notable British Trials series, Filson Young made clear that she was a woman who wanted murdering: she was a poor housekeeper, had poor taste, had gone to fat, was of suspect (Eastern European) origins, and in her showiness, was, in a word, vulgar. Pundit Arthur Binstead, editor of The *Sporting News* offered the aside that had her 'penchant for tieing velvet bows on paintings been better known a verdict of "Justifiable Homicide" would have been returned against her husband'.[34] When Ethel Le Neve first moved into the Crippen home (she asked readers of her autobiography to understand and sympathise), she found 'evidence . . . of the character of Mrs Crippen here'. The house was 'furnished in a higgledy-piggledy way'; not only was there 'scarcely anything that matched', but the 'extraordinary litter' made it 'almost impossible to keep it as tidy as I would like' what with 'masses of cheap stuff . . . and trumpery nicknacks, cheap vases, china dogs'.[35] Prosecutor Sir Travers Humphreys (charged, we should remember, with securing Crippen's conviction) later speculated that 'in another country he would I feel sure have been given the benefit of "extenuating circumstances"'.[36]

In almost every detail, Cora Crippen became 'one of the trashy, flashy girls . . . calling themselves "ladies"' who had moved beyond their 'natural station', swelling and infecting suburbia, to debase middle-class values and emasculate their husbands. Apart from reports of an untidy house furnished in questionable taste, however, the evidence was scant, not to mention irrelevant. In early reports of the crime, Cora's friends gave warm testimonials to a generous and caring woman. In her neighbourhood, tradesmen found her 'very charming . . . a very well dressed lady, . . . very quiet'. The milkman thought her 'very pleasant . . . always very nice . . . beautiful . . . and about the last woman I should ever think would be murdered'.[37] Others shared letters indicating a warm-hearted, affectionate nature, a woman who bore as her private pain her inability to have children. Crippen's business partner spoke of 'her charming manners', adding 'what passes my understanding is how Crippen could have thrown her over in favour of his typist'.[38] Such views, however, were entirely erased, made superficial and uninformed, when the more conclusive evidence of the interior of the home was offered.

When newspaper reporters began looking for personal reminiscences, they found one Adeline Harrison, an acquaintance eager to share her judgements of the Crippen home. Her account of domestic squalor became so authoritative that Filson Young reprinted a large portion of it in his introductory essay to the trial transcript. With relish, Mrs Harrison detailed grimy windows, and in the kitchen a state of dirt and disorder with 'dirty crockery, edibles, collars of the doctor's, false curls of her own, hairpins, brushes, letters, a gold jewelled purse, ... The kitchener and gas stove were brown with rust and cooking stains. The table was littered with packages, saucepans, dirty knives, plates, flatirons, a washing basin, and a coffee pot.' In the midst of the rubble, 'thrown carelessly across a chair', she recalls with attentive detail, 'was a lovely white chiffon gown embroidered with silk flowers and mounted over white *glacé*'. She completes the kitchen scene with a suggestive addendum, recalling an untidy female cat in the house 'scratching wildly at a window in a vain attempt to attract the attention of a passing Don Juan'.[39]

The slide from bad taste to poor housekeeping to sluttish sexuality was, in most reports and in the trial, 'natural'. That there was no evidence of sexual promiscuity (as opposed to the several years of Crippen's and Le Neve's adulterous affair) made little difference to the summary of her character that Chief Justice Alverstone delivered in his charge to the jury. She was a woman, he told them, 'who had had a past'; thus 'a woman making very warm friendships, very popular, very vivacious' lacked appropriate reticence and relished adornment 'such as a person in that class of life would be fond of'. He called special attention to evidence that was as telling of the victim as of the crime. There were strands of bleached hair wrapped around hair curlers found in the grave, and fragments of an undervest, 'a woman's vest with lace on the arms . . . which, of course, you know only adorns the garments of women who like that sort of adornment'.[40] What Alverstone expressed with minimal restraint, Filson Young's influential narrative interpreted explicitly. Her 'exceptional liveliness' was a 'vitality of that loud, aggressive, and physical kind that seems to exhaust the atmosphere around it'; her charitable work was only 'the impulsive kindness of heart which is characteristic of people of her type'; she sought attention through dress to secure 'little social triumphs among her friends' who apparently shared 'her florid taste'. 'We must remember what she was', Young counsels, 'because this can help us measure the extent of Crippen's delicacy: – always considerate, you see . . . . He had decided it would be better that she should cease to exist; and his ingenuity and consideration hit upon the most merciful and the safest poison he could have used.'[41]

The virulent misogyny directed against Cora Crippen was precise and particular; it was not directed against Crippen's typist and lover, Ethel Le Neve, but against the inadequate suburban wife. Indeed, Ethel Le Neve escaped an equally ready categorisation – the adulterous office siren. Instead the typist, 'neat and always to time', became the woman adequate to choosing appropriate window treatments, a woman safely elevated to suburbia. The remarkable affection shown Crippen along with the suppression of doubts about Le Neve are comprehensible only when the portrait of Cora Crippen is placed in the context of vaguely defined but pervasive class anxiety attached to the perception of the New Suburbans.

Notes

1. The Crippen case has been summarised in Edwardian legal memoirs, in popular histories and has been the subject of plays and films. See for example, Tom Cullen, *Crippen: The Mild Murderer* (1977); Jonathan Goodman, *The Crippen File* (1985); Filson Young, (ed.), *The Trial of Hawley Harvey Crippen*, Notable British Trials Series (1920).

2. Young, *The Trial* p. 40.

3. Edward Marjoribanks, *The Life of Sir Edward Marshall Hall* (1934), p. 284.

4. Donald J. Olsen, *The Growth of Victorian London* (1976); H. J. Dyos, *Victorian Suburb: A Study of the Growth of Camberwell* (Leicester, 1961).

5. G. S. Layard, 'A hundred-and-fifty a year' *Cornhill* (May 1901), reprinted in E. Royston Pyke, *Busy Times: Human Documents in the Age of the Forsytes* (New York, 1970), p. 162.

6. Charles Booth, *Life and Labour of the People in London* 17 Vols, 3rd Series: *Religious Influences* (1902–1904; N.Y., 1970), 1, pp. 150–151.

7. *The Suburban Homes of London: A Residential Guide to Favourite London Localities* (1881), p. 294.

8. Hermann Muthesias, *The English House* (1904; N.Y., 1979), p. 8.

9. See, for example, John Ruskin, *The Seven Lamps of Architecture* (1849), Ch. 3.

10. H. G. Wells, *Tono-Bungay* (1909), p. 98.

11. *Ibid.*, pp. 98–99.

12. P. F. William Ryan, 'Going to business in London' in George R. Sims (ed.), *Living London* (3 Vols, 1902; reprinted as *Edwardian London* 4 Vols, 1990), 1, p. 202.

13. Shan Bullock, *Robert Thorne, the Story of a London Clerk* (1907), p. 249.

14. Richard Church, *Over the Bridge* (1956), p. 62.

15. Quoted in P. J. Waller, *Town, City, and Nation: England, 1850–1914* (Oxford, 1983), p. 148.

16. Arthur Conan Doyle, 'A case of identity' *The Annotated Sherlock Holmes* (2 Vols, N.Y., 1967), 1, p. 404.

17. George R. Sims, 'In London's shadowland' in Sims, *Living London* 3 (1990), pp. 275–280.

18. George and Weedon Grossmiths' *The Diary of a Nobody* first ran serially in *Punch* and was then separately published in 1892. Like Crippen, Pooter lived in Holloway.

19. Doyle, 'A case of identity' p. 405.

20. Cited in Waller, *Town, City* p. 148.

21. *Spectator* (9 Feb. 1895); reprinted in P. Coustillas and C. Partridge (eds.), *Gissing: The Critical Heritage* (1972), p. 239.

22. T. W. H. Crosland, *The Suburbans* (1905), p. 7.

23. *Ibid.*, p. 203.

24. *Ibid.*, p. 202.

25. *Ibid.*, pp. 76–77.

26. George Gissing, *In the Year of Jubilee* (1894, 1994), p. 39.

27. *Ibid.*

28. *Ibid.*, p. 5.

29. *Ibid.*, p. 8.

30. *Ibid.*, p. 40.

31. *Ibid.*, p. 142.

32. Philip Gibbs, *The New Man: A Portrait Study of the Latest Type* (1913), pp. 70–71.

33. R. H. Best, W. J. Davies and C. Perks, *Brassworkers of Berlin and Birmingham* (1910). Compare Mrs Hugh Bell, *At the Works* (1907); Ernst Duckerstoff, *How an English Workman Lives* (1899). All are cited by Peter N. Stearns, 'Working-class women of Britain' in Martha Vicinus (ed.), *Suffer and Be Still: Women in the Victorian Age* (Bloomington, IN, 1973), pp. 102–103.

34. Cited in Cullen, *Crippen* p. 162.

35. Ethel Clara Le Neve, *Ethel Le Neve: Her Life Story with the True Account of their Flight and her Friendship for Dr Crippen* (Cowes, 1910), p. 21.

36. Sir Travers Humphreys, *Criminal Days* (1946), p. 113.

37. *StPC* 15 July 1910, reprinted in Goodman, *The Crippen File*, p. 8.

38. *DM* 16 July 1910, reprinted in Goodman, *The Crippen File*, p. 17.

39. *JB* 10 Dec. 1910, quoted in Young *Trial*, pp. xxx–xxxi.

40. Young, *Trial*, pp. 165–166.

41. *Ibid.*, p. xxvii.

CHAPTER ELEVEN

The trial of Madame Fahmy: Orientalism, violence, sexual perversity and the fear of miscegenation

LUCY BLAND

In the speculation following the death of Princess Diana in a car crash in August 1997, one conspiracy theory declared that her sexual relationship with an Arab had become such an embarrassment and threat to the Royal Family that she needed to be removed. The rumour that she was pregnant by Dodi al Fayed, who died with her, demonstrated that fear of miscegenation was alive and well. Back in 1923, the death of another multi-millionaire Egyptian 'playboy' was also front-page news, as was the 'unsavouriness' of miscegenation – in this instance, the marriage of twenty-two-year-old Ali Kamel Bey Fahmy to thirty-two-year-old French woman Marie Marguerite. In the early hours of 10 July 1923, during a violent thunderstorm, Mme Fahmy shot her husband dead in London's Savoy hotel.

During the subsequent Old Bailey trial, in September of that year, Mme Fahmy admitted to the killing, but in defence claimed, firstly, that it was an accident, believing that she had disengaged the pistol earlier in the evening, and secondly, and somewhat contradictorily, that it was an act of self-defence, as he had threatened to kill her. The third plank to her plea, which only became established as the trial proceeded, was that she was 'driven to desperation' by the 'brutality and beastliness' of her Oriental husband.[1] The six-day trial ended in a verdict of 'not guilty' not simply to murder, but to manslaughter as well, even though evidence that the shooting was either accidental or that she acted in self-defence, was, to say the least, unconvincing. So what were the determinants of the trial's outcome? Puzzling too was the fact that, of the huge numbers attending the court, the majority were women: 'fashionably dressed', who 'drove up in motor-cars', 'wearing earrings and ropes of pearls'. Some behaved disgracefully: 'Several women sought to secure front positions by climbing over the back of the seats.'[2] It was not just 'fashionable' women who were present; on the third day of the trial, according to a shocked *Daily Express*: 'After the luncheon interval the first three rows of the public gallery were filled by young girls who were unmistakably shop assistants.'[3] If my first question was 'what were the determinants of the trial's outcome'?, my second question is: 'what was the particular fascination of this murder trial for women?' I will be suggesting that Orientalism is the key to the answers to both these questions. Orientalism, as defined by Edward Said in his ground-breaking book of that name,[4] was (and still is) a discourse in which the West's 'knowledge' about the Orient is fundamental to its domination over it. Analysis of the Fahmy case – the 'most remarkable of modern trials' (also described by the same newspaper as 'the most disagreeable'[5]) – is important for the light it sheds both on Orientalism in operation during this period and on the contemporary fears of miscegenation.[6]

The trial opened on Monday 10 September 1923 and concluded the following Saturday. The prosecution was led by Percival Clarke,[7] while the defence was headed by the most famous (and expensive)[8] defence lawyer of the day, Sir Edward Marshall Hall. Before the trial even opened, the *Daily Mail* set the scene: Ali Fahmy (referred to disrespectfully by the *Daily Mail* simply as 'Ali') had 'built one of the most magnificent palaces in Egypt . . . [it] is surrounded by wonderful grounds and contains elegant swimming pools'.[9] Other newspapers follow suit with further references to the beautiful palace and the yacht at Luxor. But it was wealth which was at once 'Orientalised': the *Daily Chronicle*, for example, wrote of the 'luxurious surroundings that lent all the glamour of an Eastern romance', while the *Daily Sketch*'s front-page headlines read: 'From Oriental Luxury to Old Bailey Dock.'[10] It was typical of the polarisation of East and West, Orient and Occident, that was purposively constructed throughout the trial, and in which the law and the press effectively colluded.

On day one of the trial, Said Enani, Ali Fahmy's Egyptian secretary, who had travelled to England with the Fahmys, was subjected to a four-hour cross-examination. Enani was asked by Marshall Hall about Fahmy's brutality; Enani admitted to recollecting that Fahmy had once dislocated Mme Fahmy's jaw, but denied general cruelty. Fahmy was simply 'a bit unkind'. Enani also disavowed that earlier in the year Fahmy had sworn on the Koran to kill his wife. Fahmy's brutality was further illustrated by a letter read out in court written to his wife's sister about his wife; he referred to his being 'engaged in training her'.[11] Recounting Ali Fahmy's violence was not the only way in which Enani was deployed as a witness; he was also asked about his own relationship with Ali Fahmy. Enani admitted that he had been very attached to his employer – not in a master–servant relationship, but as a great friend; Marshall Hall, however, implied that their relationship was something more: that in Egypt their association was 'notorious'.

The extent of Ali Fahmy's 'sexual perversity' was expanded upon on day two, which saw the cross-examination of the doctor who had attended Mme Fahmy while she was at the Savoy. The doctor confirmed that she was suffering from a painful 'condition' requiring surgery, which was 'consistent with her story of her husband's cruel conduct'.[12] The *Daily Express* was a little more explicit, presenting Marshall Hall as saying that Fahmy 'attacked his wife like a raving, lustful beast because she would not agree to an outrageous suggestion he made – a suggestion which would fill every decent-minded person with utter revulsion'.[13] Yet readers might still have wondered at her 'condition'. The trial transcripts unfortunately no longer exist, and given press censorship,[14] one cannot know for certain what was actually said in court.[15] However, depositions are lodged at the Public Record Office and here the evidence of two doctors clarifies her medical problem: external haemorrhoids, one of which was described as 'thrombosed', and a fissure of the anus.[16] Clearly Mme Fahmy's husband demanded buggery, as later press references to 'unnatural sexual intercourse' imply.

Once established as a sexual pervert – engaging both in homosexual relations and in buggery with his wife – Fahmy's 'sadism' was elaborated upon. The 'sadist', defined by Marshall Hall as 'the man who enjoyed the sufferings of women'[17] was also Orientalised, as we see in Marshall Hall's reconstruction of the fatal night. According to Marshall Hall, Fahmy had made a vile suggestion, and when his wife had refused, he had rushed at her and attempted to strangle her. 'Then in sheer desperation, as he crouched for the last time – crouched like an animal, like an Oriental . . . she put the pistol to his face . . .'. Fahmy was a 'treacherous Eastern beast'.[18] Explicitly, the Oriental male was being defined here as inherently bestial. As for the claim that Mme Fahmy killed in self-defence, no reference was made by Marshall Hall to the night porter's evidence of the previous day that Ali Fahmy was shot just after having been observed stooping down in the corridor, whistling to a little dog, and not, as she maintained, as he attacked her in her bedroom. But already the die was cast and the establishment of Fahmy as sexually perverse and ruthlessly cruel – central tropes in the West's construction of the Oriental male – acted to render marginal any evidence contrary to the developing verdict: the guilt of Ali Fahmy, rather than that of the defendant.

On day three Marshall Hall managed an extraordinary *coup de main*. On hearing that Clarke intended to question Mme Fahmy about her relations with other men in order to prove her immorality, Marshall Hall called for a point of law. On the dismissal of the jury, he managed to persuade both Clarke and the judge, Justice Rigby Swift, that all such questioning should be rendered inadmissible, since it would 'prejudice the jury unfavourably'.[19] Justice Swift agreed that cross-examination should focus solely on Mme

Fahmy's relations with her husband. Yet Clarke, as prosecution counsel, had lost a vital weapon: Mme Fahmy had indeed had a shady past. When aged sixteen, she had borne a daughter out of wedlock; later she had been divorced, she had had numerous affairs with wealthy men, and she had lived with Ali Fahmy before marriage. But it appears that Clarke never insisted on his right to investigate such matters. Why was he willing to acquiesce?

Marshall Hall's cross-examination of Mme Fahmy concentrated on the ways in which she had been brutalised and her civil liberties denied. The conditions under which her husband had made her live were presented as insupportable and as inherently Oriental – in contradistinction to the freedoms of the West. On his yacht, she was locked in and guarded: 'alone on board and surrounded by black men.'[20] (The contradiction within this statement appears to have gone unrecognised; many in the courtroom might well have subscribed in some sense to Ali Fahmy's own view of his black servants. When his wife complained about a black valet who regularly entered her room while she was dressing, Fahmy replied: 'He does not count. He is nobody.'[21]) Mme Fahmy was not simply involuntarily confined, she was effectively reduced to the same status as her guards, for 'he demanded a slave-like obedience'.[22] Should she think of disobeying, there was the threat of Costa, a powerfully built black servant who Fahmy claimed was beholden to him for saving his life. Costa, Fahmy warned, would disfigure her should Fahmy so order, and should she escape, Costa would always seek her out.

Her situation was presented as unacceptable precisely because it was not the Western way of doing things. To quote Marshall Hall: 'The curse of this case is the atmosphere which we cannot understand. The Eastern feeling of possession of the woman, the Turk in his harem, the man who is entitled to have four wives if he liked for chattels ...' '... which to we Western people with our ideas of women is almost unintelligible'.[23] As it happened, Fahmy had had only the one wife, but it was the status of women within Islamic marriage which was objected to, fuelled by Western misunderstanding of the harem.[24] Although Mme Fahmy had tried to insert a clause into her marriage contract giving her the right to divorce, she had been persuaded by Fahmy's relatives to sign without it. 'She had no right to divorce her husband whatever he did and he could divorce her by repudiating her.'[25] (England's Divorce Act of that year may at this point have come to people's minds, for at last divorce had been equalised between the sexes.) 'We in this country put our women on a pedestal', boasted the judge disingenuously, 'but in Egypt it is different.'[26] Mme Fahmy's helplessness in the face of Eastern tyranny was underscored by the defence and the press's frequent references to the fragility of her appearance. Over the East–West divide were superimposed the similarly polarised stock characterisations of melodrama – the overpowering male villain and the weak female victim. Mme Fahmy was described, not just as beautiful and elegant, but also as small, frail, frightened and cowered, given to almost constant weeping, with the press repeatedly referring to her as 'pale and drooping'.

In Marshall Hall's summing-up, the issue of the gun and the specific details of the killing were not key to the defence's case. The gun expert cross-examined on day two had been adamant that the pistol, a Browning automatic, could *not* go off accidentally. Mme Fahmy, who claimed never to have fired a gun until the night of the killing, insisted that she had believed her earlier dislodging of a cartridge had rendered the gun inoffens-ive, and that she had 'often' [*sic*] seen her husband unload his own pistol in this manner. However, there was still no denying that she had fired at Fahmy three times. As for her claim of self-defence, there was the porter's evidence of the incident of Fahmy and the dog, which directly contradicted her story. In the end, what was largely responsible for condemning Ali Fahmy and vindicating his wife was not the claim of accidental shooting or her act of self-defence, but his vilification as an Oriental. 'I dare say Egyptian civilisation is one of the oldest and most wonderful civilisations in the world', suggested Marshall Hall sarcastically, 'but if you strip off the external civilisation . . . you get the real Oriental underneath.'[27] Yet perhaps Marshall Hall's most quotable statement concerned the danger of miscegenation. 'Her great mistake – possibly the greatest mistake a woman could make – was as a woman of the West in marrying an Oriental.'[28] It was a logical conclusion to the demonisation of the Orient, which had been propagated throughout the trial.

The East–West binary was rolled out once again in Marshall Hall's theatrical finale. He reminded the jury of 'that wonderful work of fiction written by Robert Hichens, Bella Donna'.[29] This was a popular novel, set in Egypt, which had also been turned into a play.

> You will remember the influence of Mahmoud over the Englishwoman, who, under his inspiration, poisons her English husband. You will remember the final scene where this woman goes out of the garden into the dark night of the desert. Members of the jury, I want you to open the gates where the Western woman can go – not into the dark night of the desert, but back to her friends . . . let this Western woman go back into the light of God's great Western sun.[30]

Marshall Hall's 'reading' of the text was very misleading. The English woman does not attempt to poison her husband under the inspiration of the Egyptian Mahmoud Baroudi; it is all her own idea. As for the representa-tion of the desert as darkness and despair, the book on the contrary presents the desert as a site of freedom, light and spirituality. As one of the first 'desert romances', the romance is more with the landscape than with its inhabitants. But Marshall Hall chose quite deliberately to misrepresent, for it served as a dramatic reinforcement of the East–West divide.

To return to my first question – the determinants of the trial's outcome – I have suggested that the mobilisation of negative representations of the Orient and its inhabitants were crucial. However, I do not think this explanation is sufficient. I propose that it was the *combination* of Fahmy's Oriental racial 'otherness', his sexual perversity, and the act of miscegenation which, in effect, overdetermined the outcome. If the negative representations of the Orient evident in the trial drew on a repertoire of tropes which had been in circulation for over a century,[31] in relation to Egypt there was an additional, more contemporary negative referent. Egypt, which had been under British control since 1882, had seen nationalist revolution in 1919, leading in the year previous to the trial to a state of nominal independence.[32] To the British establishment, Egyptians were politically troublesome.

Troublesome too was the 'sexual pervert'. Attitudes towards 'sexual perversity' had been formed in part by the Oscar Wilde trials of 1895 (the spectre of the decadent homosexual)[33] and more recently by the notorious 1918 libel case brought by well-known dancer Maud Allan against the maverick MP Noel Pemberton-Billing for his accusation of lesbianism. The wide press coverage of the trial, which involved extensive discussion of various sexual perversions, further 'informed' the general public about the 'beastliness' of unconventional sex.[34] Yet sexual perversity was already racialised – seen as the preserve of the racially 'other'. Orientals were assumed to be inherently perverse; any explicit detail, as in the Fahmy case, confirmed and reinforced dominant assumptions.

The third element in this trichotomy of sins, namely miscegenation, had also been in the news of late. Many of the non-white men in Britain at this time were sailors, hit by the dramatic increase in job competition after postwar demobilisation. The 1919 'race riots' that took place in a number of ports throughout Britain,[35] although largely due to economic factors, were blamed in part on white men's 'understandable' fury at black men's relationships with white women. The press was vocal in its opposition. To quote just two examples, one from 1919: 'the consorting of black men and white women . . . exhibits either a state of depravity or a squalid infatuation; it is repugnant to all our finer instincts'; the other from 1920: 'To the ordinary Briton there is something repulsive about inter-marriage or its equivalent between white and coloured races.'[36]

Ali Fahmy's actions may have been indefensible, but the odds stacked against him went much deeper than anything relating to his actual behaviour. As other chapters in this volume have argued, British courts regularly discounted the seriousness of British men's violence against their wives and partners. Ali Fahmy's violence was seen as exceptional and unacceptable because it transgressed certain taboos: it was perpetrated by an Oriental man on an Occidental woman, and it was combined with sexual perversity. I would suggest that Percival Clarke's willingness to forego his right to interrogate Mme Fahmy on her past was due precisely to his subscribing to such a view.

Turning to my second question, namely why did the trial hold such a fascination for women, 'A Psychologist' in the *Daily Express* thought he/she had the answer: these 'female ghouls', who 'rejoiced' and 'gloated' in listening to the 'unprintable evidence', 'want an outlet for their own repressed vileness'.[37] A more helpful approach, I would suggest, lies with considering Orientalism's multiplicity. Edward Said has been criticised for implying a homogeneous Orientalist discourse[38] and one as ahistorical as the 'timeless' Orient portrayed by Orientalists. I would argue, likewise, that if we look at the period of the Fahmy trial, namely the 1920s, Occidental views of the Orient did not solely consist of the negative representations mobilised within the trial; the latter coexisted with what one could call more 'positive' representations of the imaginary Orient, knowledge of which would also have informed the reading of the trial, and may have constituted part of the appeal. I subdivide these into what I call a series of Oriental romances.

Firstly, there was a romance of place – a romance of landscape, where the desert is the central love object, the site of symbolic freedom and spiritual quest[39] but also a romance of location more generally.[40] Under this heading, one can include the West's fascination with ancient Egypt. This romance had had a recent fillip. Tutankhamen's tomb had been discovered the year before the Fahmy trial – the first unplundered tomb, demonstrating something of the extent of ancient Egypt's wealth and splendour. But this romance had its negative side: interest in ancient Egypt was decidedly different from interest in the Egypt of the 1920s. Ancient Egypt was pre-Islamic and reputedly non-Arab. One argument from the nineteenth century declared that the ancient Egyptian rulers were Caucasian – Aryans from India.[41] Another claim was that Egypt's decline had been due to miscegenation – adulteration of Caucasian blood.[42] It is unlikely that the appeal of Egyptology alone drew the crowds to the trial.

Secondly, there was a romance with Eastern dress: the recent popular commodification of the East as demonstrated in early twentieth-century Oriental fashion for Western women.[43] But if women flocked to the Old Bailey in order to see Orientals dressed in traditional wear, they would have been disappointed. Newspapers commented frequently on the presence of Orientals in the court, where, to quote the *People*, 'East and West sat cheek by jowl',[44] but they were all in European garb. Yet, many of the papers carried photographs of Mme Fahmy wearing a veil, captioned 'Egyptian dress', which undoubtedly added to the trial's allure. The veil was and still is one of the key symbols of the 'otherness' of the Orient.[45] When Mme Fahmy wore a veil in court, however, it was of the short, European style.

Thirdly, there was a romance with the Oriental male. On the one hand, there was homoerotic romance, fuelled by Richard Burton's 1880s translation of the Arabian Nights,[46] and expanded upon with the reports of T. E. Lawrence's Arabs, depicted as traditional, primitive, but courageous fighters and, above all, sexually uninhibited.[47] They were the repositories of the escapist sexual fantasies of European homosexual men, such as the socialist Edward Carpenter and the novelist E. M. Forster, who journeyed to the East in search of the liberatory 'other', freed from Western sexual taboos.[48] On the other hand, and most pertinent for this discussion, there was heterosexual romance, which in the early twentieth century took the form of a new sub-genre developed for the female reader, desert romances.[49] Faced with a shortage of young men after the carnage of the Great War, and with those men still alive often physically or psychologically damaged, the soldier hero of much wartime romantic fiction was superceded by an alternative masculinity. Although desert romances increasingly depicted the hero as not wholly or even partly of Arab descent – the most famous example, then and now, being Ahmed in E. M. Hull's 1919 *The Sheik*, who is revealed late in the book to be the son of a Spanish woman and a Scottish aristocrat[50] – some of the heroes of the earlier texts are pure blood Arabs. Joan Conquest's best-selling 1920 *Desert Love* for example, has as her hero Hahmed, Camel King, who wins the heart and hand of seventeen-year-old English woman Jill Carden, a classic desert romance heroine: young, beautiful, independent and wealthy, but sexually inexperienced. Hahmed is a powerful and civilised Arab, who has spent many years in England, but still insists on women's absolute submission. He kills easily, anyone or anything who displeases him, and when aged fourteen, had strangled the young female lover of his eleven-year-old betrothed, and supported the latter's stoning to death. The narrative shocks Jill, but it does not lessen her adoration, and the book ends with her giving birth to his child in the desert.[51] The hero of these novels is handsome, rich, educated, meticulously clean, priapic, domineering and brutal. The heroine falls for all these qualities, surrendering herself finally to her seduction (in the case of *The Sheik* her rape) thereby permitting sexual response without the burden of responsibility. Her new awareness of her sexuality (in the first instance thrust upon her by the hero's penetrating gaze) also marks her entry into full womanhood.[52]

The women spectators at the Fahmy trial are likely to have been familiar with at least some of this literature. Hull's *The Sheik* was the best-seller of the day, and its hugely popular Hollywood version, starring heart-throb Rudolph Valentino,[53] opened in London the same year as the trial.[54] What one cannot fail to note are some of the obvious parallels between the classic, desert romance narrative and that of the Fahmys. Like the typical desert romance heroine, Mme Fahmy was a beautiful European woman who was independent and rich (although not born into wealth, she was already wealthy on meeting Fahmy). Like the fictitious heroine, once she was under the spell of the Oriental male, she was violated and locked up, unable to escape. Ali Fahmy, likewise, met many of the criteria of the desert romance hero. He was handsome, very rich, educated (he spoke both French and English), brutal and sexually rapacious (although not in the manner appropriate to the fictitious hero). He inspired complete loyalty from servants, at least from Costa and Said Enani, and he engaged himself in 'training' the Western woman into submission, another trope of the desert romance novel, in which analogy is made to the breaking in of a horse. A letter from him to her read out in court displayed great devotion,[55] and she herself during the trial said that she had not hated him, 'only what he wanted me to do', and that on the contrary, she had loved him.[56] They had lived together in great grandeur, in palaces and yachts. In all these ways then, the story of the Fahmys could be read as a desert romance.[57] There were of course important differences. She was older than him by ten years (something else that the prosecution counsel could have made much of, had he chosen to), she was most definitely not sexually inexperienced, and, most significant of all, once violated and confined, she did not submit, but rebelled and killed.

The Fahmy trial and its re-presentation in the press stand as a microcosm of certain dominant discourses in the 1920s concerning the Orient, miscegenation and 'abnormal' sexual practices. From the early nineteenth century until the end of the Second World War, Britain and France dominated the Orient (the 'Orient' in this period referred to what is today called the Middle-East). The three domains were 'represented' in the trial: Britain by the legal counsel, France by the defendant, and the Orient by the dead Egyptian husband. In practice, differences between Britain and France were submerged, and the defendant was taken as emblematic of 'Western Womanhood', standing against the brutality of the East. In reading the reportage of the trial today we are stunned by the blatant racism; in the 1920s, the ideas expressed were part and parcel of common parlance. Mme Fahmy was aided and abetted by cultural fears[58] – of the 'otherness' of the Orient, of sexual perversity, of miscegenation.

In the aftermath of the trial, it was not only Marshall Hall who spoke against miscegenation; the *Daily Mirror* was keen to reinforce the message, its editorial proclaiming that 'the moral of the case' is 'the undesirability of the marriages which unite Oriental husbands to European wives'. It knew where to lay the blame:

> Too many of our women novelists, apparently under the spell of the East, have encouraged the belief that there is something specially romantic in such unions. They are not romantic, they are ridiculous and unseemly; and the sensational revelations of the trial . . . will not be without their use if they bring that fact home to the sentimental, unsophisticated girl.[59]

However 'unseemly', the fantasy of such unions did not diminish in the years following the trial, for desert romances remained highly popular into the 1930s. What the *Daily Mirror* editorial failed to realise was that the Fahmy narrative was *itself* a desert romance.[60] The ending might have been unfortunate, but, hey, she got away with it, and when did the endings to a narrative ever fully dissuade one from the power and pleasure of its telling?

Notes

Thanks to Laura Doan for responding with immediate and very helpful comments.

1. Sir Edward Marshall Hall, defence lawyer, as quoted in the *DMr* 12 Sept. 1923, p. 2. There are few secondary sources on this trial, but see the interesting analysis by Anette Ballinger, 'The guilt of the innocent and the innocence of the guilty: the cases of Marie Fahmy and Ruth Ellis', in Alice Myers and Sarah Wright, (eds.), *No Angels: Women who Commit Violence* (1996). She argues that the verdict was due to Mme Fahmy's use of 'appropriate' femininity – presenting herself as a frail, helpless, dazed and grieving victim. Although Ballinger acknowledges the role of Orientalism, she does not see this as central, and ignores both Fahmy's sexual perversity and the issue of miscegenation.

2. *EN* 15 Sept. 1923, p. 1; *DC* 13 Sept. 1923, p. 1.

3. *DE* 13 Sept. 1923, p. 1.

4. Edward Said, *Orientalism* (1978).

5. *IPN* 20 Sept. 1923, p. 2.

6. See Paul Rich, *Race and Empire in British Politics* (Cambridge, 1986).

7. Percival Clarke was the son of Sir Edward Clarke, QC, who had unsuccessfully defended Oscar Wilde in 1895.

8. He was paid 652 guineas in this particular case. Edward Marjoribanks, *Famous Trials of Marshall Hall* (1950), p. 365.

9. *DM* 10 Sept. 1923, p. 6.

10. *DC* 11 Sept. 1923, p. 1; *DS* 12 Sept. 1923, p. 2; and see *DE* 11 Sept. 1923, p. 1.

11. Fahmy to Yvonne Alibert, 18 Jan. 1923, PRO CRIM 1/247.

12. *EN* 11 Sept. 1923, p. 1.

13. *DE* 12 Sept. 1923, p. 8.

14. For example, *DS* 12 Sept. 1923, p. 2: 'much that he [Marshall-Hall] indicated could not be printed.'

15. There was censorship there as well, according to the *People* 16 Sept., p. 7: 'the actual details of his [Fahmy's] conduct were too sordid and disgusting to be minutely described even in court.'

16. Depositions of Dr Gordon and Dr Morton, PRO CRIM 1/247.

17. *Times* 12 Sept. 1923, p. 7; also in *DM* 12 Sept. 1923, p. 1. See Lucy Bland, 'Trial by sexology? Maud Allan, *Salome* and the "Cult of Clitoris" case' in Lucy Bland and Laura Doan (eds.), *Sexology in Culture* (1998) for discussion of the first use of the term 'sadism' in an English court.

18. *Times* 12 Sept. 1923, p. 7; *DE* 12 Sept. 1923, p. 8.

19. *Times* 13 Sept. 1923, p. 7.

20. *Ibid.*

21. *DMr* 13 Sept. 1923, p. 2; *DC* 13 Sept. 1923, p. 1; *DS* 13 Sept. 1923, p. 1. What would of course have horrified the British public was the thought of a *white* woman's nakedness open to the gaze of a black man, or indeed of an Oriental – the reversal of the usual representation of an Eastern woman on display to an observer from the West.

22. *DMr* 12 Sept. 1923, p. 2.

23. *Times* 14 Sept. 1923, p. 7; *DC* 14 Sept. 1923, p. 1.

24. See Leila Ahmed, 'Western ethnocentrism and perceptions of the harem' *FS* 8 (1982).

25. *Times* 14 Sept. 1923, p. 7.

26. *EN* 15 Sept. 1923, p. 1.

27. *DC* 14 Sept. 1923, p. 10; and see the *People* 16 Sept. 1923, p. 7.

28. *Times* 14 Sept. 1923, p. 7; There are similar versions of this statement in other newspapers, see *DS, DE, DM, DC*, all for 14 Sept.

29. *Bella Donna* was written in 1909, with a popular version appearing in 1911; it was reprinted many times.

30. *DMr* 15 Sept. 1923, p. 2; similar versions of this speech in *EN, DS, DC*.

31. See Said, *Orientalism*; Rana Kabbani, *Europe's Myths of Orient* (1986); John M. Mackenzie, *Orientalism: History, Theory and the Arts* (Manchester, 1995).

32. See R. L. Tignor, *Modernisation and British Colonial Rule in Egypt, 1882–1914* (Princeton, 1966); John Darwin, *Britain, Egypt and the Middle East* (1981).

33. See H. Montgomery Hyde (ed.), *The Trials of Oscar Wilde* (1948); Alan Sinfield, *The Wilde Century* (1994).

34. See Bland, 'Trial by sexology?'; Philip Hoare, *Wilde's Last Stand: Decadence, Conspiracy and the First World War* (1997).

35. See Peter Fryer, *Staying Power* (1984); Jacqueline Jenkinson, 'The 1919 riots' in Panikos Panayi (ed.), *Racial Violence in Britain in the Nineteenth and Twentieth Centuries* (Leicester, 1996).

36. *WM* 6 June 1919; *EN* 5 Oct. 1920.

37. 'A Psychologist', 'In the Stalls of the Old Bailey' *DE* 13 Sept. 1923, p. 4.

38. See Dennis Porter, 'Orientalism and its problems' in Patrick Williams and Laura Chrisman (eds.) *Colonial Discourse and Post-Colonial Theory* (1993); Aijaz Ahmad, 'Orientalism and after' in Williams and Chrisman (eds.), *Colonial Discourse*; Lisa Lowe, *Critical Terrains: French and British Orientalisms* (Ithaca, 1991).

39. We see this not simply in desert romances such as *Bella Donna*, but in travel writings, including writings by women. See Hsu-Ming Teo, 'Clean spaces, dirty bodies: the Middle Eastern desert in British women's travel writing, 1890–1914' in Patricia Grimshaw and Diane Kirkby (eds.), *Dealing with Difference* (Melbourne, 1997).

40. I am thinking here of the elaborate Oriental detail that one sees in nineteenth and twentieth-century Orientalist painting, literature and theatre. See Mackenzie, *Orientalism: History, Theory and the Arts*.

41. See Martin Bernal, *Black Athena* (1987).

42. See Robert Young, *Colonial Desire* (1995).

43. See Peter Wollen, 'Fashion/Orientalism/the body' *NF* 1 (Spring 1987), pp. 5–33; Mica Nava, 'The cosmopolitanism of commerce and the allure of difference' *IJCS* 1 (1998), pp. 163–196.

44. *People* 16 Sept. 1923, p. 7.

45. See Joanna de Groot, ' "Sex" and "race": the construction of language and image in the nineteenth century' in S. Mendus and J. Rendall (eds.), *Sexuality and Subordination* (1989); Judy Melbo, *Half-Veiled Truths* (1996).

46. Richard Burton, *Plain and Literal Translation of the Arabian Nights Entertainments* (1919 [1884–1886]).

47. See Graham Dawson, *Soldier Heroes* (1994), Chs. 6–8.

48. See Parminder Kaur Bakshi, 'Homosexuality and Orientalism: Edward Carpenter's journey to the East' in Tony Brown (ed.), *Edward Carpenter and Late Victorian Radicalism* (1990); Jane L. Pinchin, *Alexandria Still: Forster, Durrell, and Cavafy* (Princeton, 1977).

49. The writings of Robert Hichens are held to be amongst the first examples of these 'desert romances'. See Robert Hichens, *The Garden of Allah* (1904); Hichens, *Bella Donna*; Billie Melman, *Women and the Popular Imagination* (New York, 1988). For reflection on how Western women are differently placed in relation to Orientalism see Reina Lewis, *Gendering Orientalism* (1996); Billie Melman *Women's Orients: English Women and the Middle East, 1718–1918* (Michigan, 1992).

50. E. M. Hull, *The Sheik* (1919); and see Patricia Raub, 'Issues of passion and power in E. M. Hull's *The Sheik*' *WS* 21 (1992), pp. 119–128; Karen Chow, 'Popular sexual knowledges and women's agency in 1920s England: Marie Stopes's *Married Love* and E. M. Hull's *The Sheik*' *FR* 63 (1999), pp. 64–87.

51. Joan Conquest, *Desert Love* (1920).

52. See Evelyn Bach, 'Sheik fantasies: Orientalism and feminine desire in the desert romance' *Hecate* 23 (1997), pp. 9–40.

53. See Miriam Hansen, 'Pleasure, ambivalence, identification: Valentino and female spectatorship' in Christine Gledhill (ed.), *Stardom: Industry of Desire* (1991); Gaylyn Studlar, 'Valentino, "Optic Intoxication", and dance madness' in Steven Cohan and Ina Rae Hark (eds.), *Screening the Male* (1993); Gaylyn Studlar, ' "Out Salomeing Salome": dance, the New Woman, and fan magazine Orientalism' *MQR* 34 (1995), pp. 487–510.

54. 'Film of the Week' *Times* 24 Jan. 1923.

55. The letter is in with the depositions, PRO CRIM 1/247.

56. *DMr* 14 Sept. 1923, p. 2.

57. Media reports themselves on occasion made such a reading, drawing intertextually on the referent of literary romance. I have already quoted the *Daily Chronicle*'s initial description of the trial – that it 'lent all the glamour of an eastern romance'. *DC* 11 Sept. 1923, p. 1. The *People* likewise suggested that 'some of the revelations were suggestive of the fanciful romances of the Arabian nights'. *People* 16 Sept. 1923, p. 7.

58. Thanks to Laura Doan for suggesting this formulation.

59. 'The Fahmy Trial' *DMr* 17 Sept. 1923, p. 7.

60. Desert romances in a sense echoed miscegenation fears, for if concern with miscegenation is about a desire to keep 'civilised' and 'primitive' separate, it is arguably also indicative of a profound longing for the 'other'. See Robert Young, *Colonial Desire: Hybridity in Theory, Culture and Race* (1995).

CHAPTER TWELVE

'The irons of their fetters have eaten into their souls': nineteenth-century feminist strategies to get our bodies onto the political agenda

CATHERINE EULER

In 1971, the year the first women's refuge opened in England, a group of women in West Yorkshire made what was for them a startling discovery. They were 'astounded' to learn that nineteenth-century feminists had even been interested in violence against women, though less astounded that they had campaigned against it:

> This then enabled us to ask questions about where did all that knowledge go? How are relationships of power structured with regard to ideas that matter? The disappearance of that knowledge felt to us, at that time, extreme. It left us all with a feeling that to keep it in the public domain we must keep working. That if we were to stop, this knowledge might disappear again.[1]

Many of the women they 'discovered' have now been written about in more depth, though some are still quite shadowy figures. More analyses of their political strategies – what worked, what didn't, and why – are still needed, especially in the light of recent scholarship.[2] There is now a very long list of nineteenth-century women who responded to a growing perception of women's oppression and male violence against women, including, for example, Elizabeth Wolstenholme-Elmy, an atheist freethinker who opposed rape in marriage, which was made illegal in the UK only as late as 1991.[3] This chapter will explore the strategies of three feminists who spent most of their lives working on these issues: Josephine Butler (1828–1906), who worked primarily on prostitution; Frances Power Cobbe (1822–1904), who is best known for her work on domestic violence, though she was also a prominent anti-vivisectionist; and Ellice Hopkins (1836–1904), a 'social purist' who called for the protection of young girls and a concomitant male chastity.

I am not going to ask the question 'where did all that knowledge go?' for much of it is now readily accessible to women who want it. Instead, I want to begin an exploration of the text-based, body-related strategies these women used to achieve political aims. I want to look also at the distinction between what they *intended* to accomplish and what *effects* their words might have had. How you decide to read a text is a choice that reflects your own theoretical and political assumptions. I have read these texts from a combined radical feminist/socialist feminist standpoint, with an emphasis on historical particularism.

When we read these nineteenth-century feminist texts it is possible to read them as texts about violence, and/or as texts about sexuality. Often they are also texts about class, gender, age and race. Women in the nineteenth century did not have the same consciousness we have. I argue that the work of Butler, Cobbe and Hopkins was primarily focused on male violence, and was not *primarily* about sexuality. Some historians have claimed these women were trying to repress something called 'sexuality', or that they were trying to put limits on something called 'desire.' Textual effects may have included constructions of desire, but that was not the main aim at the time. I argue that these women were, in fact, struggling to repress male violence and limit male sexual abuse because they understood that these things were part of both the cause and the effect of women's oppression; that they were trying to combat a 'predatory male sexuality'[4] which resulted in abuse of the women they sought to protect. They realised that violence against women was connected, web-like, to women's lack of education and the vote, as well as to the other issues which they worked on, including employment, married women's property, laws on divorce and separation, justice for poor women, animal rights, ethics, morality and spirituality.[5]

The current conflicted interpretation of nineteenth-century feminist texts centres largely on arguments about women's freedom of choice. The power of choice, or the 'will' – what the self can or cannot do, or thinks it can or cannot do – is often designated by the word 'agency'. I argue that 'agency' is also socially constructed, and that violence and abuse (or sometimes even the covert threat of these) can affect its operation.

Some believe that 'sexuality' and 'desire' are obvious expressions of individual will. Therefore, the logic goes, if someone's 'desire' is limited, their 'agency' is thus curtailed, and they are thereby disempowered. Judith Walkowitz, for example, has suggested that nineteenth-century portrayals of women as 'victims' in fact disempowered women because these portrayals were based on the notion of women's (innocent) 'passionlessness'.[6]

In this chapter, I will argue that physical violence and sexual abuse (or the threat of these) had a more damaging effect on women's agency than did the languages used by feminists, who were in fact trying to empower women.

Over the past fifteen years there has been a growing historical trend towards emphasising the power and effect of language or other symbols, rather than looking too closely at the physical realities or practices they try to represent. I have tried to interpret these texts using an emphasis on the physical body, rather than an emphasis on language. I contend that these nineteenth-century feminists used language about the damage done to women's physical bodies *as a conscious strategy* to achieve real political and social change.

Reading or hearing about violence to women's bodies (or experiencing physical violence) creates emotional reaction. Cobbe, Butler and Hopkins knew this as well as we do. In 1878, Cobbe published an article called 'Wife Torture in England' in the *Contemporary Review*. In it she appeals to chivalrous, civilised English gentlemen to act to protect women's interests. In the era before women could vote for Members of Parliament, they were dependent on male legislators to change the law. There was a power imbalance – so she was probably wise to compliment rather than condemn them! Cobbe wanted the male legislators to amend the Matrimonial Causes Bill of 1878, so that women could for the first time obtain separation orders in a magistrates' court on the grounds of cruelty.

In 1857, women had been allowed to get a divorce through the Divorce Court; this gave some property protection, but it did not include grounds of cruelty and it was a more complicated and expensive process than getting a simple separation (not a divorce) in the magistrates' courts. A few better-off, working-class women did use the Divorce Court, but not many.[7] Cobbe noticed the problems still faced by women, especially poorer women, and campaigned for the 1878 Bill as a way of remedying these.

In the early nineteenth century, if your husband was beating you and you left him, all your property still belonged to him. If you didn't own property, he still had a right to your wages. Between 1839 and 1878 husbands retained custody of all children above age seven. (Before 1839 fathers had absolute custody rights, with very few exceptions.)[8] So, to escape violence very likely meant giving up your children; and your husband retained the right to your income. Cobbe tried to make it easier for women to leave violent relationships by giving them rights to their income after separation; rights to custody of children under ten, as well as a right to alimony payments.

In her article, Cobbe constructed domestic violence as an exclusively working-class problem. Modern feminists, and even some later nineteenth-century feminists, knew that this was an untrue portrayal of the problem.

Middle and upper-class women also suffered substantially from domestic violence, as the post-1857 Divorce Court records amply demonstrate.[9] However, if we really try to keep Cobbe's time-context in mind, we would do well to remember that she was addressing middle and upper-class legislators whom she could not afford to offend. They were the only source of legal change for women. One probable *effect* of the language of the article was to help strengthen the social validity of the middle classes by constructing them as more 'virtuous' than the working classes. What Cobbe was *actually trying to accomplish* was to change the laws governing separation in a way that would actually be advantageous to working-class women. Thus, she could deploy a language of class as part of her overall strategy to accomplish what she wanted. James Hammerton maintains that the 'narrowly defined class dimensions of the debate . . . doomed the reformers to little more than half-measures'.[10] Well, yes, but this was also the case for a great many other nineteenth-century reforms, most of which came piece by piece. I don't think we can assume, as Hammerton does,[11] that Cobbe actually believed that wife-torture *only* happened in working-class homes; she may have done, but this very public, very political article is not sufficient proof of her innermost private beliefs on the matter. Again, the *effect* may have been to reinforce a particularly erroneous brand of classism, but what she *accomplished* was to change the law, partly through using one of the languages available to her at that time: the language of class.

It was not the only conscious strategy that Cobbe employed. Where (mostly) men have inflicted physical pain in private, this has had the effect of reinforcing gendered power imbalances and altering or controlling the behaviour and/or subjectivity (inner self or sense of self) of the victims. On the other hand, Cobbe used public descriptions of physical cruelty to change the behaviour and subjective emotional reactions of the lawmakers. Body and emotionality are quite powerfully linked, and Cobbe's article is a good historical example of deploying these links to achieve a feminist political end.

In the article she lists newspaper accounts of 'wife-torture' in a matter-of-fact, quasi-scientific fashion:

> James Mills cut his wife's throat as she lay in bed. He was quite sober at the time. On a previous occasion he had nearly torn away her left breast.
>
> J. Coleman returned home . . . and, finding his wife asleep, took up a heavy piece of wood and struck her on the head and arm, bruising her arm. On a previous occasion he had fractured her ribs.
>
> John Mills poured out vitriol deliberately, and threw it in his wife's face, because she asked him to give her some of her wages. He had said previously, that he would blind her.
>
> James Lawrence, who had been frequently bound over to keep the peace, and who had been supported by his wife's industry for many years, struck her

on the face with a poker, leaving traces of the most dreadful kind when she appeared in court.

Frederick Knight jumped on the face of his wife (who had only been confined a month) with a pair of boots studded with hobnails.

Richard Mountain beat his wife on the back and mouth, and turned her out of her bed and out of their room one hour after she had been confined.

Alfred Roberts felled his wife to the floor, with a child in her arms; knelt on her, and grasped her throat. She had previously taken out summonses against him, but had never attended.

John Harris . . . after vainly attempting to force her into the oven, tore off her night-dress and turned her round before the fire 'like a piece of beef' while the children stood on the stairs listening to their mother's agonised screams.

Richard Scully knocked in the frontal bone of his wife's forehead.

William White . . . threw a burning paraffin lamp at his wife, and stood quietly watching her enveloped in flames, from the effects of which she died . . . .

George Ralph Smith . . . cut his wife . . . 'to pieces' with a hatchet, in their back parlour. She died afterwards, but he was found Not Guilty, as it was not certain that her death resulted from the wounds . . . .[12]

These are extremely powerful, emotive descriptions of precise kinds of violences done to individual women's bodies. Cobbe gives several examples of this kind, and then moves swiftly on to a description of her proposed Bill. Her campaign strategy was successful. The 1878 law was a major break-through, especially for women with little or no money, who could thereafter leave abusive husbands, take their children (aged under ten) with them, retain any property gained after separation, and have a sum for mainten-ance (if their husbands could be made to pay it). Physical cruelty was, for the first time, recognised as grounds for legal separation. Divorce would not include these grounds until 1937. *Private*, domestic harm carried out to women's bodies, when articulated into *public* language, with all its accom-panying emotional impact, can and did have a *political* effect.

Cobbe also briefly touched on the issue of female agency, or power of choice, in her article – an issue that is critical to feminist understandings of resistance and empowerment. 'Of course', she writes, 'the ideas of the suf-fering wives are cast in the same mould as those of their companions . . . [this] forms the culminating proof of how far the irons of their fetters have eaten into their souls . . . surely . . . a woman who has been brought down by fear, or by her own gross passions, so low as to fawn on the beast who strikes her, is one to make angels weep?'[13] Those who today work as domestic violence officers or in women's refuges recognise that many women spend several years returning to their abusers again and again.

Physical violence affects the construction of women's sense of themselves, their own subjectivity, and their agency, or their power of choice. Women who experience extreme forms of violence within emotional and sexual relationships often report *losing themselves*. They talk about it as a loss of self, and use this language in partial explanation of why they might repeatedly endeavour to placate their torturer as a way of avoiding further physical pain. In thinking about these things I found very helpful an article by Bibi Bakare-Yusuf called 'The economy of violence: black bodies and the unspeakable terror'.[14] She discusses the torture of Black bodies under the slavery regime of the American South.[15] 'The body in pain', writes Bakare-Yusuf, 'is not able to participate fully in civic life, because pain destroys the capacity of language; the body is denied the facilities that make subjectivity possible . . . the ability to verbally express the presence of pain is unavailable to the person in pain.'[16] In women's lives, physical pain itself contributes to silencing and thus to privatising violence.

It seems almost ironic then that it was the very verbalisation of that pain which, in 1878, permitted the presence of private, wounded, female bodies in male, public, civic life. In discussing appropriate approaches to historical texts such as Cobbe's, it is very important to keep in mind this question about violence and silence, the role of speaking and writing in the construction of the self, and the role of silencing in the construction, or indeed the *loss* of the self, and how violence, or rather, how physical pain has the potential to silence. Roland Barthes talks about how certain texts can lead to a loss of self because the texts induce a form of ecstatic 'bliss', and that this loss of self is a transformative, positive event.[17] Bodily violence may induce the opposite of 'bliss', and the attendant loss of self may go beyond temporary textual and verbal silence into the permanent silence of physical death itself.

Like Cobbe, Josephine Butler also spoke and wrote about women's bodies and what men do to them, and made use of physical descriptions, during the years *she* campaigned to change the law. While living in Oxford after her marriage in 1852, Butler was shocked to hear men's casual acceptance of the double standard of sexual morality, which she felt was grossly unjust to women. After the accidental death of her young daughter, she threw herself into so-called 'rescue work', or helping women to leave prostitution. It was an area that would become the main focus of her life.

In the 1860s, Parliament passed three Contagious Diseases Acts, which allowed the police, especially in naval port cities, to detain women who they suspected of being prostitutes; these women then had their vaginas compulsorily examined for venereal disease. Ostensibly, the Acts were passed to protect troops in militarised towns and cities from becoming unwell and unfit for combat. Before the Acts were passed, the soldiers and sailors had themselves been tested.[18] To Josephine Butler, the Acts were tantamount to state complicity with the double standard of sexual morality, as well as a particular denial of women's civil rights. They singled out only women, never men, for punishment, and this seemed unjust to her. She used her considerable energy and intellectual clarity on the matter to campaign for their repeal. For over twenty years she constantly corresponded with local support groups throughout Britain, and travelled and spoke extensively, when her health permitted. Her work resulted in a European-wide, and then international, movement against trafficking in women for sexual exploitation and in the repeal of the Contagious Diseases Acts in 1886. She has often been accused of fomenting an unfounded 'moral panic' about prostitution because of her involvement in the 1885 *Pall Mall Gazette* series on 'The Maiden Tribute', but in her mind white slavery – the selling of young women for sexual exploitation – was an empirical phenomenon she had seen in both England and the Continent.[19]

Like Cobbe, she used strong images of female bodily victimisation as a strategy. She testified before the 1871 Parliamentary Inquiry into the Acts, that their main end was not the suppression of vice, but rather to 'provide clean harlots for the army and navy'.[20] She employed images of the 'instrumental rape'[21] of the medical examiner's speculum. One CD Acts campaigner described the 'torture' of 'girls unjustly seized' by the police, who were then forced to undergo medical examinations which 'caused them intense pain and suffering'.[22] Strong public images of female bodily violation helped to achieve the eventual political victory. Butler continued to campaign against 'all government and official recognition of the necessity of vice for men, and the destruction of women for this end'.[23]

The campaign focused particularly on women made vulnerable by poverty and/or seduction, but also foregrounded the negative effect on *all women* of the state's collusion with male sexual privilege. Campaigners focused on reducing male sexual privilege, rather than on promoting women's. Female sexual desire was definitely downplayed. They also used the idea of female 'innocence' as a political strategy. Butler had women who had survived prostitution living with her in her home at various times: she was not naïve about some of the characters who had survived streets and brothels; but it was essential to portray them all as ultimately 'innocent' victims in order to win the eventual political victory. (Can you be imperfect and a victim at the same time?) In order to conquer an injustice, there had to be a victim of injustice; 'guilty' women were more likely to have deserved whatever they got. Butler, after all, placed herself in direct opposition to the Victorian paradigm that often portrayed prostituted women as the effluvium of society, the source of disease and pollution, of moral decay, and the cause of all the Empire's ills.[24] She had to contend with the threats to her person and to her social status which derived from even talking about prostitution in public or associating with these women. Yet she was clear about her political aims. It was, therefore, strategic to construct prostituted women as victims of injustice, innocent of sexual desire. She manipulated the existing discourse for her own ends, just like Cobbe.

Judith Walkowitz, however, has suggested that Josephine Butler's campaigns employed language which 'set limitations on . . . female agency and desire',[25] a common criticism of women involved in what are generally categorised as nineteenth-century social purity campaigns. She even goes so far as to say that historians who repeat the narratives of violence and sexual danger risk reproducing discourses that situate and construct women as *victims* lacking agency.[26] The implication is that the very act of revealing the victimisation of some women actually constructs all women as victims.[27] By employing discourses which participated in the 'disciplining' or control of bodies and sexualities, Walkowitz implies, nineteenth-century feminists, and perhaps anyone who tries to deal with these issues, actually reproduce the power relations they are seeking to escape. However, speaking publicly about silenced private pain is also a powerful form of agency. Demonstrating how women's bodies can be exploited and beaten by men is in itself a political act – often a courageous one. Pointing out that women can be victimised more easily in a social system where men are privileged does not aim to disempower, but empower. The pro-women legislative changes of the nineteenth and twentieth centuries are but one indication of this. 'Feminist protest' was not in itself a 'politics of repression', as Walkowitz implies.[28]

I would contend that there is a logic mistake in this genre of reasoning which arises from two sources: (1) the idea that Butler and other 'social purity' campaigners were dealing with issues of sexuality and desire, rather than with violence and abuse; and, related to this, (2) the idea that desire and agency are practically identical. Walkowitz's argument implies that women are constructed as victims when their desire (and, therefore, their will, or agency) are limited by discourses of sexual danger. While sexual desire may be one manifestation of a culturally and temporally specific agency, they are not the same thing. Are Cobbe and Butler primarily discussing sexual danger or male violence? The original use to which narratives like Cobbe's and Butler's were put was to give public voice and public power to the silenced, physically attacked and exploited bodies of women, and to insist that women's low civic status was the main reason the violence and injustice were allowed to continue. Their texts may not be primarily about sexuality at all, but rather they represent some of the first feminist efforts to describe, in the most polite terms possible, certain forms of male violence, exploitation and oppression.

In approaching historical feminist responses to violence we must try to hear these sources in their own time-frame. We need to distinguish between what these 'first wave' women were (a) actually trying to accomplish and (b) what effect their words could have in practice. In its own time-frame, Butler's discourse about a single standard of sexual morality for men and women was not so much an attempt to limit the possibilities of female desire as it was an attempt to limit male violence and exploitation. Discourses may have an effect on limiting agency, but so do physical violence and abuse. Speaking of women's bodies and their victimisation may (or may not) have the effect of constructing women as victims. However, mentioning out loud that women are beaten and exploited can also have useful, powerful and beneficial political effects, as Cobbe, Butler and Hopkins discovered.[29]

Ellice Hopkins acted on her concerns by founding the Social Purity Alliance and the White Cross League. Operating within a semi-religious discourse, Hopkins wanted young men to exercise sexual restraint, and believed that a single standard of sexual morality would elevate society as a whole. She appealed to the masculine ideal of the chivalrous medieval knight in order to motivate young men to sign chastity pledges. This approach is so foreign to a post-sexual-libertarian culture that to us it sounds slightly ridiculous and classically Victorian in its supposed repressiveness. However, Hopkins simultaneously pointed to the victimisation of young girls and prostituted women. Later, religious zealots would unfortunately channel similar ideas towards a condemnation of prostituted women themselves. Hopkins, however, focused on prostituted women as victims of an exploitive, unregulated male sexuality. She also believed that some young women were more vulnerable than others to child sexual abuse and a consequent or related involvement in prostitution.

Ellice Hopkins addressed a meeting in Leeds in 1884 which was attended by a number of respectable women: the wives of clergy, industrialists, businessmen and landowners. Her talk inspired two of them to found the Leeds Ladies Association for the Care and Protection of Young Girls, sometimes also called the Ladies Association for the Protection of Friendless Girls.[30] At the group's second meeting, chaired by Ellice Hopkins, these predominantly middle-class women created five different branches of their new organisation: the Preventive, the Educational, the Workhouse, the Magdalene and the Petitioning branches. Neither the Workhouse nor the Magdalene branches were ever particularly active in working directly with prostituted women. The Petitioning Branch participated in campaigns in favour of the 1885 Criminal Law Amendment Act, which, while it criminalised male homosexuality, also raised the age of consent for girls from thirteen to sixteen, making these young women less sexually available to men. The Educational Branch distributed the religious tracts and pamphlets of the Social Purity Alliance and White Cross Society, calling for male chastity, but soon gave this up after concluding, 'the Town is as yet unprepared for these pamphlets. Several ladies spoke of the disadvantages of them being injudiciously distributed.'[31] (Perhaps the men of Leeds were scandalised by the idea that limits might be set on *their* desire.) As the other four branches dwindled in activity over time, the primary focus of the Leeds Ladies became the Preventive Branch. They founded two homes for young girls which continued as such until just after the Second World War, when they became mixed children's homes under the aegis of the new welfare state.[32]

Of the founders, Catherine Briggs and Florence Kitson, the latter was also involved in campaigning for women's careers and women's education; women of the Briggs family were, in the early twentieth century, to become some of the first female Leeds City Councillors, and the Briggs family itself was locally quite prominent. It is clear that, rather than being narrowly defined as social purity campaigners, these women must be located within the broader range of nineteenth-century feminist activity, including education and political rights. They understood that the particular vulnerability of 'friendless' working-class girls was related to the civic vulnerability of women as a whole.

Briggs and Kitson wrote the mission statement for the Leeds Ladies Association and remained heavily involved in the girls' homes for several decades. The same statement recurs frequently from 1884 to 1923, in a kind of formulaic, almost chant-like way: 'The object of the Association is entirely preventive', they wrote. 'Girls, at the most impressionable age of six to sixteen, are taken and cared for . . . the only qualification being that they are utterly friendless, or have friends who are a source of danger to them and worse than none.' Another document uses a similar phrase, 'the only recommendation being that they are entirely friendless, or in dangerous surroundings, where those who should be their friends are worse than none'.[33] While several 'rescue' cases came into the homes, the Leeds Ladies never engaged in the direct work with prostituted women that they had initially envisioned.

As a historian reading the aims of the Leeds Ladies, do I read them as a narrative about repressed Victorian sexuality, about sexual danger and moral and social purity, as middle-class meddling in working-class lives, or do I read them as an early feminist attempt to protect other, younger women from male violence and/or exploitation? When the founders, over and over again, fail to describe explicitly and exactly what they are protecting these girls against, is this a silence which one reads as a silence about sexuality or as a silence about violence? Are Josephine Butler's pronouncements about the Contagious Diseases Acts documents that should be read as being about sexuality or as being about violence? How does it affect my interpretations if I read texts about prostitution as texts about male violence?

Cecilie Hoigard and Liv Finstad, in a modern study of prostitution, conclude that 'the impoverishment and destruction of the women's emotional lives makes it reasonable, in our eyes, to say that customers practice gross violence against prostitutes'.[34] Several studies have shown that prostituted women 'suffer high rates of rape and battery . . . they are all too frequently murdered as a result of their work'.[35] Women experiencing prostitution, as with women experiencing repeated physical violence, report an acute sense of the loss of self. If self and agency are actually damaged by violence to the physical body, as Bakare-Yusef contends, to what extent does prostitution do the same? Do childhood sexual abuse and prostitution damage the operation of the will in the way physical pain can?[36] If historical, prostitution involved physical violence or childhood sexual abuse, as it frequently does now, how can it be argued that women were exercising an undamaged power of choice? Agency (power of choice) and language are linked; if agency is damaged, then silence or covert discourses can be the result. It may be that the language of the nineteenth-century social purity campaigners who set out to 'rescue' 'Magdalenes' rings so strange in our ears simply because their language was then inadequate to describe a phenomenon for which they had only religious or moral terminology. I would argue that in each of the three cases I have examined, we are looking at texts which reflect early feminist attempts to describe certain forms of male violence, rather than texts which are primarily indicative of the late nineteenth-century 'deployment of sexuality'.[37]

If we are reading about violence, we are reading about a loss of self, a loss of language and about a feminist struggle for an articulation of a language that could help reduce or reform the harmful usage of male power. If we are reading about sexuality, there are several possible interpretations. They could be texts about maintaining social order and protecting the gains of the British Empire, as Lynda Nead has suggested.[38] These texts could be simply reflections of social purity campaigns deployed by the middle classes to construct and enhance their own status and identity by alternately condemning the sexuality of either the upper or lower classes. The Leeds Ladies Association was certainly implicated in a powerful, middle-class culture that saw the young women in the homes as primarily suited for domestic service, and most of the training efforts focused on this. However, they were also trying to prevent vulnerable young girls from being abused, raped or pimped by male relatives or friends. Even if we do read these texts as being about sexuality, it is clear that the social purity campaigners were aware that a hierarchy existed in which *male* sexuality took social precedence. So what do we attempt? A neat discursive analysis of the unintended effects, or a time-aware understanding of what these women were actually trying to do? These analyses, of course, need not be mutually exclusive, but it is generally a good thing for readers and writers to be clear about their interpretive choices.

Some theorists try to position prostitution as yet another form of queer sexuality, whose very transgressiveness supposedly makes it emancipatory. They might suggest, as Judith Butler has done, that transgressing dominant discourses about sexuality is in and of itself a method of reclaiming women's agency.[39] This view again is partly attributable to the conflation of desire with agency, rather than positioning sexual desire as one temporally and culturally specific manifestation of human agency. The 'empowerment' theory of prostitution leads to the anachronistic conclusion that the social purity campaigners contributed more to women's enslavement than to women's emancipation. Walkowitz's contention that historians who repeat narratives of sexual danger revictimise women by proscribing desire is a related view. Nineteenth-century feminists were working within existing narrative forms; this does not mean they were unable consciously to subvert or manipulate these forms for their own emancipatory ends. All human beings, and especially subjugated ones, are faced with the same prospect. We cannot completely escape our social and temporal context, which is partly formed by the narratives available to us. In much of human history, women have been victims of power, not holders of power. This is our context. To point it out is to move towards power, not towards repression.

Middle and upper-class nineteenth-century feminist activists like Josephine Butler or Ellice Hopkins had every intention of proscribing the type of male desire which could involve violence against the women with whom they worked. They were not revictimising women. They were attempting to empower them using the words and methods available to them in their class at that time. These women, by working with and campaigning for the personal safety and integrity of working-class women, used their public, middle-class, privileged voice effectively. They escaped the silencing, intimidating effect of physical violence and spoke out publicly about the effect of violence on women's physical bodies, thus employing emotion as a consciously political weapon. My contribution has not explored the many other discursive strategies which they used, such as the language and arguments of religion,[40] nor have I looked at strategies which did not work so well. Obviously, much more can be done. I believe that accessible analyses of their strategies can contribute to future feminist work in these areas.

Bakare-Yusef maintains that 'the body's return to flesh is a central site for the production of . . . counter-memory'[41] for the subjugated group. Using this strategy, Butler, Cobbe and Hopkins achieved concrete political aims, while at the same time helping to articulate an emerging feminist language about male violence. When feminists in 1971 found the bones of the older texts and were 'astounded' by remembering these women's voices, they restarted a counter-memory which continues to the present day. For women of the early 1970s to discover these women was to find 'exemplars who left palms in their pathway instead of thorns'.[42]

Notes

1. Author's interview with Jalna Hanmer, 18 Aug. 1999. Transcript deposited in the Feminist Archive North, Leeds Metropolitan University. See also Jalna Hanmer, 'Violence to women: from private sorrow to public issue' in Georgina Ashworth and Lucy Bonnerjea (eds.), *The Invisible Decade: UK Women and the UN Decade 1976–1985* (Aldershot, 1985); Dale Spender, *Women of Ideas – and What Men Have Done to Them* (1982).

2. Barbara Caine, *Victorian Feminists* (1993). See also Betty Friedan, *The Feminine Mystique* (Middlesex, 1963), Ch. 4, and compare Shulamith Firestone, 'The women's rights movement in the US: a new view' in Leslie Tanner (ed.), *Voices from Women's Liberation* (New York, 1971).

3. See, for example, the extensive nineteenth-century feminist biographies and writing samples at: http://www.netsrq.com/~dbois/index.html and http://www.spartacus.schoolnet.co.uk

4. Lucy Bland, *Banishing the Beast: English Feminism and Sexual Morality 1885–1914* (1995).

5. Josephine Butler (ed.), *Women's Work and Women's Culture* (1869, British Library Microfiche, 1987), Introduction, *passim*.

6. Nancy F. Cott, 'Passionlessness: an interpretation of Victorian sexual ideology, 1790–1850' in Nancy F. Cott and Elizabeth H. Pleck (eds.), *A Heritage of Her Own* (New York, 1979), pp. 162–181.

7. A. James Hammerton, *Cruelty and Companionship: Conflict in Nineteenth-Century Married Life* (1992), p. 103.

8. Maeve E. Doggett, *Marriage, Wife-Beating and the Law in Victorian England: 'Sub Virga Viri'* (Columbia, SC, 1992), p. 29.

9. Hammerton, *Cruelty* pp. 103–107.

10. *Ibid.*, p. 67.

11. *Ibid.*, pp. 67, 106–107.

12. Frances Power Cobbe, 'Wife torture in England' *CR* (April 1878), p. 74.

13. *Ibid.*, p. 64.

14. Bibi Bakare-Yusef, 'Black bodies and the unspeakable terror' in Ronit Lention (ed.), *Gender and Catastrophe* (New York, 1998).

15. See also Elaine Scarry, *The Body in Pain: The Making and Unmaking of the World* (Oxford, 1985).

16. Bakare-Yusef, 'Black bodies' p. 176.

17. Roland Barthes, *The Grain of the Voice: Interviews 1962–1980* (Los Angeles, CA, 1991), p. 117.

18. Myrna Trustam, 'Distasteful and derogatory? Examining Victorian soldiers for venereal disease' in London Feminist History Group (ed.), *Men's Power, Women's Resistance: The Sexual Dynamics of History* (1983).

19. Deborah Gorham, 'The "Maiden tribute of modern Babylon" re-examined: child prostitution and the idea of childhood in late-Victorian England' *VS* 21, (1978), pp. 353–379.

20. Eleanor S. Reimer and John C. Fout (eds.), *European Women: A Documentary History, 1789–1945* (Brighton, 1983), p. 228.

21. Judith R. Walkowitz, *City of Dreadful Delight: Narratives of Sexual Danger in Late-Victorian London* (Chicago, 1992), p. 90, quoting a CD Acts campaigner.

22. Letter from unnamed field worker in unnamed town to Josephine Butler, 1872, Brotherton Library Collection, Leeds University, JB9.

23. Josephine Butler, *A Call to Action. Being a Letter to the Ladies of Birmingham. Supplementary to an Address Given in Birmingham. November* (Birmingham, 1881). Quoted in Sheila Jeffreys, *The Idea of Prostitution* (North Melbourne, 1997), p. 9.

24. Lynda Nead, *Myths of Sexuality: Representations of Women in Victorian Britain* (Oxford, 1988), Ch. 3.

25. Walkowitz, *City* p. 93.

26. *Ibid.*, pp. 240–245.

27. See also Christina Sommers's controversial *Who Stole Feminism? How Women Have Betrayed Women* (New York, 1995).

28. Walkowitz, *City* p. 245.

29. Butler, *Women's Work* p. xvi.

30. Records of the Leeds Association for the Care and Protection of Young Girls, Acc. 1380, Sheepscar Archives, Leeds, Envelope 17. See also Frances Power Cobbe, *Friendless Girls, and how to help them: being an account of of the Preventive Mission at Bristol* (1862).

31. Leeds Association, Minute Book 29, Nov. 1884.

32. Leeds City Library, Local History Archives, *Leeds Ladies Association for the Care and Protection of Young Girls, Annual Report* (Leeds, 1944).

33. Leeds Association, Envelope 17.

34. Cecilie Hoigard and Liv Finstad, *Backstreets: Prostitution, Money and Love* (Cambridge, 1992). Quoted in Sheila Jeffreys, *The Idea of Prostitution* (North Melbourne, 1997), p. 259.

35. Jeffreys, *The Idea of Prostitution* pp. 254–255.

36. For some women, of course, these are not always mutually exclusive categories.

37. Michel Foucault, *The History of Sexuality, vol. I, An Introduction* Engl. trans. (1979).

38. Nead, *Myths of Sexuality* Ch. 3.

39. Judith Butler, *Gender Trouble: Feminism and the Subversion of Identity* (1990).

40. Although this has to a certain extent been done elsewhere. See, for example, the bibliography at: http://landow.stg.brown.edu/victorian/gender/femrelig.html

41. Bakare-Yusef, 'Black bodies' p. 182. See also Mark Ledbetter, *Victims and the Postmodern Narrative or Doing Violence to the Body: An Ethic of Reading and Writing* (Basingstoke, 1996), pp. 9, 13, 14–15.

42. Frances Power Cobbe, 'The final cause of woman' in Butler (ed.), *Women's Work* (1869).

Class and gender

Clark, Anna, *The Struggle for the Breeches: Gender and the Making of the British Working Class* (Berkeley, 1995).

D'Cruze, Shani, *Crimes of Outrage: Sex, Violence and Victorian Working Women* (1998).

Davidoff, Leonore and Catherine Hall, *Family Fortunes: Men and Women of the Middle Class* (1987).

Davidoff, Leonore, *Worlds Between: Historical Perspectives on Gender and Class* (Cambridge, 1995).

Hall, Catherine, *White, Male and Middle Class: Explorations in Feminism and History* (Cambridge, 1992).

Kingsley Kent, Susan, *Making Peace. The Reconstruction of Gender in Interwar Britain* (1993).

Poovey, Mary, *Uneven Developments: The Ideological Work of Gender in Mid-Victorian England* (Chicago, 1988).

Family, courtship and illegitimacy

Behlmer, George, 'Summary justice and working-class marriage in England, 1870–1940' *LHR* xii (1994), pp. 229–275.

Davidoff, Leonore, Megan Doolittle, Janet Fink and Katherine Holden, *The Family Story. Blood Contract and Intimacy 1830–1960* (1999).

Davies, Margaret Lewellyn (ed.), *Maternity: Letters from Working Women* (1978).

Davies, Margaret Llewellyn (ed.), *Life As We Have Known It* (1990).

Davin, Anna, *Growing Up Poor: Home, School and Street in London 1870–1914* (1996).

Frost, Ginger S., *Promises Broken: Courtship, Class and Gender in Victorian England* (Charlottesville, VA, 1995).

Gillis, John, *For Better For Worse: British Marriages, 1600 to the Present* (Oxford, 1985).

Gillis, John, 'Servants, sexual relations and the risks of illegitimacy in London, 1801–1900' in Judith L. Newton, Mary P. Ryan and Judith R. Walkowitz (eds.), *Sex and Class in Women's History* (1983), pp. 114–145.

Gordon, Linda, *Heroes of their Own Lives: The Politics and History of Family Violence: Boston 1880–1960* (1989).

Hendrick, Harry, *Child Welfare. England 1972–1989* (1994).

Henriques, U. R. Q., 'Bastardy and the new poor law' *P&P* 37 (1967), pp. 103–129.

Holcombe, Lee, *Wives and Property: Reform of the Married Women's Property Law in Nineteenth-Century England* (Toronto, 1983).

Lewis, Jane (ed.), *Labour and Love: Women's Experience of Home and Family* (Oxford, 1986).

Norton, Caroline, *Selected Writings of Caroline Norton* (New York, 1978).

Perkin, Joan, *Women and Marriage in Victorian England* (1989).

Pinchbeck, Ivy and Margaret Hewitt, *From the Eighteenth Century to the Children Act 1948* Vol. 2, *Children in English Society* (1973).

Reay, Barry, 'Sexuality in nineteenth-century England: the social context of illegitimacy in rural Kent' *RH* 1 (1990), pp. 219–247.

Roberts, Elizabeth, *A Woman's Place: An Oral History of Working-Class Women, 1890–1940* (Oxford, 1995).

Ross, Ellen, *Love and Toil: Motherhood in Outcast London, 1870–1918* (New York, 1993).

Shanley, Mary Lyndon, *Feminism, Marriage and the Law in Victorian England 1850–1895* (Princeton, 1989).

Stone, Lawrence, *The Road to Divorce: England 1530–1987* (1992).

Wohl, Anthony (ed.), *The Victorian Family: Structure and Stresses* (1978).

Feminist perspectives on violence against women

Black, Naomi, *Social Feminism* (Ithaca, NY, 1989).

Cook, S. and J. Besant (eds.), *Women's Encounters with Violence: The Australian Experience* (California, 1997).

Hanmer, J. and M. Maynard (eds.), *Women, Violence and Social Control* (1987).

Painter, Kate, 'Different worlds: the spatial, temporal and social dimensions of female victimization' in David J. Evans *et al.* (eds.), *Crime, Policing and Place* (1992); pp. 165–166.

Smart, Carol, 'Feminist approaches to criminology or postmodern woman meets atavistic man' in L. Gelsthorpe and A. Morris (eds.), *Feminist Perspectives in Criminology* (1990), pp. 70–84.

Stanko, Elizabeth A., *Intimate Intrusions; Women's Experience of Male Violence* (1985).

Stanko, Elizabeth A., *Everyday Violence: How Women and Men Experience Sexual and Physical Danger* (1990).

Sumner, C., 'Foucault, gender and the censure of deviance' in L. Gelsthorpe and A. Morris (eds.), *Feminist Perspectives in Criminology* (Oxford, 1992), pp. 26–40.

Walklate, S., 'Can there be a progressive victimology?' *IRV* 3 (1994), pp. 1–15.

Domestic violence

Ayers, Pat and Jan Lambertz, 'Marriage relations, money, and domestic violence in working-class Liverpool, 1919–39' in J. Lewis (ed.) *Labour and Love: Women's Experience of Home and Family, 1850–1940* (Oxford, 1986).

Bauer, C. and L. Ritt, ' "A husband is a beating animal": Frances Power Cobbe confronts the wife-abuse problem in Victorian England' *IJWS* 6 (1983), pp. 99–118.

Bauer, C. and L. Ritt, 'Wife-abuse, late Victorian English feminists, and the legacy of Frances Power Cobbe' *IJWS* 6 (1983), pp. 195–207.

Clark, Anna, 'Humanity or justice? Wifebeating and the law in the eighteenth and nineteenth centuries' in Carol Smart (ed.), *Regulating Womanhood: Historical Essays on Marriage, Motherhood and Sexuality* (1992).

Cobbe, Frances Power, 'Wife torture in England' *CR* 32 (1878), pp. 55–87.

Dobash, Rebecca Emerson and Russell Dobash, *Violence Against Wives* (New York, 1979).

Doggett, Maeve E., *Marriage, Wife-Beating and the Law in Victorian England* (Columbia, S.C., 1992).

Hammerton, A. James, *Cruelty and Companionship: Conflict in Nineteenth-Century Married Life* (1992).

Lambertz, Jan, 'The politics and economics of family violence, from the late nineteenth century to 1948' (MPhil, Manchester University, 1984).

Lambertz, Jan, 'Feminists and the politics of wife-beating' in H. L. Smith (ed.), *British Feminism in the Twentieth Century* (1990), pp. 25–46.

Leneman, Leah, 'A tyrant and tormenter: wifebeating in Scotland in the seventeenth and eighteenth centuries' *C&C* 12 (1997), pp. 31–54.

Leneman, Leah, *Alienated Affections: The Scottish Experience of Divorce and Separation, 1684–1830* (Edinburgh, 1998).

May, Margaret, 'Violence in the family; an historical perspective' in J. P. Marton, (ed.), *Violence in the Family* (Chichester, 1978).

Pahl, Jan, *Private Violence and Public Policy: The Needs of Battered Women and the Response of the Public Services* (London, 1985).

Pleck, Elizabeth, *Domestic Tyranny: The Making of American Social Policy against Family Violence from Colonial Times to the Present* (Oxford, 1987).

Ross, Ellen, ' "Fierce questions and taunts": married life in working-class London, 1870–1914' *FS* 8, 3 (1983), pp. 575–602.

Tomes, N., 'A "torrent of abuse": crimes of violence between working-class men and women in London' *JSH* 11 (1978), pp. 328–345.

Wiener, Martin, 'The sad story of George Hall: adultery, murder and the politics of mercy in mid-Victorian England' *SH* 24 (1999), p. 193.

Infanticide

Arnot, Margaret L., 'Gender in focus: infanticide in England 1840–1880' (PhD, University of Essex, 1994).

Campbell, Duncan, *A Stranger and Afraid: The Story of Caroline Beale* (1997).

Higginbotham, Ann R., '"The sin of the age": infanticide and illegitimacy in Victorian London' in Kristine Ottesen Garrigan (ed.), *Victorian Scandals: Representations of Gender and Class* (Athens, 1992), pp. 257–288.

Marks, M. N., 'Characteristics and causes of infanticide in Britain' *IRP* 8 (1996), pp. 99–106.

Rose, Lionel, *Massacre of the Innocents* (1986).

Seaborne Davies, D., 'Child-killing in English law' *MLR* 1, 3, Dec. 1937, pp. 203–223.

Histories of crime and punishment

Arnot, M. and C. Usborne (eds.), *Gender and Crime in Modern Europe* (1999).

Emsley, Clive, *Crime and Society in England 1750–1900* (London, 1996).

Emsley, Clive and L. A. Knafla, 'Crime histories and histories of crime: studies in the historiography of crime and criminal justice in modern history' *H&T* 36 (1997), p. 108.

Emsley, Clive, 'The history of crime and crime control institutions' in M. Maguire, R. Morgan and R. Reiner (eds.), *The Oxford Handbook of Criminology* (Oxford, 1994).

Gatrell, V. A. C., 'Crime, authority and the policeman-state' in F. M. L. Thompson (ed.), *The Cambridge Social History of Britain, 1750–1950* Vol. 3, *Social Agencies and Institutions* (1990).

Gatrell, V. A. C., *The Hanging Tree: Execution and the English People, 1770–1868* (Oxford, 1994).

Gatrell, V. A. C. and T. B. Hadden, 'Criminal statistics and their interpretation' in E. A. Wrigley (ed.), *Nineteenth-Century Society: Essays in the Use of Quantitative Methods for the Study of Social Data* (Cambridge, 1972), pp. 336–396.

Gatrell, V. A. C., Bruce Lenman and Geoffrey Parker, *Crime and the Law: The Social History of Crime in Western Europe since 1500* (1980).

Hay, Douglas *et al.*, *Albion's Fatal Tree* (New York, 1975).

Ignatieff, Michael, *A Just Measure of Pain: The Penitentiary in the Industrial Revolution, 1750–1850* (1978).

Jones, D., *Crime, Protest, Community and Police in Nineteenth-Century Britain* (1982).

Philips, David, *Crime and Authority in Victorian England: The Black Country 1835–1860* (1977).

Taylor, H., 'Rationing crime: the political economy of criminal statistics since the 1850s' *EHR* 51 (1998), pp. 569–590.

Zedner, Lucia, *Women, Crime and Custody in Victorian England* (Oxford, 1991).

Crime and violence

Archer, John E., 'Poaching gangs and violence: the urban-rural divide in nineteenth-century Lancashire' *BJC* 39 (1999), pp. 25–38.

Bottoms, Anthony E. and Paul Wiles, 'Explanations of crime and place' in David J. Evans *et al.* (eds.), *Crime, Policing and Place: Essays in Environmental Criminology* (1992), p. 31.

Cockburn, J. S., 'Patterns of violence in English society: homicide in Kent 1560–1985' *P&P* 131 (1991), pp. 70–106.

Davies, Andrew and Geoffrey Pearson (eds.), 'Histories of crime and modernity' special issue, *BJC* 39 (1999).

Davis, Jennifer, 'The London garotting panic of 1862: a moral panic and the creation of a criminal class in Mid-Victorian England' in V. A. C. Gatrell, B. Lenman and G. Parker (eds.), *Crime and the Law: A Social History of Crime in Western Europe Since 1500* (1980).

ESRC Violence Research Programme, *Taking Stock: What Do We Know About Violence?* (1998).

Sharpe, J. A., 'The history of violence in England: some observations' *P&P* 108 (1985), pp. 206–215.

Sindall, Rob, *Street Violence in the Nineteenth Century: Media Panic or Real Danger?* (Leicester, 1990).

Stone, L., 'Interpersonal violence in English society, 1300–1980' *P&P* 101 (1983), pp. 22–33.

Stone, L., 'A rejoinder' *P&P* 108 (1985), pp. 216–224.

Young people and violence

Cox, P., 'Girls, deficiency and delinquency' in D. Wright and A. Digby (eds.), *From Idiocy to Mental Deficiency. Historical Perspectives on People with Learning Difficulties* (1996), pp. 184–206.

Davies, Andrew, 'Youth gangs, masculinity and violence in late Victorian Manchester and Salford' *JSH* 32, 2 (1998), pp. 349–369.

Davies, Andrew, ' "These viragoes are no less cruel than the lads": young women, gangs and violence in late Victorian Manchester and Salford' *BJC* 39, 1 (1999), pp. 72–89.

Humphries, Stephen, *Hooligans or Rebels? An Oral History of Working-Class Childhood and Youth 1889–1939* (Oxford, 1983).

Pearson, Geoffrey, *Hooligan: A History of Respectable Fears* (1983).

Pearson, Geoffrey, ' "A Jekyll in the classroom, a Hyde in the street": Queen Victoria's hooligans' in David Downes (ed.), *Crime and the City* (1989), pp. 11–20.

Schwarz, Bill, 'Night battles: hooligan and citizen' in Mica Nava and Alan O'Shea (eds.), *Modern Times: Reflections of a Century of English Modernity* (1996).

Weinberger, Barbara, 'Policing juveniles: delinquency in late nineteenth and early twentieth-century Manchester' *CJH* 14 (1993), pp. 43–55.

The Courts and the Law

Arnaud-Duc, N., 'The law's contradictions' in G. Fraisse and M. Perrot (eds.), *A History of Women in the West* 5 Vols (Harvard, 1993), Vol. 4, Ch. 4.

Conley, Caroline, *The Unwritten Law: Criminal Justice in Victorian Kent* (Oxford, 1991).

Davis, Jennifer, 'A poor man's system of justice: the London Police Courts in the second half of the nineteenth century' *HJ* 29, 2 (1984), pp. 309–333.

Davis, Jennifer, 'Prosecutions and their context: the use of the criminal law in later nineteenth-century London' in D. Hay and F. Snyder (eds.), *Policing and Prosecution in Britain, 1750–1850* (Oxford, 1989), pp. 379–426.

Elliot, D., *Criminal Procedure in England and Scotland* (1878).

Hale, Sir M. *The History of the Pleas of the Crown* 2 Vols (1936).

King, Peter, 'Punishing assault: the transformation of attitudes in the English courts' *JIH* 27 (1996), pp. 43–74.

Radzinowicz, L., *A History of English Criminal Law* 4 Vols (1948–1968).

Robb, George and Nancy Erber (eds.), *Disorder in the Court: Trials and Sexual Conflict at the Turn of the Century* (1999).

Simpson, Alan, *Biographical Dictionary of the Common Law* (1984).

Skyrme, T., *A History of the Justices of the Peace* 2 Vols (Chichester, 1991).

Policing

Carrier, J., *The Campaign for the Employment of Women as Police Officers* (Aldershot, 1988).

Levine, Philippa, ' "Walking the streets in a way no decent woman should": women police in World War I' *JMH* 66 (1994), pp. 34–78.

Lock, J., *The British Policewoman* (1979).

Steedman, Carolyn, *Policing the Victorian Community: The Formation of English Provincial Police Forces, 1856–80* (1984).

Storch, R. D., 'The plague of blue locusts: police reform and popular resistance in Northern England, 1840–1857' *IRSH* 20 (1975), pp. 61–90.

Storch, R. D., 'The policeman as domestic missionary: urban discipline and popular culture in Northern England, 1850–1880' *JSH* 9 (1976), pp. 481–509.

Woodeson, Alison, 'The first women police: a force for equality or infringement?' *WHR* 2 (1993), pp. 217–232.

Riot and violent protest

Bohstedt, J., 'Gender, household and community politics – women in English riots, 1790–1810' *P&P* 120 (1988), pp. 88–122.

Linebaugh, Peter, 'The Tyburn riots against the surgeons' in Douglas Hay *et al.*, *Albion's Fatal Tree* (New York, 1975).

Neal, Frank, *Sectarian Violence: The Liverpool Experience, 1819–1914* (Manchester, 1988).

Rule, J. and R. Wells, *Crime, Protest and Popular Politics in Southern England, 1740–1850* (1997).

Stevenson, J., *Popular Disturbances in England, 1700–1870* (1979).

Swift, Roger, 'Anti-Irish violence in Victorian and Edwardian England' *CJH* 15 (1994), pp. 127–140.

Swift, Roger, 'Heroes or villains? The Irish, crime, and disorder in Victorian England' *Albion* 29 (1997), pp. 399–421.

Thompson, E. P., *The Making of the English Working Class* (1965).

Thompson, E. P., 'The moral economy of the English crowd in the eighteenth century' *P&P* 50 (1971), pp. 76–136.

Walter, J. and K. Wrightson, 'Dearth and the social order in early modern England' *P&P* 71 (1976), pp. 22–42.

Wright, D. G., *Popular Radicalism: The Working-Class Experience, 1780–1880* (1988).

Yeo, E. and S. Yeo (eds.), *Popular Culture and Class Conflict, 1590–1914: Explorations in the History of Labour and Leisure* (Brighton, 1981).

Masculinity and violence

Archer, John (ed.), *Male Violence* (1994).

Baldrick, R., *The Duel: A History of Duelling* (1965).

Campbell, Ann and Steven Muncar, 'Men and the meaning of violence' in John Archer (ed.), *Male Violence* (1994).

Mangan, J. A. and J. Walvin (eds.), *Manliness and Morality: Middle-Class Masculinity in Britain and America, 1800–1940* (Manchester, 1987).

McClelland, Keith, 'Masculinity and the "representative artisan" in Britain, 1850–80' in M. Roper and J. Tosh (eds.), *Manful Assertions: Masculinities in Britain since 1800* (1991), pp. 74–91.

McLelland, Keith, 'Rational and respectable men: gender, the working class, and citizenship in Britain, 1850–1867' in Laura L. Frader and Sonya O. Rose (eds.), *Gender and Class in Modern Europe* (Ithaca, NY, 1996).

Newburn, Tim and Elizabeth A. Stanko (eds.), *Just Boys Doing Business: Men, Masculinities and Crime* (1995).

Price, Richard N., 'The other face of respectability: violence in the Manchester brickmaking trade 1859–1870' *P&P* 66 (1975), pp. 110–132.

Simpson, Anthony, 'Dandelions on the field of honour: duelling, the middle class and the law in nineteenth-century England' *CJH* 9 (1988), pp. 99–155.

Walkowitz, J., 'Jack the Ripper and the myth of male violence' *FS* 8 (1982), pp. 543–574.

Wiener, Martin J., 'The Victorian criminalization of men' in Pieter Spierenburg (ed.), *Men and Violence: Gender, Honor, and Rituals in Modern Europe and America* (Ohio, 1998).

Sexual violence

Brownmiller, S., *Against Our Will: Men, Women and Rape* (1975).

Carter, J. M., *Rape in Medieval England: An Historical and Sociological Study* (New York, 1985).

Clark, Anna, *Women's Silence, Men's Violence: Sexual Assault in England, 1770–1845* (1987).

Conley, C., 'Rape and justice in Victorian England' *VS* 29 (1986), pp. 519–536.

D'Cruze, Shani, 'Approaching the history of rape and sexual violence: notes towards research' *WHR* 1 (1992), pp. 377–396.

Elstrich, S., *Real Rape* (Cambridge, MA, 1987).

Gordon, Linda, 'The politics of child sexual abuse: notes from American history' *FR* 28 (1988), pp. 56–64.

Hooper, Carol-Ann, 'Child sexual abuse and the regulation of women: variations on a theme' in C. Smart (ed.), *Regulating Womanhood: Historical Essays on Marriage, Motherhood and Sexuality* (1992), pp. 53–77.

Jackson, Louise A., 'Family, community and the regulation of child sexual abuse: London 1870–1914' in A. Fletcher and S. Hussey (eds.), *Childhood in Question* (Manchester, 1999), pp. 133–151.

Jackson, Louise A., *Child Sexual Abuse in Victorian England* (2000).

Jackson, Stevi, 'The social context of rape; sexual scripts and motivation' *WSIQ* 1 (1978), pp. 27–39.

Jones, Joanne, 'Male violence against women in Manchester and its representations in the local press, 1870–1900' (PhD, Lancaster University, 1999).

Kelly, L., *Surviving Sexual Violence* (Cambridge, 1988).

Lees, Sue, *Carnal Knowledge: Rape on Trial* (1996).

Olafson, E., D. Corwin and R. Summit, 'The modern-history of child sexual abuse awareness – cycles of discovery and suppression' *JCAN* 17 (1993), pp. 7–24.

Smart, Carol, 'A history of ambivalence and conflict in the discursive construction of the "child victim" of sexual abuse' *SLS* 8 (1999), pp. 396–397.

Smart, Carol, 'Reconsidering the recent history of child sexual abuse, 1910–1960' *JSP* 29 (2000), pp. 55–71.

Soothill, Keith, Sylvia Walby and Paul Bagguley, 'Judges, the media and rape' *JL&S* 17 (1990), pp. 211–233.

Temkin, Jennifer, *Rape and the Legal Process* (1987).

Sexuality

Bartley, Paula, *Prostitution: Prevention and Reform in England, 1860–1914* (2000).

Bland, Lucy, *Banishing the Beast: English Feminism and Sexual Morality 1885–1914* (1995).

Bland, Lucy, 'In the name of protection: the policing of women in the First World War' in J. Brophy and C. Smart (eds.), *Women in Law. Explorations in Law, Family and Sexuality* (1985).

Brookes, Barbara, *Abortion in England 1900–1967* (1988).

Edwards, Susan, *Female Sexuality and the Law* (Oxford, 1981).

Humphries, Steve, *A Secret World of Sex. Forbidden Fruit: The British Experience 1900–1950* (1988).

Jackson, Margaret, *The Real Facts of Life: Feminism and the Politics of Sexuality c. 1850–1940* (1994).

Jeffreys, Sheila, *The Spinster and Her Enemies: Feminism and Sexuality 1880–1930* (1985).

Jeffreys, Sheila, *The Idea of Prostitution* (North Melbourne, 1997).

Kingsley Kent, Susan, *Sex and Suffrage in Britain, 1860–1914* (Princeton, NJ, 1987).

Mahood, Linda, *The Magdalenes: Prostitution in the Nineteenth Century* (1990).

Marcus, S., *The Other Victorians; A Study of Sexuality and Pornography in Mid-Nineteenth Century England* (1966).

McHugh, P., *Prostitution and Victorian Social Reform: The Campaign against the Contagious Diseases Acts* (1980).

McLaren, Angus, *Reproductive Rituals: The Perception of Fertility in England from the Sixteenth Century to the Nineteenth Century* (1984).

Smart, Carol, *Regulating Womanhood: Historical Essays on Marriage, Motherhood and Sexuality* (1992).

Terrot, Charles, *The Maiden Tribute: A Study of the White Slave Traffic of the Nineteenth Century* (1959).

Walkowitz, Judith R., *City of Dreadful Delight: Narratives of Sexual Danger in Late-Victorian London* (Chicago, 1992).

Walkowitz, Judith R., 'Dangerous sexualities' in G. Fraisse and M. Perrot (eds.), *A History of Women in the West* 5 Vols (Harvard, 1993), Vol. 4, Ch. 14.

Sociohistorical Context

Beddoe, Deirdre, *Back to Home and Duty: Women Between the Wars 1918–39* (1989).

Best, Geoffrey, *Mid-Victorian Britain 1851–75* (1985).

Booth, Charles, *Life and Labour of the People in London* 17 Vols, 3rd series (1902–1904; NY, 1970).

Boyce, G., J. Curran and P. Wingate (eds.), *Newspaper History from the Seventeenth Century to the Present Day* (1978).

Braybon, Gail and Penny Summerfield, *Out of the Cage. Women's Experiences in Two World Wars* (1987).

Brown, L., *Victorian News and Newspapers* (Oxford, 1985).

Burnett, J., *Destiny Obscure* (1982).

Caine, Barbara, *Victorian Feminists* (1993).

Chinn, C., *They Worked All Their Lives: Women of the Urban Poor in England, 1880–1939* (Manchester, 1988).

Davies, Andrew, *Leisure, Gender and Poverty; Working-Class Culture in Salford and Manchester, 1900–1939* (Buckingham, 1992).

Digby, Anne, *Pauper Palaces* (1978).

Dyhouse, Carol, 'Driving ambitions: women in pursuit of a medical education, 1890–1939' *WHR* 7 (1998), pp. 321–341.

Dyhouse, Carol, 'Women students and the London medical schools, 1914–39: the anatomy of a masculine culture' *G&H* 10 (1998), pp. 110–132.

Dyos, H. J., *Victorian Suburb: A Study of the Growth of Camberwell* (Leicester, 1961).

Finlayson, Geoffrey, *Citizen, State and Social Welfare in Britain, 1830–1990* (Oxford, 1994).

Gaffin, Jean and David Thomas, *Caring and Sharing: The Centenary History of the Cooperative Women's Guild* (Manchester, 1983).

Harrison, Brian, *Drink and the Victorians: The Temperance Question in England 1815–1872* (1971).

Horn, Pamela, *The Rise and Fall of the Victorian Domestic Servant* (2nd edn., Gloucester, 1986).

Knott, John, *Popular Opposition to the 1834 Poor Law* (1986).

Levine, Philippa, *Victorian Feminism 1850–1900* (Miami, FL, 1994).

Midwinter, E., *The Development of Social Welfare in Britain* (Buckingham, 1994).

Olsen, Donald J., *The Growth of Victorian London* (1976).

Richards, Jeffrey, *Happiest Days: The Public School in English Fiction* (Manchester, 1988).

Rowbotham, Judith, *Good Girls Make Good Wives. Guidance for Girls in Victorian Fiction* (Oxford, 1989).

Scott, Gillian, *Feminism and the Politics of Working Women: The Women's Cooperative Guild, 1880s to the Second World War* (1998).

Sims, George R. (ed.), *Living London* 3 Vols (1902; reprinted as *Edwardian London* 4 Vols, 1990).

Tebbutt, M., *Women's Talk: A Social History of Gossip in Working-Class Neighbourhoods, 1880–1960* (Aldershot, 1995).

Thane, Pat, *Foundations of the Welfare State* (1982).

Vicinus, Martha (ed.), *Suffer and Be Still: Women in the Victorian Age* (Bloomington, IN, 1973).

Vincent, D., *Bread, Knowledge and Freedom* (1980).

Walker, Linda., *The Women's Movement in Britain 1790–1945* (1998).

Waller, P. J., *Town, City, and Nation: England, 1850–1914* (Oxford, 1983), p. 148.

White, J., *The Worst Street in North London: Campbell Bunk, Islington, Between the Wars* (1986).

Williamson, Lori, *Power and Protest: Frances Power Cobbe and Victorian Society* (1998).

Theoretical and interdisciplinary texts

Connell, R., *Gender and Power* (Cambridge, 1987).

Cordess, Christopher and Murray Fox (eds.), *Forensic Psychotherapy: Crime, Psychodynamics and the Offender Patient* (London and Bristol, 1996).

Foucault, M., *Discipline and Punish: The Birth of the Prison* (1991).

Freud, Anna, *The Ego and the Mechanisms of Defence* (1936, Engl. trans., 1937).

Freud, Sigmund, 'Studies on hysteria' written with Josef Breuer (1895) in *The Standard Edition of the Complete Psychological Works of Sigmund Freud* (trans. and ed. James Strachey, 1953).

Gay, Peter, *Freud for Historians* (Oxford, 1985).

Klein, Melanie, *Envy and Gratitude and Other Works 1946–1963* (1988).

McNay, L., *Foucault and Feminism* (Cambridge, 1992).

Meyers, Diana Tietjens, *Feminists Rethink the Self* Feminist Theory and Politics Series (Boulder, CO, 1997).

Ramazanoglu, C. (ed.), *Up Against Foucault; Explorations of Some Tensions Between Foucault and Feminism* (1993).

Sawicki, J., *Disciplining Foucault: Feminism, Power and the Body* (1991).

Scarry, Elaine, *The Body in Pain: The Making and Unmaking of the World* (Oxford, 1985).

Scheper-Hughes, Nancy, 'The cultural politics of child survival' in her *Child Survival: Anthropological Perspectives on the Treatment and Maltreatment of Children* (Reidel, Dordrecht and Lancaster, 1987).

Weedon, C., *Feminist Practice and Poststructuralist Theory* (Oxford, 1987).

INDEX

adolescence, 129, 130, 162–3
  working-class girls, 207–8
adultery, 145–7
agency, women's, 109, 199, 202, 205,
    208
alcohol, 12, 28, 34, 47, 48, 49
  victims of sexual violence, 112, 115,
    155–6, 164–5
  women, 165–6
Allan, Maud, 190
Allen, Mary, 119
Archer, John, 219
Archer, John E., vii, 2, 14, 15, 217
Arnot, Margaret, 2, 16, 216
Arnaud-Duc, N., 92, 218
assault, see fighting; violence, physical
Ayers, Pat, 136, 215

Bagguley, Paul, 220
bailiffs, 47
Bakare-Yusuf, Bibi, 203, 209
Baldrick, R., 219
Barthes, Roland, 203
Bauer, C., 215
Becker, Lydia, 36
Beddoe, D., 221
Beerbohm, Max, 175–6
Behlmer, George, 213
belts (as weapons), 46, 74, 79
Besant, S. J., 214
Best, Geoffrey, 221
Birmingham, 70
Black, Naomi, 214
Blair, Lois, 126
Bland, Lucy, 3, 13, 14, 95, 98, 126,
    136, 221
body, 95, 146, 200, 201
  pain, 203, 204

Bohstedt, J., 219
Booth, Charles, 131, 173, 174, 221
Bottoms, Anthony, 217
Boyle, Nina, 119
boys, 159
  see children, youth gangs
Braddon, Mary, 162
Braybon, Gail, 221
breadwinner, 29, 30, 34
  see also separate spheres; domesticity
Breuer, Josef, 223
Brierly, Thomas, 28
Bristol, 120
British Crime Surveys, xi
The British Workman, 34
Brookes, Barbara, 61, 221
Brown, L., 222
Brownmiller, S., 220
buggery, 187
Bullock, Shan, *Robert Thorne,* 175
Burnett, Jacky, 3, 17
Burnett, John, 222
butchers, 51
Butler, Josephine, 131, 198, 203–5,
    207, 209
Butler, Judith, 209

Caine, Barbara, 222
Cameron, D., 108
Campbell, Ann, 219
Campbell, Duncan, 216
capital punishment, 4, 5, 171
Caputi, Jane, 105
Carpenter, Edward, 192
Carrier, J., 218
Carter, J. M., 220
Central Criminal Court (Old Bailey),
    32, 55, 56, 57, 58, 61, 97

Morgan, R., 216
Morris, A., 214
Mother's Union, 141, 142
motherhood, 58, 143, 148
  punishment of children, 163
  and social welfare, 121
  see also domesticity; household;
    wives; women
Mrs Halliburton's Troubles, 160
Mulvey, Laura, 64
Muncar, Steven, 219
murder, 3, 13, 33, 46, 96, 104
  Crippen case, 170–2, 180–1
  Fahmy case, 185–9, 193
  by scuttlers, 73, 79
  see also homicide; manslaughter

Napier, Caroline, 35
National Society for Prevention of
    Cruelty to Children, 119, 121,
    126, 130
National Union of Women Teachers,
    124
Nead, Lynda, 208
Neal, Frank, 219
neighbourhood, *see* space
le Neve, Ethel, 170, 171, 180
Newburn, Tim, 220
newspapers, 106
  see also press reporting
Norton, Caroline, 35, 214

Oates, Dr Margaret, 62
Olafson, E., 220
Oldham, 124, 125
Oliphant, Margaret, 98
Olsen, Donald J., 222
orientalism, 3, 186, 187, 190–1
  the veil, 192
Ouida, 162

Pahl, Jan, 215
Painter, Kate, 214
Pall Mall Gazette, 95, 204
Pankhurst, Christabel, 146
Parker, G., 216, 217
Pearson, Geoffrey, 15, 71, 217, 218
penal system, 5

Perkin Joan, 214
philanthropy, 15, 107, 120
  Lad's Clubs, 70, 71
Philips, Davis, 41, 42, 216
physical violence, *see* violence, physical
Pinchbeck, Ivy, 214
poaching, 50
police, 7–9, 47, 49, 50, 80–1, 93,
    218–19
  and domestic violence, 31
  Metropolitan, 121
  and sexual violence, 113, 114, 123
  women police, 3, 119, 120, 128,
    140–1, 172
    discrimination against, 122–4
    Liverpool Women's Police Patrols,
      126–7
    Policewomen's Regulations (1933),
      126
  women police surgeons, 3, 119,
    125–6, 127, 131, 132
Poovey, Mary, 213
poverty, 58, 148
  and domestic violence, 29
  see also domesticity; household
power, 2
pregnancy, 32, 146
  concealment of, 55–6, 58–9
  physiological knowledge, 60
  suppression of symptoms, 65
  see also infanticide; motherhood;
    quickening
press reporting, 7, 71, 74, 82
  assigning responsibility for violence,
    111
  narrative construction, 107–8
  sensational, 104
  sexual violence, 89–101, 104–16
  The Times, 3, 59, 89–91, 98
  see also discourse; newspapers
Preston, 50
Price, Richard, N., 220
prosititution
  and physical violence, 208
  and sexual violence, 110, 113, 114,
    204
  white slave trade, 95, 99
provocation, 33, 48